The Forgotten Creed

The Forgotten Creed

Christianity's Original Struggle against Bigotry, Slavery, and Sexism

Stephen J. Patterson

OXFORD

UNIVERSITY PRESS

Oxford University Press is a department of the University of Oxford. It furthers the University's objective of excellence in research, scholarship, and education by publishing worldwide. Oxford is a registered trade mark of Oxford University Press in the UK and certain other countries.

Published in the United States of America by Oxford University Press
198 Madison Avenue, New York, NY 10016, United States of America.

Library of Congress Cataloging-in-Publication Data
Names: Patterson, Stephen J., 1957– author.
Title: The forgotten creed : Christianity's original struggle against bigotry, slavery, and sexism / Stephen J. Patterson.
Description: New York, NY : Oxford University Press, 2018. |
Includes bibliographical references and index.
Identifiers: LCCN 2017050017 | ISBN 9780190865825 (hardcover : alk. paper) |
ISBN 9780190865849 (epub) | ISBN 9780190879037 (oso)
Subjects: LCSH: Bible. Galatians, III, 28—Criticism, interpretation, etc. |
Identity (Psychology)—Religious aspects—Christianity—Biblical teaching. |
Identification (Religion)—Biblical teaching. | Equality—Religious aspects—
Christianity—Biblical teaching.
Classification: LCC BS2685.52.P38 2018 | DDC 227/.406—dc23
LC record available at https://lccn.loc.gov/2017050017

3 5 7 9 8 6 4

Printed by Sheridan Books, Inc., United States of America

For you are all children of God in the Spirit.
There is no Jew or Greek;
There is no slave or free;
There is no male and female.
For you are all one in the Spirit.

The First Creed

"They called me everything but a child of God."

Curt Flood
On playing in the Carolina League
as a black ballplayer in 1957

CONTENTS

Introduction

The Unbelievable Creed

On a warm, June Sunday in St. Louis I wandered with an old friend through the church where, earlier that morning, my children had been baptized. We came to the baptismal font, around which our family had gathered for the ceremony during the regular Sunday service. It was about four feet high, just low enough for my daughter to reach up and fiddle her fingers in the water and watch the droplets dribble back into its shallow pool. My friend, who had grown up in a secular upper-class home in Tito's Yugoslavia, had little knowledge of fonts and baptism and the goings-on that morning. So he asked, what does it mean, baptism?

The question gave me pause. When you baptize a baby, it is a kind of naming ceremony, like those found in many societies. When you are baptized, like I was, on the eve of puberty, it is a coming-of-age ceremony, a *rite de passage*—again, a common practice across cultures. Sometimes, though rarely, an adult is baptized. Then it signals a religious conversion, the culmination of a profound personal transformation. I rambled. "But what do *you* think it means?" he asked. It was a fair question. I had just seen my own children baptized.

"It means," I said, "you're a child of God." "So you're saved?" No. That's not what I meant. That *is* what most people assume it means. That is what most people think the Christian religion is all about: salvation. But that is not really it. Earlier that morning the minister had used words from an ancient, nearly forgotten credo once associated with baptism. "You are children of God," she said. "There is no Jew or Greek, no slave or free, no male and female." The words were from a letter of Paul the Apostle, who had taken them, in turn, from an ancient baptismal creed he had come to know through the Jesus movement. That is what it's about—being a child of God. Ethnicity (no Jew or Greek), class (no slave or free), and gender (no male and female) count neither for you nor against you. We are all children of God. He was skeptical. An early Christian creed about race, class, and gender? Unbelievable.

Why not be skeptical? What has Christianity ever had to say about race, class, and gender? I suspect that most people would think nothing good. Sunday morning is still the most segregated hour in American life. From the time African slaves first began to convert to the religion of their masters, whites prohibited blacks from worshipping with them—still true in most American churches until after the civil rights era. Then, in the 1960s, white churches began to "open their doors" to African Americans and—surprise—most blacks said "thanks, but no thanks." This wasn't major league baseball, after all. Most African Americans preferred to worship in the churches their ancestors had built of necessity, theirs, now, by choice, rather than join churches that had shunned them for more than a century. The story of race and religion in America is pocked with indignities large and small. So, while police departments, public schools, restaurants, the United States military, and baseball have all become racially integrated, America's churches have not. It may be that the church is the last truly segregated public space in America.

How about class? Does Christianity have anything helpful to say about class? Perhaps. You might hear "blessed are the poor" on any given Sunday, but more likely you will hear "blessed are the poor in spirit." The words of Jesus are assumed to be about your spiritual life, not your finances—unless, of course, you attend one of the larger, far more successful churches where the "prosperity gospel" is preached, where the word is always about your finances. If you believe, keep the right company, straighten out your life, and tithe, you will prosper. The millionaire preaching these words to you is a witness to his own truth. The faithful definitely will prosper. And what of those who do not? Well, anyone can read those tealeaves. In today's fastest-growing churches, the gospel is all about class.

And gender? Simply put, the church is the last, greatest bastion of gender bias in American society. The Catholic Church does not ordain women as priests and probably never will. Neither do the Orthodox churches. The largest Protestant denominations do not ordain women as ministers, nor do most of the historically black churches. Only the small denominations once known as the "mainline" churches ordain women—and these are the churches that are in decline. My own United Church of Christ, the oldest church in the United States, which ordained the first woman minister in the mid-nineteenth century, now has fewer than a million members. Today the Mormons outnumber the church of the Pilgrims seven to one—and the Mormons are not ordaining any women. The church is the last institution in America where it is still legal to discriminate on the basis of gender.

So, an ancient Christian credo declaring solidarity across ethnic lines, class division, and gender difference sounded a little unbelievable to someone who had come to see the Christian church as more a symbol of social ills than of starry-eyed utopian dreams. And that these words could have come from the Apostle Paul—to anyone with a passing familiarity with Christianity—would have seemed more incredible still. Most people today assume that Paul is the father of Christian anti-Semitism, was profoundly misogynistic, and was authoritarian when it came to slavery. Let wives be submissive and slaves be obedient, he taught. Or so they think. And why not? Clear statements to that effect appear in the New Testament letters claiming the great apostle's authorship—Colossians, Ephesians, 1 Timothy, and Titus. But every beginning student of the Bible learns that these letters are pseudonymous, forgeries. Paul did not write them. On the other hand, Paul himself did indeed write the Epistle to the Galatians, including the remarkable words of Galatians 3: 26–28:

> For you are all children of God through faith in Christ Jesus;
> for as many of you who have been baptized have put on Christ:
> there is no Jew or Greek;
> there is no slave or free;
> there is no male and female;
> for you are all one in Christ Jesus.

The debate about the meaning and significance of this passage began already in the early twentieth century. In 1909, the German Catholic scholar Johannes Belser noticed it and its remarkable claim and argued that Paul could not have meant anything social or political by it.[1] It simply meant that everyone is equal in the sight of the Lord. But the Protestant Liberal Heinrich Weinel, who helped to found something called the *Freie Volkskirche* (the Free People's Church), a hotbed of theological liberalism and social democratic reform in early-twentieth-century Germany, saw it

---

1. "Die Frauen in die neutestamentliche Schriften," *Theologische Quartalschrift* 90 (1909): 321–51.

differently. He argued that Galatians 3:28 was at the heart of Paul's radical social vision—even if his own nerves would not quite tolerate the fullness of that vision in real time.[2] Today, most scholars do not deny the radical social and political implications of the saying, but they also do not assign the verse directly to Paul. To be sure, Paul wrote it into his Galatian letter, but for reasons that I shall explain in chapter 1, most students of Paul believe that he was drawing upon an ancient creedal statement originally associated with baptism. Paul knew it and quoted it, but he did not compose it. That honor belongs to some early Christian wordsmith now long forgotten.

The credo itself has also been mostly forgotten. The current, state-of-the-art scholarly treatment of the earliest Christian statements of faith scarcely mentions it.[3] A recent nine-hundred-page study of baptism in the New Testament refers to it only in passing.[4] Again, why not? In the long history of Christian theology, spanning centuries and continents, this creed has played virtually no role. How could it? The church became a citadel of patriarchy and enforced this regime wherever it spread. It also endorsed and encouraged the taking of slaves from the peoples it colonized. And within a hundred years of its writing, "no Jew or Greek" became simply "no Jews," as the church first separated from, then rebelled against its Jewish patrimony, eventually attempting patricide.

But thoughtful and sensitive scholars still studied the creed. I recall first engaging students with it through the work of Elisabeth Schuessler Fiorenza, whose book, *In Memory of Her* (1983),[5] introduced my generation of scholars to the hidden histories of women in early Christian texts. Schuessler Fiorenza insisted that you had to read between the lines, and sometimes just read the lines critically and carefully, to see what years of patriarchy had obscured from view. This ancient creed is a good example of how her methods could bear fruit. If you read the third chapter of Galatians, you'll barely notice the creed. The chapter is all about faith, and how faith has replaced the need for the Jewish Law. Paul brings in the creed to shore up his idea that the Law no longer separates Jew from Gentile—"there is no Jew or Greek." The other parts of the creed—"there is no slave or free,"

---

2. Heinrich Weinel, *Paulus. Der Mensch und Sein Werk* (Tübingen: J. C. B. Mohr [Paul Siebeck], 1904), 212–15.

3. Larry Hurtado, *Lord Jesus Christ: Devotion to Jesus in Earliest Christianity* (Grand Rapids, MI: Eerdmans, 2003).

4. Everett Ferguson, *Baptism in the Early Church: History, Theology, and Liturgy in the First Five Centuries* (Grand Rapids, MI: Eerdmans, 2009), 147–48.

5. Elisabeth Schuessler Fiorenza, *In Memory of Her: A Feminist Theological Introduction* (New York: Crossroad, 1983).

"no male and female"—are irrelevant to the argument and scarcely register. But if you pause long enough to examine Galatians 3:28 carefully, you quickly see its formulaic qualities. You might even guess that it was a creed of some sort. In the first chapter, I will do a methodical close reading of the text to unearth the whole creed from its textual surroundings. The point is, this creed is part of a hidden history, but not just of women and gender. Here was another take on slavery quite radical for its day. And "there is no Jew or Greek" was perhaps the most challenging claim of the three.

As I began to think about this creed more and more over the years, it gradually occurred to me that if it was actually a pre-Pauline formula, then it would belong to the earliest attempts to capture in words the meaning of the Jesus movement. There are no Christian writings older than Paul's letters. Therefore, anything embedded in these letters could lay claim to the title of "first." Was this the first Christian creed? Arguably, yes. What does Christianity have to say about race, class, and gender? *Everything*, apparently, at least originally. Before Revelation made Christianity a set of arcane apocalyptic predictions; before the gospels told the story of Jesus as God's persecuted righteous Son; before Paul could argue that human beings are justified by faith, not by works of the Law—before any of that, there was first this elegant credo and the utopian vision it contained. It says nothing about theology proper. It asks one to believe nothing about God or the nature of Jesus Christ, nothing about miraculous births or saving deaths, nothing about eternal salvation. It says everything, though, about identity. We human beings are naturally clannish and partisan: we are defined by who we are not. *We* are not *them*. This creed claims that there is no us, no them. We are all one. We are all children of God.

In Christ Jesus. Ah, the caveat! Daniel Boyarin, the last scholar to explore this creed in great depth, would be eager, and right, to point this out.[6] Boyarin, an Orthodox Jew, urged caution before we all go running off down the road to the utopia where all are one. "There is no Jew or Greek" *in Christ Jesus* just means that there is no longer Jew. Unity under the banner of Christ may sound good to everyone already under the banner of Christ, but to those who are not and do not wish to be, "we are all one in Christ Jesus" sounds more totalitarian than utopian. Quite so. Boyarin was concerned mostly about Paul, who wrote these words into his Epistle to the Galatians, and about the long-term impact Paul turned out to have on Western civilization, especially for Jews. But again, Paul did not compose the creed. He

---

6. Daniel Boyarin, *A Radical Jew: Paul and the Politics of Identity* (Berkeley: University of California Press, 1994).

borrowed it, and in so doing, he changed it, adapted it. For Paul, indeed, it was all about being "in Christ Jesus." But those words are part of Paul's adaptation of the creed, not the creed itself. On the face of it, that must surely sound like special pleading. Believe it or not, though, there are very sound critical arguments for saying this, which I will lay out, anon, in chapter 1. But even without these scholarly gymnastics, one can see that the creed was not originally about cultural obliteration. "There is no Jew or Greek" stands alongside "no slave or free" and "no male and female." These are not distinctions of religion and culture, but of power and privilege. In the world of Greek and Roman antiquity, free men had power and agency, slaves and women did not. As we shall learn, the creed was originally built on an ancient cliché that went something like this: I thank God every day that I was born a native, not a foreigner; free and not a slave; a man and not a woman. The creed was originally about the fact that race, class, and gender are typically used to divide the human race into us and them to the advantage of *us*. It aimed to declare that there is no us, no them. We are all children of God. It was about solidarity, not cultural obliteration.

I live my life on a college campus, where a claim like this is really not so remarkable. In fact, it is a place so comfortable and proud of its ideals of inclusion and acceptance that we have already pressed on into increasingly finely tuned postmodern explorations of the limitations of oneness and solidarity. In that sense, what I am about to lay out in the chapters to follow may seem just a tad quaint to those on the leading edge of this conversation. I am putting the finishing touches on this manuscript, though, in the aftermath of a historic American presidential election in which the newly elected president rode into office by telling white, middle-class Americans who their enemies really are: foreigners, who are taking their jobs; the poor, who are soaking up their tax dollars on the public dole; and women, who do not know their proper place. This message found a special resonance with Christians, most of whom voted for him: 58 percent of Protestants, 60 percent of (white) Catholics, 61 percent of Mormons, and 81 percent of (white) evangelicals. White evangelicals made up more than 25 percent of the American electorate in 2016.[7] Without their record turnout and overwhelming support, Donald J. Trump would not have been elected president of the United States. Suddenly, we find ourselves living in a white Christian nation, in which race, class, and gender do matter after all. Difference does matter. There *is* an "us" and a "them." How far we will go down this road to

---

7. The data and figures come from the Pew Research Center, "How the Faithful Voted," last modified on November 9, 2016, http://www.pewresearch.org/fact-tank/2016/11/09/how-the-faithful-voted-a-preliminary-2016-analysis/.

fascism is, for now, anyone's guess. Are we fools now to fear the worst, or will we become fools to our descendants because we did not worry more?

Whatever the future holds for our little world, with its big fish like Trump, it is time now more than ever to tell the story of this forgotten first creed. History reminds us again and again that it has always been easier to believe in miracles, in virgin births and atoning deaths, in resurrected bodies and heavenly journeys home, than something so simple and basic as human solidarity. Here, then, is an episode of our history from a time long past, when foreigners were slaughtered, captives sold as slaves, and women kept in their place, when a few imaginative, inspired people dared to declare solidarity between natives and foreigners, free born and slaves, men and women, through a ceremony and a creed. This is the story of that first, unbelievable creed.

CHAPTER 1

⚬◡⚬

Christianity's Forgotten First Creed

Sometime in the middle of the first century, somewhere in the lands lying along the northern coast of the Mediterranean Sea, Paul of Tarsus went looking for his scribe. Paul—the Apostle Paul—was about to write an angry, aggressive, snarky missive that would eventually land in, of all places, the Bible. Had he known that he was writing scripture, that his words would one day be parsed as the Word of God—indeed, that his words would someday be read by anyone other than the unsuspecting readers who were to be this explosive letter's first recipients—perhaps he would have softened his tone. But he didn't. Instead, he loaded up and let them have it with both barrels. Much of it is pretty hard to read, but not all of it. Some of the things Paul thought to put in this letter were, in fact, beautiful. And so it is that one of the real gems from the earliest days of nascent Christianity came to be nestled in one of the angriest pieces of literature from the ancient world. We know this letter today as Paul's Epistle to the Galatians. Among its sharp rhetorical jabs, its dripping sarcasm, and thinly veiled threats there is, alas, an ancient creed, a beautiful thought, an idea that might have changed much of human history, had it not been ignored and forgotten by the generations that came after Paul and learned to revere him, in spite of his thorny personality. So how is it that we still have this lost and forgotten creed—possibly the oldest in the history of Christianity?

THE BACKSTORY

The Apostle Paul, of course, was a follower of Jesus. Originally, though, he was not. When Paul first heard about the Jesus movement, he did not like it. He had not known Jesus personally, though they might have been roughly the same age. Jesus was not a well-known public figure in his own lifetime. His reputation and fame would spread only many years later. So Paul missed out on hearing or meeting Jesus for himself. Whether or not that would have made a difference, we cannot know. But when Paul encountered the followers of Jesus, his reaction must have been severe. In this letter, Galatians, he himself says that back then he "persecuted the church of God and violently and tried to destroy it" (Gal 1:13). He does not say why he was so opposed to it—and all speculation about why is mere guesswork. He says only that one day all that changed. And we are just as in the dark about how and why this happened too. Paul himself says only— quite mysteriously—one day God chose "to reveal his son in me" (Gal 1:16). Many years later, the author of the biblical book of Acts would use his imagination to create one of the most iconic scenes in biblical history. Paul—in this story referred to by his Jewish name, "Saul"—was bound for the city of Damascus, "breathing threats and murder against the disciples of the Lord," and armed with letters to arrest any followers of "the Way" he might find there. Acts relates what happens next:

> Suddenly a light from heaven flashed around him and he fell to the ground and heard a voice saying to him, "Saul, Saul, why do you persecute me?" And he said, "Who are you, Lord?" And he said, "I am Jesus, whom you are persecuting. Get up and go into the city and you will be told what to do." Those traveling with him stood speechless, for they heard the voice but saw no one. Saul got up from the ground. When he opened his eyes he could see nothing, so they took him by the hand and brought him to Damascus. And for three days he was blind, and ate and drank nothing.
>
> Acts 9:3–9

In Acts' colorful account, a disciple named Ananias is directed in a vision to go to Saul, lay hands upon him, and restore his sight. And so, Acts says, the "scales fell from his eyes," and Saul—Paul—was baptized.

Paul's own account of this event is much the sparer. He says only that God "chose to reveal his son in me, *that I might preach about him among the Gentiles*" (Gal 1:16). And that, it turns out, was really the passion awakened in Paul that day. Today Paul is known for declaring to sinners the world over that they are justified by their faith. But Paul was not really so concerned with saving sinners, in his day or ours. This is not what drew him finally to the Jesus movement. He was interested in *Gentiles*—non-Jews.[1] Paul, a Jew, became convinced that Jesus was the long-awaited Jewish messiah. If this was so, he reasoned, Gentiles too ought to be told. Others in the Jesus movement were also interested in evangelizing Gentiles. Most of them assumed, however, that followers of the Jewish messiah would of course need to be observant Jews and follow the laws and customs laid out in the Torah. But Paul hatched a more novel idea: that Gentiles could be included even if they did not wish to observe the Jewish Law. Paul suspected that if Gentiles were required to be Law observant, they just would not participate. The problem was not the several holidays, the dietary rules, or the Ten Commandments. Thou shalt not steal, after all, is only common-sense morality. The problem was the practice of circumcision. The Jewish Law required that all Jewish males—and male converts to Judaism—be circumcised. Genital mutilation is no small thing. So Gentiles wishing to associate with Jews usually chose to do so informally, without being circumcised. Jews referred to these Jewish sympathizers respectfully with the Greek term *theoseboi*—"God-fearers"—but they were not really Jews. Most of the first followers of Jesus also took this view: Gentiles who wished to be included fully in all the promises associated with following the Jewish messiah would need to be circumcised. But Paul disagreed. He believed that in the messianic age dawning, Gentiles should rightly follow the messiah *as Gentiles*,[2] without circumcising their genitals. And that is why he was writing the letter that would one day become the biblical Epistle to the Galatians.

"The Galatians" were actually a small cluster of "churches" that Paul had founded in south central Anatolia (modern Turkey). These were not churches in the modern sense, but small communities devoted to following Jesus, as interpreted to them by Paul, their founding father, so to speak. They are, in fact, something of a mystery to scholars. We do not really know where they were, how many there were, or when Paul organized them. At

1. That Paul was interested primarily in the question of Gentiles and their inclusion in his communities is the insight of Krister Stendahl. His book, *Paul Among Jews and Gentiles* (Philadelphia: Fortress Press, 1976), sparked something of a revolution in the way scholars now see Paul, a perspective sometimes referred to as "the New Paul." An excellent recent and thorough discussion of this new perspective on Paul is Pamela Eisenbaum's book, *Paul Was Not a Christian* (San Francisco: HarperOne, 2009). A more recent take on what it would mean for Paul to advocate for Gentiles in the Epistle to the Galatians is offered by Brigitte Kahl in *Galatians Re-Imagined: Reading with the Eyes of the Vanquished*, Paul in Critical Contexts (Minneapolis: Fortress Press, 2010). I will discuss all of this further in chapter 4.

2. See esp. Eisenbaum, *Paul Was Not a Christian*, 254–55.

this point it would be customary to insert a long discussion about the "north Galatian hypothesis" and the "south Galatian hypothesis," the two competing theories about the location of these churches.[3] In fact, it might be more important to note simply that they were "Galatian" churches; that is, they were made up of Gauls. Gauls were Gentiles, true, but they were also *Gauls*, in many ways the quintessential barbarians where Romans were concerned. They were an enemy race, once feared, but now subdued. Their homeland was far to the west, in what is now France. But in Paul's day Gauls lived in scattered enclaves across the Roman Empire—the Galatian diaspora, we might say. Jews too were a conquered people living in diasporic communities throughout the empire. So for Paul, a Jew, to reach out to Gauls in solidarity would have meant something more than simply bridging the religious divide separating Jews from Gentiles.[4] Paul was an apostle of a new empire, the Kingdom of God once proclaimed by Jesus of Nazareth, and he believed this new empire would arrive soon and replace the empire that had reduced these Gauls to foreigners living in a foreign land. Paul, it seems, was all in on a project that was deeply subversive and far more risky than it might first appear. So how did he come to the Gauls of Anatolia in the first place?

Paul's change of heart about the Jesus movement took place somewhere in the eastern Roman Empire. Acts locates the event on the "road to Damascus"—and Damascus may indeed have been one of Paul's early home bases.[5] But this is unimportant. What is important, and remarkable, is that the Apostle Paul spent the better part of fifteen years preaching in the Roman East with very little success. There are no known churches on the Pauline model from Arabia, Damascus, or Syria and Cilicia—all the places Paul names from those early years.[6] There must have been something quite challenging and worrisome about Paul's interpretation of the Jesus movement. In fact, he seems to have been out of sync even with the rest of the movement, especially its leadership in Jerusalem. His conflict

---

3. Those with an interest in such matters might consult one or two commentaries on Galatians, such as Hans Dieter Betz's *Galatians: A Commentary on Paul's Letter to the Churches in Galatia*, Hermeneia (Philadelphia: Fortress Press, 1979), esp. 3–5, or J. Louis Martyn's *Galatians: A New Translation with Introduction and Commentary*, Anchor Bible 33A (New York: Doubleday, 1997), 15–17.

4. This insight comes from Kahl, *Galatians Re-Imagined*, and Davina Lopez, *Apostle to the Conquered: Reimagining Paul's Mission*, Paul in Critical Contexts (Minneapolis: Fortress Press, 2008).

5. See Gal 1:17.

6. See Gal 1:17, 21.

with Jerusalem came to a head in Antioch,[7] a coastal city a few hundred miles to the southeast of the Galatian communities—modern-day Antakya in southeastern Turkey. Paul had argued in Antioch that Jews and Gentiles could have common meals together without strict observance of the Jewish Law. Apparently, his argument initially prevailed and the experiment of mixed Jewish–Gentile table fellowship worked for a while. But soon leaders of the Jesus movement in Jerusalem got wind of it and sent word that the practice had to be stopped. Paul calls the delegation that brings this news "the circumcision people" (Gal 2:12), so we may assume that this was their issue. Jews, they argued, should not eat with Gentiles unless they agreed to be circumcised. Why this was will have to wait for another chapter, for it seems that Jews did not generally eschew eating with the uncircumcised (how would one know, after all). In any event, when the pro-circumcision people arrived, Paul was discredited, his allies abandoned him, and the whole experiment of mixed table fellowship fell apart. In his brief account of this debacle—scholars call it "the Antioch affair"—Paul indulges himself in a moment of *esprit de l'escalier*—as Paula Fredricksen once put it—and delivered one of those "I really told them!" speeches. He says, "In front of everyone I said to Cephas (Peter), 'If you, a Jew, live like a Gentile, how can you insist that Gentiles live like Jews?!'" (Gal 2:14).

The speech Paul actually delivered must not have sounded quite so good, for he ever so discreetly neglects to mention anything about what happened next. Presumably, his side did not prevail and he was sent packing. If so, he likely would have headed off west, where his route would have taken him up into central Anatolia, where he first encountered the Gauls in diaspora. In the letter to the Galatians he says that his first stay among them came about because he had become ill there.[8] So we might speculate that Paul left Antioch, got as far as south central Anatolia, and got sick. As it happens, he was nursed back to health by a community of Galatians, and so he stayed on long enough to establish a handful of "churches" among those strangers who had befriended him. These churches would have been constituted now on Pauline terms: both Jews and Gentiles associating together around common tables, circumcised and uncircumcised together. Paul eventually moved on west, to places more familiar to readers with more than a passing familiarity with the Bible: Ephesus, Philippi, Thessalonika, and Corinth.

7. A thorough discussion of the conflict in Antioch may be found on pp. 129–77 of Magnus Zetterholm's book, *The Formation of Christianity in Antioch* (London and New York: Routledge, 2003).
8. See Gal 4:13.

Paul, however, kept in touch with these Galatian communities. One day—we don't know when exactly—Paul learned that others had come to the Galatians and begun to say that Paul had been wrong. The Gentiles did have to be circumcised after all. For Paul this must have seemed like Antioch all over again. He was furious. Would they too abandon him and his principal claim, that Gentiles could be included without being circumcised? And if they did, what would become of those communities? What would become of the solidarity he had so carefully forged there between Jews and Gauls? Would any of the Gauls even stay connected? Paul seems to have taken this all very personally. So, when he went looking for his scribe to "take a letter," he was primed for a fight.

PAUL'S ARGUMENT

Paul wrote the Epistle to the Galatians to win back these churches to his point of view. His first tack was to go autobiographical. His antagonists had apparently cast aspersions on his story and character, so he goes back to set the record straight (by his own lights, of course).[9] He tells the Galatians how he became a follower and why, and how he acquitted himself by working independently as an evangelist in Arabia and Syria; how he went to Jerusalem, not once, but twice, to parlay with the leaders there; and how he worked out a deal with them—that he would preach to the Gentiles, while Peter preached to the Jews. That long story, told in Galatians 1:11–2:14, is how we know about Paul's early efforts in the East, including the dreadful affair at Antioch. But, of course, Paul had not really won the day at Antioch, so he soon takes a new tack.

Perhaps his scribe, who would have known a little about rhetoric, coached him to go for a biblical illustration. He chose the story of the patriarch Abraham, whom God regarded as a good and just person simply because he had trusted God.[10] As the story is told in Genesis, chapters 12 through 25, God commands the aging, childless, homebody Abraham to pull up stakes and go to a new place, a new land, where God intends to bless him with countless descendants. For Gauls living in diaspora, this must have seemed a fine illustration. In it, Abraham believes God, he *trusts*

9. Most of the moves Paul makes in this letter are actually carefully executed elements in a sophisticated rhetorical model, the details of which are described by Betz in his commentary on Galatians (see note 2, earlier). The first part of the letter is the *narratio*, that is, a telling of the whole story to get the relevant facts on the table.
10. See Gal 3:6–14.

him, and he does as he is told. Because of this trust, this *faith*, God judges Abraham to be a good and just person. If this was true for Abraham, why would it not be true for other pagans, like the Galatians? This, by the way, is the origin of Paul's signal idea of "justification by faith." It was all about including Gentiles without the need for circumcision.

Now, this was not a bad argument, but it did have one little problem—the ending. After the uncircumcised Abraham demonstrates his fidelity to God, God comes up with a ritual to mark their new relationship. The ritual? Circumcision![11] In fact, this is the myth of origins for the Jewish practice of circumcision. Paul never mentions this inconvenient fact, but instead veers off into some fancy exegetical footwork on Abraham and other Old Testament figures, on whether Abraham will have descendants plural or *a* descendant, and on other arcane matters that are difficult to follow, even for the modern biblical scholar.[12]

By now his scribe might have been telling him that he needed an argument that is very practical, very clear, very rooted in the life and experience of the people to whom he was writing. What Paul writes next is the whole point of this long digression into Paul's argument in Galatians. Here is how you would encounter it in the New Revised Standard Version of the Bible:

> [23]Now, before faith came, we were imprisoned and guarded under the Law until faith would be revealed. [24]Therefore, the Law was our disciplinarian until Christ came, so that we might be justified by faith. [25]But now that faith has come, we are no longer subject to a disciplinarian, [26]for in Christ Jesus you are all children of God through faith. [27]As many of you as were baptized into Christ have clothed yourselves with Christ. [28]There is no longer Jew or Greek, there is so longer slave or free, there is no longer male and female; for all of you are one in Christ Jesus.
>
> Gal 3:23–28

THE CREED

"There is no longer Jew or Greek." "All of you are one in Christ Jesus." Nice. It is to the point. It works. It may be Paul's finest moment in the letter. But now allow your gaze to travel back over these words for a second look. Is there not more here than is needed? In verse 28 there is no longer Jew

---

11. See Gen 7.
12. See Gal 3:10–22.

or Greek—yes—but Paul adds to this two other, nearly identical statements: "there is no longer slave or free" and "there is no longer male and
female." Nothing in the letter necessitates these added clauses. The issue
at hand is not slavery or gender roles, but the equal standing of Jew and
Greek. There are three statements where only one is needed. And why are
the superfluous words in verse 28 so neatly arranged, in parallel, almost
rhythmic clauses? And, if one looks closely, it is clear that these are not
the only parallel clauses in these verses. This is even clearer in the original
Greek of the passage: verses 26 and 28d are also worded just alike. "*For you
are all* children of God . . ." // "*For you are all* one . . . ," and then, in each, "*in
Christ Jesus.*" If one looks at this passage long enough, it behaves like an
autostereogram—one of those computer-generated pictures that looks like
random designs until suddenly it resolves into a three-dimensional horse
or castle or space ship. Galatians 3:26–28 is not simply a prose argument, a
paragraph. Here it is once again, this time laid out to highlight the remarkable formulaic quality of these verses more clearly:

[26]*For you are all* children ("sons"[13]) of God through faith *in Christ Jesus.*

[27]As many of you who have been baptized into Christ

have been clothed in Christ:

[28a]*There is no longer* Jew *or* Greek,

[28b]*There is no longer* slave *or* free,

[28c]*There is no longer* male and female.

[28d]*For you are all* one *in Christ Jesus.*

Obviously, this is no ordinary speech. Sometimes people talk like this,
but usually this sort of thing is the product of deeper thought and pla-
nning. The parallelism in verse 28 is almost perfect. No longer a or b. No
longer c or d. No longer e and f. And the binary sets are well selected.
Jew or Greek—there's ethnicity. Slave or free—that's class. Male and
female—there's gender. Race, class, gender—that is a compact, but fairly
complete list of the ways by which human beings divide themselves one
from another. Someone thought about that for a long time. And here is a
little detail easily overlooked: it goes Jew or Greek, slave or free, but male
and female. And, by the way, it's *male* and *female*, not *man* and *woman*.

---

13. The word in Greek is *huioi*, literally "sons." I will use the word "children" in my
discussion of it because when Paul uses it we can usually tell from the context that
he is applying it to both men and women. Indeed, this text in particular advocates a
departure from the androcentric perspective that made the male word "sons" seem
perfectly normal, even when applied to women. When the discussion requires more
nuance, I will use "son/sons" to translate the word, but otherwise I will use "children."

This precise wording was not randomly selected. As many have noticed, it repeats exactly a version of Genesis 1:27 that literate, Greek-speaking Jews of the Mediterranean world might have known quite well. In the account of creation found in the common Greek version of Genesis, when God makes the first human being, it says, "He made him in his own image, *male and female* he made them" (Gen 1:27). When the third binary set slips into a slightly different form, it is for a reason: to capture that specific reference to Genesis.[14] That is all very well thought out. So Galatians 3:28 is a deeply thoughtful, carefully worded, formulaic collection of sentences. It has all the makings of a creedal formula. Indeed, virtually every scholar of this material agrees that this is exactly what it is: an early Christian creed. But a creedal formula has to have an occasion, a time when people would have repeated it. That brings us to verse 27.

Galatians 3:27 is about baptism. This is not a particularly attention-grabbing detail, for most people assume that early followers of Jesus were baptized. Why shouldn't Paul mention it? But students of Galatians usually note that this particular reference to baptism seems to come from out of the blue. The letter does not otherwise discuss or even mention baptism. The matter that separates Paul from his opponents in Galatia is the question of circumcision, not baptism. Must Gentiles be circumcised? What does baptism have to do with this? Nothing. We nowhere learn that Paul's antagonists in Galatia have another view of baptism that he felt he must correct or dispute. Nor does Paul here or anywhere else argue that baptism could replace circumcision, as a few scholars have assumed must have been the case.[15] The argument in Galatians simply is not about baptism. So why bring it up? Paul brings up baptism in 3:27 because Galatians 3:26–28 formed the heart of a *baptismal* creed. The great scholar of Galatians, Hans Dieter Betz, avers that Paul probably took these verses from an early Christian baptismal liturgy.[16] In the argument about whether Gentiles ought to be circumcised, Paul apparently wanted his readers to remember these particular words from a baptismal liturgy with which they may have been familiar: "there is no longer Jew or Greek." The other clauses—"no

14. This detail, often noted, was pointed out by Krister Stendahl in 1966 in *The Bible and the Role of Women: A Case Study in Hermeneutics* (Philadelphia: Fortress, 1966), 32.

15. E.g., Rudolf Schnackenburg, *Baptism in the Thought of St. Paul* (Oxford: Blackwell, 1964), 70–71. The idea that baptism could be a kind of circumcision "not made with hands" is found in Col 2:11–13. But Colossians is a later, pseudonymously written text, not from Paul's own hand.

16. Betz, *Galatians*, 184; the idea goes back at least to the 1940s: see, e.g., Franz Leenhardt, *La place de la femme dans l'église d'après le Nouveau Testament*, Études théologiques et religieuses 23/1 (Montpelier: La Faculté Libre de Théologie Protestante, 1948), 31.

longer slave or free" and "no longer male and female"—simply came along for the ride.

WHERE DID IT COME FROM?

So where did Paul get this creed?[17] Could he have created this formula himself to use when he baptized new followers of Jesus? Possibly. But this is not very likely. "No longer Jew or Greek" went to the heart of Paul's efforts, but not so much "slave or free" and "male and female." Not to mislead, Paul was not the slave-oppressing, woman-bashing misogynist he is often assumed to be. This view of Paul comes largely from New Testament texts that are attributed to Paul, but which he did not actually write. So, for example, Paul seems to say in 1 Timothy: "Let all who are under the yoke of slavery look upon their masters as worthy of all honor, so that the name of God and the teaching might not be blasphemed" (1 Tim 6:1). This is pretty clear: slaves should remain docile and obedient to their masters. But that is not actually Paul. 1 Timothy was written fifty to a hundred years after Paul's death by someone wishing to appropriate Paul's authority for his own views. The author of 1 Timothy is just as discouraging when it comes to women:

> Let a woman learn in silence and all submission. I will permit no woman to teach or to exercise authority over men; she must keep silent. . . . Woman shall be saved through bearing children, provided she continues in faith and love and holiness with modesty.
>
> 1 Tim 2:11–15

These words are not Paul's. Nor are the similar statements found in Colossians, Ephesians, and Titus.[18] These epistles are all forgeries committed in the name of Paul after the apostle was long dead and gone.[19] In the

---

17. Students of the passage have answered the question variously; for a survey see Dennis R. MacDonald, *There Is No Male and Female: The Fate of a Dominical Saying in Paul and Gnosticism*, Harvard Dissertations in Religion 20 (Philadelphia: Fortress Press, 1987), 9–14.

18. See Col 3:18, Eph 5:22–33, and Titus 2:4–5.

19. The theory that 1 Tim, 2 Tim, and Titus, as well as Col, Eph, and 2 Thess, were written under Paul's name by someone else, writing some years after Paul's death, is widely held by critical scholars of the New Testament. A recent and thorough explanation of the theory is in Bart Ehrman's popular book, *Forged* (San Francisco: HarperOne, 2011); a more technical version of this same argument is in his *Forgery and Counterforgery: The Use of Literary Deceit in Early Christian Polemics* (Oxford and New York: Oxford University Press, 2012). Ehrman argues that "forgery" is the proper term for these books. Since the nineteenth century, scholars have called them "pseudepigraphical,"

late first and early second centuries, Paul's star was rising and many people tried to appropriate his voice to bolster their own views. Some even took to editing Paul's original letters to include such ideas. One very famous example is 1 Corinthians 14:33b–36:

> As in all the churches of the Saints, the women should keep silence in the churches. For they are not permitted to speak, but should be subordinate, even as the Law says. If there is anything they wish to know, let them ask their husbands at home. For it is shameful for a woman to speak in church. What! Did the Word of God begin with you, or are you the only people it has reached?

Most scholars agree that these words were added to 1 Corinthians at about the same time 1 Timothy was composed.[20] All of this has served to ruin Paul for many reasonable, thinking people today. But of course, for most of Christian history, these forgers made Paul very useful to those who would shepherd the church into the patriarchal form it finally took, and still takes for most of the world even today. Even the liberal Pope Francis will not be ordaining any women to the priesthood.

Paul himself did not take this view. Women not only spoke in the churches he frequented but also were leaders in them. Phoebe, the subject of Romans 16, was likely the head of the church at Cenchreae. Paul calls her the patron (*prostatis*) of many, and his own patron.[21] In the same letter he greets a certain Junia, "my kinswoman and fellow prisoner," whom he describes as "prominent among the apostles" (Rom 16:7). In Philippians he asks Euodia and Syntyche (both women) to come to some agreement. These women, whom Paul calls his "fellow workers" (Phil 4:2), must have been among the leaders of that church, which, according to Acts, was first hosted by a woman named Lydia.[22] Their disagreement is apparently causing a rift

a benign term for the same thing. This will be discussed further in chapters 6 and 7, where it will be very important to distinguish Paul's views from the later forgers'.

20. The theory that 1 Cor 14:33b–36 is a late interpolation into Paul's original letter goes back to the German scholar Wilhelm Bousset, "Der erste Brief an die Korinther," *Die Schriften des neuen Testaments* (Göttingen: Vandenhoeck & Ruprecht, 1908), 141–42. It was widely held at one time, but now may be more disputed. Some scholars have cried foul, saying that this is simply a liberal attempt to cleanse Paul from a view distasteful to many moderns. Others have argued that Paul wrote these words but meant them ironically, adding "What! Did the word of God originate with you?" in verse 36. For a discussion of the alternatives and their relative merits, see Antoinette Clark Wire, *The Corinthian Women Prophets: A Reconstruction Through Paul's Rhetoric* (Minneapolis: Fortress Press, 1990), 229–32.

21. Rom 16:2.

22. See Acts 16:11–15.

in the community. In 1 Corinthians, Paul reprimands certain women for praying and prophesying with hair unbound—and yet, they are still to pray and prophesy, *not* to keep silent.[23] For this reason critical scholars have revised their view, not only of Paul, but also of the role of women in that first generation of nascent Christianity, generally speaking—a topic about which we will have much more to say later.[24] For now, it is enough to know that Paul did not hate women.

Yet, his views did not extend quite as far as "there is no longer male and female." A hint that Paul had his limits in this arena appears in 1 Corinthians, chapter 11—the place where Paul speaks of women praying and prophesying, but does not silence them. As it turns out, though, this part of 1 Corinthians is not just about women. In it Paul addresses both women *and men* who pray and prophesy in Corinth. In another chapter we'll have time to explore this curious passage in greater depth.[25] For now, it is important only to know that Paul's problem with the Corinthian prophets was that when they prayed and prophesied, their appearance blurred the gender distinctions between the male and female participants. They were engaged in liturgical gender-bending, so to speak, apparently enacting precisely the principle that in Christ "there is no male and female."[26] This crossed a line for Paul. "In the Lord," he admits, "woman is not different from man, nor is man different from woman" (1 Cor 11:11). But that does not mean, he says, that men and women should not look like men and women. Finally he just says, no one else is doing this, so don't argue with me.[27]

What about "no longer slave or free"? How comfortable was Paul with this sentiment? Again, Paul's views on slavery were not those expressed in Colossians, Ephesians, 1 Timothy, and Titus, where slavery is endorsed and slaves are commanded to obey their masters.[28] None of these letters was

23. See 1 Cor 11:2–16.

24. See esp. Elisabeth Schuessler Fiorenza's classic work, *In Memory of Her: A Feminist Theological Reconstruction of Christian Origins* (New York: Crossroad, 1988), or a very fine collection of essays on the topic edited by Ross Shephard Kraemer and Mary Rose D'Angelo, *Women and Christian Origins* (Oxford and New York: Oxford University Press, 1999). I will treat this subject more thoroughly in chapter 6.

25. I will also discuss the liturgical gender benders in 1 Cor 11:2–16 in more detail in chapter 6. For now, consult an essay by Jerome Murphy O'Connor to see why the issue is not really why women should veil themselves, but why women and men should wear their hair in a way that was conventional for the time: "Sex and Logic in 1 Cor. 11:2–16," *Catholic Biblical Quarterly* 42 (1980): 482–500.

26. For the view that the prophets were engaged in an exercise that illustrated the principle "no male and female," see Wayne Meeks, "The Image of the Androgyne: Some Uses of a Symbol in Earliest Christianity," *History of Religions* 13 (1973–74): 165–208.

27. See 1 Cor 11:16.

28. See Col 3:22–25, Eph 6:5–8, 1 Tim 6:1, and Titus 2:9–10.

written by Paul. Forgers created them generations later to muster Paul's authority for their own views. Paul's views on slavery are not so clear. In a later chapter we will delve into this matter more thoroughly, but for now it is enough to point out that when Paul writes about slaves and slavery, he is decidedly guarded.

Consider the matter of Onesimus, the slave who is the subject of Paul's very short letter to Philemon. Philemon owned Onesimus, who had (perhaps) run away. At some point he met up with Paul and they became friends. This was awkward, because Paul knew Philemon, a member of one of his churches. So Paul wrote a letter to Philemon about what to do about Onesimus. One would expect Paul to tell Philemon that he should free Onesimus, for in Christ "there is no longer slave or free." But he does not. Or does he? What he asks is that Philemon take him back "no longer as a slave, but more than a slave, a beloved brother" (Philm 16). Does this mean that he wants Philemon to free Onesimus, or just to treat him better? Paul's intentions in Philemon are simply not clear. Recently, scholars have even pointed out that at one point in the letter Paul seems to imply that he wants Philemon to give Onesimus to him, so that Onesimus can serve Paul on behalf of Philemon.[29] Does Paul want Onesimus as his own slave? However we might understand this, Paul does in fact send Onesimus back to his owner, Philemon, preferring to risk the welfare of Onesimus to risking his friendship with Philemon. Paul is kind and magnanimous, but certainly not revolutionary.[30]

The point is not that Paul had no backbone when it came to equality for women and slaves. From our place in the twenty-first-century Western world, where slavery and gender bias are both condemned, criticizing Paul on this score would be pointless easy virtue. But here is the historical point: *if Paul had set out to create a baptismal creed, he probably would not have composed the one we find in Galatians 3:26–28.* He was passionate about "no longer Jew or Greek" and went to the mat for this principle whenever it was challenged. But he was not really passionate about "no longer slave or free" and "no longer male and female." These are ideas about baptism that he inherited from the Jesus movement and he embraced them as

---

29. See Philm 11–14.

30. I will discuss the issue of Onesimus's status and Paul's intentions more in chapter 5. A summary of current views on Onesimus's status may be found in Caroline's Osiek's commentary on *Philippians and Philemon*, Abingdon New Testament Commentaries (Nashville: Abingdon Press, 2000), 126–31, and Demetrius Williams, "'No Longer a Slave': Reading the Interpretation History of Paul's Epistle to Philemon," in *Onesimus Our Brother: Reading Religion, Race, and Culture in Philemon*, ed. Matthew Johnson et al. (Minneapolis: Fortress Press, 2012), 11–46.

others did, to an extent. But they did not drive him like the issue of Jew and Gentile did.

So Paul did not create the baptismal creed embedded in Galatians 3:26–28. The creed, then, must have preceded Paul. But there is not very much in the New Testament that precedes Paul. His voice is the first voice we hear from the nascent Christian movement. *That makes Galatians 3:26–28 one of the oldest statements of faith in all of the New Testament, perhaps even the first such statement in all of Christian history.*

If truth be told, that claim might attract criticism from specialists. A more typical claim would be that 1 Corinthians 15:3–7 is the earliest Christian creed,[31] or perhaps Romans 4:25.[32] Fair enough. These formulas are also pre-Pauline and very early. But if you go now and read them, you will not be very surprised. These are statements about Jesus's death and resurrection, or about the vicarious nature of his suffering and death. No one needs to be reminded of the importance of these concepts for the history of Christianity. But the existence of the baptismal creed we are about to explore usually comes as a surprise to most people. It sounds so contemporary. It is surprising to learn that people have been thinking about race, class, and gender for a very long time, and the followers of Jesus in fact were trying to undermine these pernicious gauges of human worth right from the beginning. The first followers of Jesus were taking on race, class, and gender. A surprise like that is worth exploring.

THE ORIGINAL CREDO

If Paul did not create this creed, but simply used it in his Epistle to the Galatians, are we looking at the original form of the creed in Galatians 3:26–28? Are these the words that people actually repeated in the ritual of baptism, or has Paul given us a loose adaptation of the creed? It is certainly possible that this iteration of it is an exact rendition of the original as Paul learned it. After all, ancients did place a good deal of value on repeating their prayers and incantations with great precision. We would expect accuracy in an actual situation of worship or sacred ceremony. But this is not that. Paul often makes use of older formulas, hymns, and other pieces of

---

31. See Hans Conzelmann, *1 Corinthians: A Commentary on the First Epistle to the Corinthians*, Hermeneia, trans. James W. Leitch (Philadelphia: Fortress, 1975), 251–54, esp. the literature cited in note 54.

32. So, e.g., Ernst Käsemann, *Commentary on Romans*, trans. Geoffrey W. Bromiley (Grand Rapids, MI: Eerdmans, 1980), 128.

tradition in his letters, and when he does, he seldom fails to leave behind his own distinctive fingerprints. Are there any clues, then, indications that what we see in Galatians 3:26–28 is the result of Paul's creative adaptation of an older, creedal formula?

I will begin by looking once again at the sentences Paul wrote. This time, however, instead of a standard translation from an English Bible, I will render them as closely as possible to the original Greek, so that the clues will be a little more obvious. Here is Galatians 3:26–28 once again, this time rendered very literally:

> [26]For you are all sons of God through faith in Christ Jesus.
> [27]For as many of you as were baptized into Christ have put on Christ.
> [28a]There is no Jew or Greek,
> there is no slave or free,
> there is no male and female;
> [28b]For you are all one in Christ Jesus.

Let us begin with the three dyadic statements in verse 28a. They form the heart and soul of the creed. They are very formulaic and repetitive, as we have noted. They are a set. But we have also seen that Paul probably would not have composed the entire set. His interest is in the first dyad, not the other two. He is passionate about overcoming the Jew/Greek distinction, but less so when it comes to the slave/free and male/female distinctions. He embraces these ideas, but probably would not have come up with all three of them on his own. Here, then, is the solid core of the original creed. It consisted of these three dyads: no Jew or Greek; no slave or free; no male and female.

Notice, however, that in this literal translation they look a little different from how they appear in the New Revised Standard Version, or most other translations. There we read, "There is *no longer* Jew or Greek, *no longer* slave or free, *no longer* male and female." Why *no longer*? It has to do with the way Paul introduces the creed in the context of Galatians. Recall, Paul was arguing that Jews once lived under the Law, as a kind of guardian, but now *no longer*.[33] Paul literally says "we are *no longer* [*ouketi* in Greek] under a guardian." Because Paul introduces the creed to further this point, most translators go on and translate the creed as though it says the same thing—there is *no longer* Jew or Greek, and so forth. But the creed does not actually say this. It says "there is no [in Greek: *ouk eni*] Jew or Greek,"

33. See Gal 3:23–25.

and so forth. The difference may seem slight, but it is important. The little phrase *ouk eni* (actually short for *ouk enesti*) means "there does not exist." It implies, in fact, that whatever it is referring to cannot exist—it is simply impossible.[34] Paul believes that because Christ has come, these distinctions *no longer* exist. But the creed claimed that these distinctions simply *do not* exist. Did not, do not, will not. Baptism did not make this true; baptism, in this tradition, simply signified that it is true. There is no Jew or Greek, slave or free, male and female. These are false distinctions that have no basis in reality. That is what the original credo claimed.

So here was the heart of the original creed. There is no Jew or Greek, no slave or free, no male and female. Even though human beings very typically make distinctions based on race, class, and gender, they in fact do not rest on anything real. Gender is a construct; class is a conceit; race is not real.

What about the rest of verses 26–28? Do they too belong to the creed, or has Paul added them to adapt the creed to his context?

VERSE 27, ORIGINAL OR ADDED?

The first thing that stands out is verse 27, the second line: "For as many of you as were baptized into Christ have put on Christ." The first line (verse 26) and the last (verse 28b) are almost exactly the same—in Greek they are even closer than they seem in English. And, as we have seen, the three dyadic statements in the middle (verse 28a) are also formulated in a nice repeating pattern. This all seems very formal and creedlike. But verse 27 is different. It stands out by itself, apart from any repeating patterns. So it may not have been part of the original creed. Some think it was, and some think it wasn't. I think it wasn't.

First, verse 27 is a kind of explanation. It reveals that the creed has to do with baptism—it is through baptism that these distinctions are exposed as false. Now, let us suppose that the creed does have to do with baptism— that it was used, say, in a baptismal ceremony. When they were actually using the creed in that context, would anyone have needed to explain that it had to do with baptism? They were baptizing—while saying the creed. Most people would have caught on. But when it is plucked out of its original setting and used in a letter, then an explanation is needed. None of the other, more formulaic clauses refers to baptism, so Paul tells them: it is

34. *L.S.J.*, s.v. *eneimi.*

in baptism that all are united as one, that all are seen as children ("sons") of God.

Second, the explanatory nature of the verse is also indicated by its syntax; it begins with the word "for"—*gar* in Greek. Greeks used the word *gar* to attach an explanatory sentence or clause. Notice that verse 26 begins with this same word, "for," or *gar*. That is because Paul is using the creed in its entirety to say why Gentile Christ followers can be included by virtue of their faith. That makes our second *gar* in verse 27 stand out all the more. That is just one too many *gars*—an explanation of an explanation. It works, but it is just a little awkward—enough to signal that Paul is adding explanations to the original creed.

A third reason for seeing verse 27 as an addition to the creed is its very different register. The first line, verse 26, says, "You are all children of God. . . ." Notice the tense: present. Notice also to whom the line is spoken: "you . . . all" (you, *plural*). It is as though the speaker is addressing a group of initiates about to be baptized. That is indeed how it was probably used. But verse 27 is different. It speaks not of "all," everyone, but "as many of you as were baptized," as though others are present who were not baptized. Furthermore, it does not use the present tense, but the Greek aorist, or simple past tense. This line, then, speaks to a group of people, some of whom (but not all) had been baptized sometime in the past. In other words, it does not presuppose the original setting of the creed, a baptismal ceremony, but the setting of the letter itself. In this sentence, Paul interrupts the creed to address the Galatians, some of whom would have been baptized sometime in the past.

Finally, the statement that one is baptized "into Christ" has a very distinctive Pauline ring to it. When Paul speaks of the followers of Jesus, he very often uses the phrase "in Christ" to describe them, as in "there is no judgment for those who are *in Christ*" (Rom 8:1). Scholars sometimes refer to this as Paul's "participation" theology, a phrase coined by E. P. Sanders.[35] Paul thought of the followers of Christ as somehow participating in Christ's continuing existence. One way Paul imagined it was to see the community of believers as the new body of Christ, inhabited by Christ's spirit. To be baptized "into Christ" meant being baptized into his "body." Consider how Paul expresses the concept in 1 Corinthians:

> For just as the body is one and has many members, but all the members of the
> body, though they are many, are one body, so it is also with Christ. For in one

---

35. See esp. E. P. Sanders, *Paul and Palestinian Judaism: A Comparison of Patterns of Religion* (Philadelphia: Fortress, 1977), 453–63.

spirit *we all were baptized into one body*—Jews or Greeks, slaves or free—and all were made to drink of the one spirit. . . . But you all are the body of Christ and each of you is a part of it.

1 Cor 12:12–13, 27

Another way he thought about it was to imagine that the life of Christ and the life of the believer had somehow merged and become one. Consider:

For the love of Christ possesses us, for we have decided on this: that one man has died for all; therefore, all have died. And he died for all, so that those who live might live no longer for themselves, but for the one who died for them and was raised. . . . So, *if anyone is in Christ*, he is a new creature.

2 Cor 5:14–15, 17a

In this passage Paul alludes to another interpretation of baptism, which he discusses more fully in Romans 6. There he says, "Don't you know that as many of you as were baptized into Christ Jesus were baptized into his death?" (Rom 6:3). Notice how the first part of this statement is almost exactly the same as Galatians 3:27. This is just how Paul typically talks about being a follower of Jesus—and how he talks about baptism. The Christ followers exist *in Christ*. Therefore, when they are baptized, they are baptized *into Christ*. That is a pretty firm Pauline fingerprint and all of this adds up to a fairly clear picture: verse 27 was not part of the original creed. Paul added it to make the creed work better in the context of the letter.[36]

VERSES 26 AND 28B

What about verses 26 and 28b? Are they original to the creed, or did Paul add them too? Some scholars see them as Paul's way of wedging the creed into the letter; they are transition lines, so to speak, written by Paul.[37] But they really aren't. The words "For you are all sons of God" do not actually connect with anything in the letter prior to 3:26. They do not transition

---

36. Other views of this verse are common. Betz (*Galatians*, 186–87) agrees that the verse is "an explanatory insertion," but thinks Paul was not its author. MacDonald (*No Male and Female*, 8, 9) thinks most of it comes from Paul, but a line referring to "putting on Christ" might have been in the original creed.

37. See, e.g., MacDonald, *No Male and Female*, 7–8.

from anything. After the creed, Paul does turn briefly to the idea that all who follow Jesus are "sons" of God. But verse 28b does not really lead into this discussion. If that had been Paul's intention, he probably would have repeated the words "for you are all sons of God." But instead he writes, "for you are all one." And that theme—unity—does not come up at all in the rest of the letter. So, verse 28b does not transition *to* anything. Verses 26 and 28b are not transition lines penned by Paul to fit the creed to its context. They are part of the creed itself. That is why they are identical in structure: "For you are all ____." In verse 26 the baptized are all children ("sons") of God; in verse 28b they are all "one." These are simply two different ways of stating the creed's central claim: they are all united in solidarity with one another. Verses 26 and 28b were originally the opening and closing lines of the creed, composed carefully to mirror one another in structure and content.

But are they completely free of Paul's editorial activity? Probably not. Notice how the opening line goes "For you are all sons of God *through faith* in Christ Jesus." Now look at the last line: "For you are all one in Christ Jesus." The words "through faith" are missing; they are not paralleled in the otherwise repeating line. Were these words, then, also part of the original creed? Did the first statement say that unity comes *through faith* in Christ Jesus, and the last that unity comes (simply) in Christ Jesus? No. To most students of the letter, the words "through faith" appear to bear Paul's strong imprint. Paul's major theme and the focus of his life was working out how Gentiles could become part of the Jesus movement without needing to follow the Jewish Law. His solution, often repeated in his letters, is that they can be seen as "just" in the eyes of God by dint of their faith. This is Paul's famous doctrine of justification by faith. So this is just the sort of adaptation Paul would have made to this creed, especially in the letter to the Galatians, where the theme is exactly that: how Gentiles are justified before God *through faith*.

There is one other likely modification to the creed that came from Paul's hand when he wrote it into the Galatian letter. It is a little harder to spot, however, because both the first and the last lines have it: "in Christ Jesus." But perhaps this phrase does sound a little odd. Isn't it supposed to be "Jesus Christ," not "Christ Jesus?" "Jesus Christ" is the expression Christians normally use in their creeds, because it is an extremely common phrase in the New Testament. But one of Paul's distinctive speech patterns is to reverse the order of Jesus Christ to yield "Christ Jesus." Outside of the letters attributed to Paul it is very rare. The gospels, Matthew, Mark, Luke, and John, never use it. It may appear one or two times in Acts in stories about Paul, but in each case some of the original manuscripts have "Christ

Jesus," while others have "Jesus Christ," making it hard to tell which reading was the original. It does not occur in Hebrews, the letters attributed
to Peter or John or Jude or James, or in Revelation. On the other hand, it
occurs dozens and dozens of times in Paul's letters. Later, writers who tried
to imitate Paul picked up on the phrase. The author of 1 and 2 Timothy and
Titus noticed it in Paul's authentic letters and decided to use it to mimic
Paul's style. With modern reference tools scholars can see that Paul actually goes back and forth between "Christ Jesus" and "Jesus Christ." But the
author of the Pastoral Epistles, as these texts are called, overdoes it in his
zeal to imitate Paul and uses it all the time. In any event, the phrase "Christ
Jesus" is in fact very distinctive of Paul. He is especially fond of the phrase
"*in* Christ Jesus."[38]

All of that makes us look at this phrase in the creed with a critical
eye. Could "in Christ Jesus" also be an editorial adaptation of the creed
from Paul's own hand? I think it is. The decisive evidence, though, is Paul
himself. As we have already seen, Paul actually alludes to our creed in
another letter, 1 Corinthians, even though he does not quote it outright.
He does it in chapter 12, when he is trying to argue that the existence
of ecstatic religious experiences, or "spiritual phenomena" as Paul calls
them,[39] should unite the group rather than divide it. To that end he says,
"For in one spirit we all were baptized into one body—Jews or Greeks,
slaves or free—and all were made to drink of the one spirit" (1 Cor
12:13). Again, although the third diad of our creed, "male and female,"
is conspicuously absent, he is clearly referring to the creed, including
the context in which it was used, baptism. But here he does not say, as
the creed states in Galatians, that all are made one "in Christ Jesus."
Instead, he says that their unity is achieved through the *spirit*. They were
baptized "in one spirit," says Paul, not "in Christ Jesus." Since "in Christ
Jesus" is such a favorite phrase of Paul, I am inclined to think that "in
one spirit" probably reflects the actual wording of the original creed. As
we shall see, followers of Jesus who practiced baptism associated it very
strongly with spiritual experiences. And if the original creed went something like "For you are all children of God in the spirit . . . you are all one
in the spirit," it is easy to imagine why Paul would have thought of the
creed at this point in the Corinthian letter, where unity and spiritual
experiences were the issue.

---

38. A few examples: Rom 3:24; 8:1, 2, 39; 15:17; 1 Cor 1:2, 4, 30; 4:15, 17; 15:31;
16:24; Gal 2:4; 5:6; Phil 1:1, 26; 2:5; 3:14; 4:7, 19, 21; 1 Thess 2:14; 5:18; Philm 23.
39. See 1 Cor 12:7–11.

If that all makes sense, the original credo would have read something like this:

For you are all children (sons) of God in the Spirit.
There is no Jew or Greek,
there is no slave or free,
there is no male and female;
For you are all one in the Spirit.

This is my best guess on how the original creed went, but it is by no means the only way to imagine it. Perhaps verse 27, which I have omitted, was in fact original. Perhaps verses 26 and 28b, which I think are original, were added by Paul. On these details I could be wrong. I am not wrong, though, about the heart of the creed. *Everyone* agrees that the three dyads in verse 28 are its central feature, its basic claim. Baptism exposes the follies by which most of us live, defined by the other, who we are not. It declares the unreality of race, class, and gender: there is no Jew or Greek, no slave or free, no male and female. We may not all be the same, but we are all one, each one a child of God.

If you are interested in the origins of Christianity, in those first ten to twenty years when the memory of Jesus was still fresh, before Paul came along and made his distinct and decisive impact on the Jesus movement, and long before literate storytellers took pen in hand and began to create the story of Jesus after the pattern of God's suffering, righteous martyr, before the advent of most of what every believer takes for granted as central to Christian faith, before the concept of faith itself, this remarkable creed should be of interest to you. In the earliest years of the Jesus movement it was repeated again and again by people who were baptized as followers of Jesus. It is a statement about the convictions of the Jesus people. It is not a statement about God, or about the mysteries of Christ. It is about people and who they are, really. In baptism they were committed to giving up old identities falsely acquired on the basis of baseless assumptions—Jew or Greek, slave or free, male or female—and declared themselves to be children of God.

Where did these ideas come from?

CHAPTER 2

༄

The Oldest Cliché

"There is no Jew or Greek, no slave or free, no male and female." Why these three pairs in particular? It is a fairly complete accounting of the ways by which human beings divide themselves into *us* and *them*: race,[1] class,[2] and gender.[3] Many ancients must have thought this too, for it turns out that these binaries together constitute something of a cliché in the annals of ancient bigotries. Here is how the pre-Socratic philosopher Thales deployed it (or was it Socrates himself?):

> Hermippus in his *Lives* refers to Thales the story, which is told, by some, of Socrates, namely, that he used to say there were three blessings for which he was grateful to Fortune: "First, that I was born a human being and not one of

---

1. Race or ethnicity? Both are terms denoting socially constructed categories of difference and very often used interchangeably. I have chosen to go with "race," as this more often connotes the imposition of an inferior identity on another to justify structures of injustice and domination. Ancients engaged in this form of human "othering" just as moderns do, even though they did not generally use skin tone as a deciding factor. For a discussion see Denise Eileen McCoskey's *Race: Antiquity and Its Legacy* (London and New York: Oxford, 2012), 27–34.

2. I have chosen the term "class" in spite of the fact that the ancient world was not a class-divided society like the industrial and postindustrial West. There was at least this single class divide in all of antiquity: the difference between slave and free.

3. Why "gender" and not "sex"? I assume that gender refers to the way people perform the role of "man" or "woman," which includes, but is not limited to, the way each is expected to engage in sexual activity. The creed is not particularly concerned with sexual activity, but with gender and gender roles more broadly understood.

the brutes; next, that I was born a man and not a woman; thirdly, a Greek and not a barbarian."[4]

Thales's first pair, "a human being and not one of the brutes," reads literally "not one of the *animals*" (*therion*). That was not a particularly common way of referring to "slaves," but it fits the ancient mindset quite well. A more common word for slave would have been *andrapodon*, or "human-footed one," coined as a riff on *tetrapodon*, or "four-footed one," meaning an animal or livestock.[5] Slaves were livestock that walked on two feet, like humans do. The reporter here, by the way, is Diogenes Laertius, who wrote his *Lives of the Philosophers* in the third century CE. That would have been more or less contemporaneous with the Jewish *Tosephta*, which offers the same cliché with a Jewish twist, attributed now to Rabbi Judah, who lived roughly a century earlier:

There are three blessings one must pray daily:
Blessed (art thou), who did not make me a Gentile;
Blessed (art thou), who did not make me a woman;
Blessed (art thou), who did not make me uneducated.[6]

"Uneducated" here translates the Hebrew word *bôr*, which means something like "hick" or "boor." But when Rabbi Meir is credited with the same three blessings in the Talmud, he offers an alternate version of the final clause: "blessed (art thou) who did not make me a slave" (*'ebed*). His interlocutor then asks, "Is that not the same as a woman?", to which Meir replies, "A slave is more contemptible."[7] Slaves, women, and foreigners were all essentially the same to ancient men—contemptible. They were all *other*.

BARBARIANS

"Thank God I am not a barbarian." The first other is perhaps the most obvious symbol of otherness of the three: the foreigner. Surely our ancestors must have regarded the foreigner as dangerously other as early as *Homo sapiens* began grouping into tribes to hunt mastodon and other *Homo*

---

4. Diogenes Laertius, *Lives* 1.33 (R. D. Hicks trans., LCL, 2 vols. [Cambridge, MA: Harvard University Press, 1925]).
5. The detail comes from Paul Cartledge, *The Greeks: A Portrait of Self and Other*, rev. ed. (Oxford and New York: Oxford University Press, 2002), 151.
6. *t. Ber.* 7:18.
7. *b. Menaḥ.* 43b.

sapiens. In the civilization that grew up around the Mediterranean Sea, Jews, Greeks, and Romans each in their turn offer many contemporaneous examples.[8]

Ancient Jews were actually as much xenophilic as they were xenophobic. The Jewish scriptures often assert God's regard for the foreigner and instruct the Israelites to feed and clothe the alien among them, "for you were once strangers in the land of Egypt" (Deut 10:18–19). On the other hand, when the Jews were recolonizing the land of Israel after the Babylonian exile, some became so obsessed with Jewish purity that they insisted any man who had married a non-Jewish wife must send her away, together with her children.[9] Nehemiah (writing during this period) says of foreign women, "I cursed them and beat some of them and pulled out their hair" (Neh 13:25). He really hated foreign women. Over time, the land of Israel was often imagined as an ethnically pure place for Israelites only, but just as often it was an ethnically diverse place where Edomites, Moabites, Ammonites, and others might live peacefully side by side.[10] But always the world was divided into Jew and Gentile. Difference did matter. You were either Jewish or *other*—sometimes welcome, sometimes not.

Greeks were equally uncompromising in dividing the world into Greeks and barbarians. The Greek word *barbaros* is onomatopoetic. Greeks could talk, but *barbaroi* could only make uncouth sounds like "bar-bar-bar." Greeks were particularly spooked, though, by Persian *barbaroi.* Cyrus the Great, the Persian king who, in the sixth century BCE, freed the Jewish captives from exile in Babylon, was the same Cyrus who conquered the Greek city-states of Ionia in the sixth century and so initiated the long struggle between Greeks and Persians immortalized in countless cultural remnants from the classical age. At the Battle of Marathon in 490 BCE, a small band of heroic Athenians turned back Darius the Great's invasion of the Greek mainland and, according to legend, Thersipus (or Erchius, or Eucles) ran the whole 26.21 miles back to Athens to announce the victory.[11] The recent

---

8. For the Greek and Roman othering of barbarian, see Cartledge, *The Greeks*, 51–77, and McCoskey's excellent volume, *Race: Antiquity and Its Legacy*; also J. P. V. D. Balsdon, *Romans and Aliens* (London: Duckworth, 1979/Chapel Hill: University of North Carolina Press, 1980); Benjamin Isaac, *The Invention of Racism in Classical Antiquity* (Princeton, NJ, and Oxford: Princeton University Press, 2004); and A. N. Sherwin White, *Racial Prejudice in Imperial Rome* (Cambridge and New York: Cambridge University Press, 1967). For Jewish attitudes toward the Gentile other, see the relevant essays in David Sim and James S. McLaren, *Attitudes to Gentiles in Ancient Judaism and Early Christianity* (London: Bloomsbury, 2013).

9. See Ezra 9–10.

10. See, e.g., Deut 2.

11. According to Plutarch, *Mor* (*Bell Ath*) 347C. The original story, in Herodotus, *Hist* V, is quite different, but not as iconic.

film, "The 300," depicts the legendary Battle of Thermopylae, where three hundred Spartan soldiers allegedly held off more than three hundred thousand Persians before, finally, giving way to the barbarian horde. The filmmaker, Jack Snyder, could not resist emulating the intense Orientalism of the original Greek memories of this event, depicting Xerxes as dark and exotic and (especially) effeminate, surrounded by thousands of primatelike minions whose servile character make them far inferior in battle to the chiseled and handsome free men of Sparta.

This was always the Greek take on Persians: they weren't real men. A famous Attic red-figure wine jug commemorates the Greek victory over these stereotyped foes. The Eurymedon Vase (ca. 460 BCE) depicts a Greek soldier, erect phallus in hand, approaching a Persian victim from behind as the latter bends over in horror.[12] While these Greeks drank to their victories, they liked to remember how they really gave it to those Persians, so to speak.

On a higher plane, Aristotle theorized that barbarians raised in the overly hot climate of Asia were intelligent enough but had no spirit. Celts to the north had plenty of cold-induced spirit but suffered from climatically induced stupidity. The moderate climate of Greece, on the other hand, yielded just the right combination of spirit and intelligence to produce a proper ruling class, the Greeks themselves.[13] He, no doubt, used something like this logic to persuade Alexander the Great to invade the Persian Empire in the fourth century. The ideology of otherness shaped the ancient world as we know it.

The Greeks shared some of their stereotypical barbarian boogiemen with the Romans, who succeeded them. And some were not boogie*men*. Greeks and Romans shared, for example, a curious fascination with Amazons. Here were women uncowed and untamed by men, bare-breasted warriors who could hold their own in battle with any man.[14] They inhabited, according to legend, the wilds of northern Anatolia in the hinterlands just south of the Black Sea and permitted no men to live among them. To avoid extinction, once a year they visited the neighboring tribe of Gargareans to

---

12. In the Museum für Kunst und Gewerbe Hamburg (1981.173). An inscription reads "I am Eurymedon, I stand bent forward." It is taken as a reference to the Battle of Eurymedon River mentioned by Thucydides (1.100), in which the Athenians defeated the Persians in 466 BCE.

13. Aristotle, *Pol* 1.1327b. The more original source of this thinking was the tract *Airs, Waters, and Places*, ostensibly authored by Hippocrates in the fifth century BCE (discussion, see McCoskey, *Race*, 46–49).

14. Lately, see Adrienne Mayor's study, *The Amazons: Lives and Legends of Warrior Women Across the Ancient World* (Princeton, NJ: Princeton University Press, 2014).

have sex with their men.[15] They kept the female offspring from this annual mating season and raised them as Amazons, but the males they exposed—thus reversing the more common ancient practice of exposing more female children than male.

A woman who is like a man is perhaps the very definition of otherness. But is that a good thing or a bad thing? Amazonian tombs were purportedly venerated throughout the ancient world, including in Athens itself.[16] Athenian girls may have even played with Amazon dolls.[17] But the overwhelming material presence of the Amazon legend comes in the form of dozens of Amazonomachies—those ubiquitous battle scenes depicting the defeat of the Amazons by the Athenians. A famous one, now in the British Museum, was once spread out across the west metopes of the Parthenon, but they seem to be everywhere. So the most important thing ancients wanted to remember about the Amazons is that they were savagely slain—on the Parthenon; on the famous Mausoleum of Halicarnassus; on countless temples, tombs, sarcophagi, cups, and shields; and now, in the exhibit halls of the British Museum. It is the battle of the sexes, literally. We will recall this once again when considering the third of our binaries, male and female.

Romans focused their fears of the stranger, though, on a foe more real and actually threatening—the Gauls, or Celts. In Roman art there seem to be as many Celtomachies as Amazonomachies. The Gauls inhabited what is now France and Belgium and parts of Germany and the Netherlands, as well as that most northern part of Italy, just south of the Alps, then called Cisalpine Gaul. They were to the Romans what Persians were to the Greeks. But Greeks feared them too, and some of the artistic representations of Gauls in defeat were Roman copies of Greek originals. This is true, for example, of the famous statue known as "The Dying Gaul," in the Capitoline Museum in Rome.[18] A Gallic warrior reclines naked on the battlefield, staunching the blood from his wounded leg, his sword, shield, and broken battle horn lying useless beneath him on the ground. If he evokes sympathy, it is because the only good Gaul is a dying Gaul. The Romans also borrowed iconic Gallic battles from the Greeks to give expression to their own hopes for final victory over these foes. Gauls, for example, sacked the famous oracular site at Delphi in 279 BCE, but were ultimately repelled by the Greeks with (according to legend) the help of Apollo, Artemis, and

15. Thus, Strabo, *Geog* 11.5.1.
16. Pausanias, *Description of Greece* 1.2.1.
17. Mayor, *The Amazons*, 33.
18. See Iain Ferris, *Enemies of Rome* (Stroud: Sutton, 2000), 6–8.

Athena.[19] A century later, Romans would count this mythic triumph on Greek soil as a Roman victory and depict it on a frieze that decorated a temple at Civita Alba, in modern Umbria. The frieze, now in the Museo Civico in Bologna, depicts a route of the alien enemy—but more important, the victory of civilization over unchecked barbarism.[20] Such public art offered the Roman illiterate public a vision of the world divided into us and them, the civilized *we* and the uncivilized *they*.

We turn once again to Jews, now in the Roman period—their generally low view of the Gentile other persists in this period as well.[21] They were idolaters, chiefly, but this somehow synced up with what Jews considered to be the most revolting Gentile flaw: sexual deviance.[22] This was such a stereotype that even Paul, who wished to include Gentiles in his Christ communities *as Gentiles*, couldn't resist a little Gentile bashing in his Epistle to the Romans. His rant in Romans 1:18–32 is very calculated, though: he wants his Roman audience to know that this rogue apostle who mixes freely with Gentiles actually knows the score—he's no Gentile lover. It culminates in a flourish about the "unnatural" sexual practices of Gentiles. Because they worship idols, he says,

> God therefore gave them up to the impurity of dishonoring their bodies among themselves in the lusting of their hearts. . . . For this reason God gave them up to dishonorable passions. Their women exchanged natural sex for unnatural, and their men also gave up natural sex with women and were consumed with passion for one another, men committing shameless acts with men and receiving in themselves the due penalty for their error.
>
> Rom 1:24, 26–27

These words, by the way, so often invoked in the modern culture wars to condemn gay and lesbian sexuality, were actually less about gay sex and more about the insatiable lust Jews believed was the downfall of all Gentiles. "Unnatural sex" was, for women, anal intercourse, which avoided nature's result.[23] Male-on-male sex also would not have indicated to Paul

19. Diodorus Siculus 22.9.

20. Ferris, *Enemies of Rome*, 13–14.

21. The subject deserves nuance, as Christian characterizations of Jews as clannish, tribal, or "particularistic" (as opposed to Christian universalism) have often been all too self-serving. Terrance Donaldson resets the discussion in *Judaism and the Gentiles: Jewish Patterns of Universalism (to 135 CE)* (Waco, TX: Baylor University Press, 2008).

22. See Martti Nissinen, *Homoeroticism in the Biblical World* (Minneapolis: Fortress, 1998), 89–102.

23. See esp. Jeramy Townsley, "Paul, the Goddess Religions, and Queer Sects: Romans 1:23—28," *Journal of Biblical Literature* 130 (2011): 710–16.

a same-sex orientation (a modern concept unknown to ancients), but just typical Gentile male over-the-top horniness. Gentile men are so consumed with passion, he thinks, that women alone are not enough to satisfy them. So they give full reign to their lust and get busy with men as well. This is all very typical *othering*, this time Jew on Gentile.

So Jews *othered* non-Jews, Greeks *othered* non-Greeks, and Romans *othered* non-Romans. Each divided the world into us and them, where "them" is always wild, violent, unmanly, servile, dirty, stupid, lazy, horny, and yet scary. That was, of course, because they were not actually wild, violent, unmanly, and so forth, but they were actually scary. Persians scared the hell out of the Greeks, Gauls terrified the Romans, and Jews had every reason to fear Gentiles, as anyone living under Roman imperial rule did. All this ethnic othering had to do finally with trying to put a finger on that fear factor. Why are we so afraid? No reason to be, really. See how we kicked their Gaulish arses back over the Alps and into the dark, dark forest. Foreigners are really no match for us after all, right?

A TOOL WITH A VOICE

Slavery in the ancient world was the ultimate class distinction. A free man in the Roman Empire had a name, patrimony, power, and agency, even if none of that came with money. A slave had none of those things. A slave's name was given by his or her master; his or her family was that of his or her master. He or she had no right to claim a father, or even a father*land*. This deracination of the slave is the beginning of what Orlando Patterson famously called the "social death" of the slave.[24] In the ancient world, one's power derived from one's social place. A slave had no place, and thus no power, no agency. And yet, every human being actually does have agency. So the slave must be made to think, to *believe* that he or she does not. That is another of Patterson's insights about slave societies: they all construct an image of the slave, a slave *persona*, that is something less than human. This social construction of the slave as subhuman takes a collective multigenerational effort deploying all the power of society itself, from its language, to its laws, to its customs and practices.

Consider how ancients spoke of slaves. The most common circumlocutions for "slave" (*doulos*) in Greek are so telling. I have already mentioned

---

24. Orlando Patterson, *Slavery as Social Death* (Cambridge, MA: Harvard University Press, 1982).

one: *andrapodon*, meaning "manfooted" (as opposed to *tetrapodon*, or "four-footed") beast.[25] Slaves were livestock. Note, by the way, the gender of this word. In a language that recognizes three genders, male, female, and neuter, this noun came out neuter, even though its constituent parts (*aner* and *pous*) are both masculine. Other terms included *pais* (boy), *katharma* (garbage), and *mastiga* (rogue). Romans thought of their slaves as "tools." A slave was an *instrumentum vocale*, a "tool with a voice."[26] But by far the most common slang for "slave" was simply *soma* (body). A slave was a body. In her revelatory work *Slavery in Early Christianity*, Jennifer Glancy shows that this was more than mere terminological denigration.[27] The slave was a kind of surrogate body placed at the disposal of an owner to do with as he or she pleased. Masters used their slave bodies for all sorts of things, including manual labor, of course, but not only this. A slave was a surrogate body in every sense. Slaves could receive corporal punishment on behalf of his or her master; a slave could be imprisoned instead of his or her master. Conversely, attacking a person's slave was tantamount to attacking his or her master. Slaves performed the duties of a hit man, leading to various legal puzzles about culpability—when was the slave liable, and when the master? Slave gangs could be deployed as private armies. Female bodies had their own special uses—milk, for one. As Glancy notes, the slave wet nurse was a stock character in generations of Greek and Roman literature.[28] Sex, for another—although one should not assume this to have been a burden borne only by female bodies. Greek and Roman men also made use of their male bodies in this way. Glancy points out that the young boys idealized in Roman love poetry for their beauty are usually slaves.[29] Brothels, of course, were usually staffed by slaves, both male and female.[30]

But what made a slave merely a body? Aristotle puzzled this out for Greeks in his *Politics*.[31] The question before him was whether a slave was a slave by nature or merely by convention. Presumably there were others in his circle who believed that slavery was merely a convention, that slaves were human beings like anyone else. But Aristotle believed that slaves were servile by nature. His argument went like this: In this world it is completely natural that there are rulers and subjects. The soul rules over the body.

25. Cartledge, *The Greeks*, 151.
26. Cartledge, *The Greeks*, 135.
27. Jennifer Glancy, *Slavery in Early Christianity* (Minneapolis: Fortress Press, 2006), esp. 9–38.
28. Glancy, *Slavery*, 18–19.
29. Glancy, *Slavery*, 23–24.
30. Glancy, *Slavery*, 54–57.
31. See *Politics* 1.1253b–1255b; for a discussion, see Cartledge, *The Greeks*, 135–43.

Human beings rule over animals. Men rule over women. Why? Because the soul is superior to the body. Human beings are superior to animals. Men are superior to women. What if this were not so? What if the body ruled over the soul, or animals over human beings, or—heaven forefend!—women over men? Disaster and dysfunction! It is just so with slavery, he says. As animals are inferior to human beings, and therefore should be ruled by them, likewise, slaves are inferior to masters and must be ruled by them.

In what sense are they inferior?

> A person who is able to belong to another person is by nature a slave (for that is why he belongs to someone else), and participates in reason only so much as to recognize that it exists, but not so much as to have it himself.[32]

Aristotle is talking about his own anthropological theories here. To his way of thinking, the human being consisted of a body and a soul, but the soul was itself divided into higher and lower elements. The higher part of the soul was thought to be the seat of reason, the lower part the seat of passions. Animals, in his scheme, have the lower part of the soul, but not the higher, reasoning part. This is true of slaves too. They have just enough reason to know that there is reason, but not enough to actually possess it. They can follow orders, but not give them. That is why, he goes on to say, we use slaves more or less like we use animals. They are simply bodies we use to provide the basic necessities of life. This natural state of things is reflected in the bodies of slaves themselves. They are typically strong and well suited to the difficult manual labor they must perform. The bodies of free people are quite different. "Upright," he calls them, better suited to the activities of citizenship. So what of slaves who have tall, upright bodies, and free persons who have strong bodies? Would that not give the lie to this entire way of thinking? No, says Aristotle, for the outward appearance of the body can be deceiving. It is the soul—the seat of reason—that really counts, and that is harder to see. Free persons have it, but slaves (animals, women) do not, regardless of the appearance of their bodies. Slaves are slaves by nature. Therefore, he concludes, "it is both expedient and just for slaves to be slaves."[33]

Such arguments, of course, boggle the modern mind with their circularity and false premises. But Aristotle lived in a world in which slavery was a given and this fed the conservative manner in which he usually argued.

32. *Pol* 1.1254b.
33. *Pol* 1.1255a.

Nature, for Aristotle, was the given state of things—convention, the normal, the widely assumed verities of human opinion. If slavery exists and is so ubiquitous, there must be a good reason for it. Could there be exceptions to the norm? Surely, and Aristotle admits of them. For example, he knew full well that slaves were often captives taken in war. When this happened, he says, then we're dealing with a legal principle that anything (or anyone) captured in war belongs to the victor. But even in these cases, he says, the victor must have had some superior quality that made him more fit to rule than the vanquished.[34] This all comes from the father of modern science, whose arguments for the justice of slavery persisted well into the nineteenth-century slave-holding culture of the United States.

As the Greek culture of Aristotle declined and the Roman Empire rose to power, slavery was one reality that endured. Romans, though, did not generally think of slavery in Aristotle's naturalistic terms. Slavery was not a matter of nature for Romans, but of convention—*legal* convention. The Justinian *Digest* of Roman law defines slavery as "an institution of the common law of peoples by which a person is put into ownership of some-body else, *contrary to the natural order*."[35] The *Digest* goes on:

> Slaves (*servi*) are so called because commanders generally sell the people they capture and thereby save (*servare*) them instead of killing them. The word for property in slaves (*mancipia*) is derived from the fact that they are captured from the enemy by force of arms (*manu capiantur*).[36]

In other words, Aristotle's exception became for Romans the general rule. Indeed, as the Roman Empire gradually expanded into Gaul, Spain, Britain, Asia Minor, and North Africa through military conquest, thousands, eventually millions of slaves were incorporated into the empire. A slave was someone whose life had been lost on the battlefield. Gone were his honor, his name, his history and patrimony. Enemy women and children were simply taken from their homes and sold—again, all an illustration of what Patterson calls the "social death" of the slave. Through the later years of the Republic and the early Principate, Rome became a slave culture. Everything—farming, mining, milling, manufacturing—was gradually turned over to slave labor. Roughly 20 to 30 percent of the population

---

34. *Pol* 1.1255a.

35. Justinian's *Digest* 1.5.4, in Thomas Wiedemann, *Greek and Roman Slavery: A Sourcebook* (Baltimore: Johns Hopkins University Press, 1981), 15.

36. *Digest* 1.5.4, in Wiedemann, *Greek and Roman Slavery*, 15.

of Roman Italy was enslaved at any one time.[37] If you add to that the number of slaves who had gained freedom through manumission, but still remained in the quasi-slave status of "freedman" or "-woman," that number would be doubled. Everyone was now classified as either slave or free. The second-century jurist Gaius summarizes the Roman legal situation succinctly in his textbook on Roman law, the *Institutes*: "The principal distinction made by the law of persons is this, that all human beings are either free persons or slaves."[38] Slave versus free was the basic class distinction in the Roman world.

Roman law, however, went even further to categorize different sorts of slaves and freedmen, based on their origin and circumstances of enslavement. For example, a slave who had been a combatant against Rome could eventually be freed, but he could never become a citizen, and when released, he could not reside within a hundred miles of the city of Rome.[39] He had, after all, once taken up arms against Rome! Legislation sometimes prohibited male citizens and freedwomen from marrying on the grounds that the freedwoman could not be presumed "virtuous"[40] (though at other times such marriages were common). And so it went. The extensive legal system that arose around slavery served to integrate foreigners into Roman society on terms that Romans could live with. The expanding empire could not help but incorporate foreigners. Incorporating them as slaves, though, was one way of keeping them foreign, inferior, and "other."

If the recognition that slavery was a state contrary to nature seems like a step in the right direction—that is, toward more humane treatment of slaves—that turns out not to have been the case. To the contrary, the legal regulation of slavery created a matter-of-factness about slavery that seems to have had the opposite effect. Handbooks were written to instruct masters in how best to manage their slaves along with their livestock and other property.[41] Galen advised slaveholders to refrain from beating their slaves, not for the slaves' benefit, but to exercise better self-control. Get someone else, a professional, to do it.[42] Juvenal remarks that some slaveholders kept a professional torturer on staff.[43] Or this unpleasant task

37. Sandra Joshel, *Slavery in the Roman World*, Cambridge Introductions to Roman Civilization (Cambridge: Cambridge University Press, 2010), 54–56.

38. Gaius, *Institutes*, 1.1, in Wiedemann, *Greek and Roman Slavery*, 24.

39. Gaius, *Institutes* 1.1, in Wiedemann, *Greek and Roman Slavery*, 25.

40. Glancy, *Slavery*, 27.

41. These include Cato the Elder's *On Agriculture* (third–second century BCE), Varro's *On Agriculture* (second century BCE), and Columella's *On Agriculture* (first century CE).

42. Joshel, *Slavery*, 122–23, referring to Galen's work, *On Diseases* 4.

43. Juvenal, *Satires* 6.480.

could be hired out to contractors, such as to these professionals in Roman Puteoli:

> (Posted) If anyone wishes to have a slave—male or female—punished privately, he who wishes to have the punishment inflicted shall do as follows. If he wants to put the slave on the cross or fork, the contractor must supply the posts, chains, ropes for floggers and the floggers themselves. The person having the punishment inflicted is to pay 4 sesterces for each of the operatives who carry the fork, and the same for the floggers and for the executioner. . . . The contractor is to set up crosses and supply without charge nails, pitch, wax, tapers, and anything else that is necessary for this in order to deal with the condemned man.[44]

Chillingly pedestrian: "Make sure the nails are included. Last time they charged me extra." If a slave really aggravated you, it was perfectly legal to kill him or her. But sometimes the sadism in this went too far, even for a notorious sadist like Gaius Caligula, who became outraged by one Roman patrician's practice of keeping a pond in the garden of his estate stocked with lampreys, into which he liked to throw insolent slaves. Caligula made him fill in the pond and get rid of the eels.[45]

Slaves were, legally speaking, nonpersons, so they did not have the right to fall in love, marry, have children, and so forth. Still, they were people and did fall in love, have sex, and have children. This all had to be incorporated into the efficient management of slaves.[46] The handbooks speak of this too. Male slaves were given access to female slaves, for a well-sexed slave is a happy slave. When slaves did fall in love or had children, these relationships could be used to minimize the risk of flight and to enforce good behavior.[47] Managers also took an interest in slave breeding to increase the livestock holdings, so to speak, of the estate.[48] Female slaves were encouraged to have children by the promise of freedom. The handbooks advise to grant freedom to women over thirty who have borne four children or more.[49] Women who bore children were lucky, under any circumstances, to make it that far, so this would never have cost the slave owner very much. Hope could buy you a lot of new slave flesh at little cost to the estate.

Slaves did, of course, often run away, so advice is given on how to build effective *ergastula*, the prisonlike barracks used to house gang slaves on

---

44. *L'Année épigraphique* 1971, no. 88, trans. J. F. Gardener and T. Wiedemann (as cited by Joshel, *Slavery*, 121).
45. Pliny, *Nat Hist* 9.39.77.
46. See Joshel, *Slavery*, 124–26, on the management of slaves.
47. Varro, *On Agriculture* 1.17.5; Columella, *On Agriculture* 1.8.5.
48. Varro, *On Agriculture* 2.10.6.
49. Columella, *On Agriculture* 1.8.19.

farms or in the mines. Place the windows high, to let in light, but to discourage escape.[50] The Romans also developed ingenious devices to manacle slaves that would not impede their ability to work. When slaves fled, slave catchers were hired to fetch them back. When runaways were captured, after being beaten and tortured, they were collared with a permanent tag reading simply TMQF. Apparently everyone knew what it meant ("Tene me qua fugio"—"Hold me for I am a runaway"). Or a runaway might simply be branded on the forehead with the letters FUG (i.e., *fugitivus*—"runner").[51]

Such brutality was of course calculated to manage Rome's large slave population by instilling in it a constant state of fear and vulnerability. But if slaves feared their masters, masters feared their slaves no less. Seneca quotes a saying—apparently common—to his friend, Lucillius: *totidem hostes esse quot servos* ("You have as many enemies as you have slaves").[52] To wit: Pliny the Younger tells the story of how the ex-Praetor of Rome, Larcius Macedo, was attacked by his slaves in the public baths and nearly killed[53]—one of many such episodes, no doubt. Under cover of the steam, they jumped him, beat him till they thought he was dead, then threw him onto the blistering hot floor of the *calderium* to make sure he was. He faked it, though, and when they carried him out, pretending that he had died of exhaustion, he came to and accused them all of attempted murder. The slaves were executed; he later died. Roman law stipulated that in such cases any slave within earshot of the incident was to be tortured and killed, "since no household would be safe if slaves were not forced by the threat of danger to their own lives to protect their masters against enemies both internal and external."[54] But this principle sometimes stretched even the capacious Roman tolerance for brutality. After another incident, in which an ex-Praetor of Rome was murdered by one of his slaves, all four hundred of his household slaves were rounded up to be executed. On this occasion the Senate did gather to debate the justice of the situation, but eventually it decided to execute them all—"since no household would be safe" otherwise.[55]

Did Jews hold slaves in antiquity? Certainly. There were no real exceptions to this practice in the Mediterranean world. The Hebrew scriptures do make overtures to more humane treatment of slaves, if they are *Hebrew* slaves. Leviticus actually prohibits the holding of Hebrew slaves; they are

50. Joshel, *Slavery*, 119; instructions for a proper secure slave quarters (*ergastulum*) is found in Columella's *On Agriculture*, 1.6.3.
51. See illustration in Joshel, *Slavery*, 119–20.
52. *Letters* 47.
53. *Letters* 3.14.
54. Ulpian, *On the Edict*, book 50, in Wiedemann, *Greek and Roman Slavery*, 169.
55. Tacitus tells the story in *Annals* 14.42–45.

to be treated as indentured servants rather than slaves.[56] The book of Deuteronomy presupposes that Jews did hold fellow Jews as slaves, but it limits their time of servitude to six years, after which they must be released.[57] Moreover, when you free a Hebrew slave, you are to provide him with a dowry of sorts—food, wine, livestock, and so forth. If a slave should wish to remain a slave, "because he loves you and your household," then Deuteronomy states that "you shall take an awl and thrust it through his earlobe into the door, and he shall be your slave forever."[58] Jews, apparently, did not wish to see too many Jewish slaves among them. As for foreign slaves, none of this applied. Foreign slaves were regarded and treated like all slaves were treated in the Ancient Near East. Later, under Roman rule, Jews seemed to have adapted to the world of their surroundings. In the Roman period Jews could, and did, hold other Jews as slaves, and for an indefinite period.[59] Jewish slaves became, as it were, foreigners to their own people.

NOT QUITE MALE

Race, class, and now, gender. Consider this, by now perhaps famous, artifact from the scrap heaps of ancient Oxyrhynchus, a letter from Hilarion, a migrant laborer in Roman-era Alexandria, to his beloved wife, Alis, who stayed home in Oxyrhynchus:

> I send you warmest greetings. I want you to know that we are still in Alexandria.
> And please do not worry if all the others come home but I remain in Alexandria.
> I beg you and entreat you to take care of the child and, if I receive my pay soon,
> I will send it up to you. If you have a baby before I return, if it is a boy, let it live;
> if it is a girl, expose it. You sent a message with Aphrodisias, "Don't forget me."
> How can I forget you? I beg you then, not to worry.
>
> The 29th year of Caesar, Pauni 23[60]

"Expose it" refers, of course, to the ancient practice of abandoning infant children to wait for whatever fate might come—death by the elements or

56. See Lev 25:39–43.
57. Deut 15:12.
58. Deut 12:15–17.
59. See Catherine Hezser, *Jewish Slavery in Antiquity* (Oxford and New York: Oxford University Press, 2005), 271.
60. POxy 744, published in A. S. Hunt and C. C. Edgar, *Select Papyri*, LCL, 3 vols. (Cambridge, MA: Harvard University Press, 1932), #105.

wild animals, or rescue by passersby on the lookout for exposed babies whom they might raise as slaves and later sell. If Hilarion in fact had a daughter, he would no doubt love her as he loves Alis. He might even one day say to her in all affection, "How could I forget you?" But in the abstract potential of childbirth, the female child is not yet a daughter. She is merely a gender, and therefore expendable. A male baby is worth raising; a female baby is not. Did Alis agree? Hilarion knows her better than we do and he assumes she does.

Here, then, is our problem. No one who has read widely in ancient literature will question why an ancient man might thank Fortune that he was born a man and not a woman. And yet, there are so many exceptions to the rule that it may seem a little hard at first to bring the issue into focus. Men love and treasure individual women and girls, but they devalue, disrespect, and even despise the female as female. Or consider Cleopatra VII, the last great Ptolemaic ruler of Egypt. She was the most powerful person in the eastern Mediterranean, charming, intelligent, who, according to Plutarch, could speak fluently to "Ethiopians, Troglodytes, Hebrews, Arabians, Syrians, Medes or Parthians" in their own tongues.[61] Julius Caesar allied with her, as did Anthony later, for her power. And yet we generally remember her as the Romans did, as a seductress and opportunist, if not merely the concubine of powerful men. Her model was, perhaps, Berenice II (ca. 273–221 BCE), the warrior queen, who rode a horse into battle as well as any man, and even entered her horses in the Olympian games and won. Her power in Egyptian politics was such that her son finally had her killed to make way for his own ambitions.[62] There are plenty of examples in Roman politics as well. The women of the Julii were often just as powerful as the Julii themselves, but they were always the women *behind* the throne, not sitting upon it.[63] Through all the centuries of the Roman Republic, and later, the Empire, there was never a female senator, never a tribune, never a consul. The very idea lies beyond the pale.

Money could bring power to women in the private sphere of commerce, as well as recognition in the public sphere of benefactions. Phile, a woman of Priene, paid for the city water system there. For this she was made the first woman in Priene to hold the office of *Stephanephorus*—the "crown

---

61. Plutarch, *Life of Antony* 27.2.

62. On Cleopatra and Berenice see "The Hellenistic Period: Women in a Cosmopolitan World," in *Women in the Classical World: Image and Text,* ed. Elaine Fantham et al. (Oxford and New York: Oxford University Press, 1994), 136–82.

63. Annelise Friesenbruch, *Caesars' Wives: Sex, Power, and Politics in the Roman Empire* (New York: Simon and Schuster, 2010).

bearer" (whatever that means).[64] We do not know where her money came from. Eumachia of Pompeii inherited her wealth from her father, a brick manufacturer, which she used to pay for additions to the building where the Fullers Guild met. They honored her with dedications inscribed over each entrance to the building and a statue, which now stands in the Museo Archaeologico Nazionale in Naples.[65] And Junia Theodora was a major benefactor in Corinth during the time the Apostle Paul was active there, and was honored with an elaborate public dedication.[66] Clearly, wealth could mitigate the disadvantages of gender. But these examples all stand out as unusual against the hundreds of such dedications routinely made to men.

So, what of the women who lived as most did—poor and far removed from the halls of power? Was there really no reason for any man to thank Fortune that the gods had made him male and not female? Let us follow the life course of a typical peasant woman to see what lies in store for her. First there is the moment of birth. As we learn from Hilarion, it was more common to expose girls than boys—so much so that free men had difficulty finding eligible women to marry. Caesar Augustus fixed this by allowing male citizens to marry former slaves—earlier Roman law had banned this.[67] By Augustus's day there just were not enough women to go around.

So let us say you are girl who is not exposed, but grows to become a child. Poor children, like poor families in general, lived at subsistence level and were often hungry. For this reason there were many public and private assistance programs. Most, however, benefited boys only, and when girls were included, their dole was substantially less than that of boys. They also ended earlier. Boys could stay on the dole until they reached majority at age eighteen, but girls only until age fourteen. Why the difference? Girls were expected by then to have been married.[68]

---

64. H. W. Pleket, *Epigraphica II: Texts on the Social History of the Greek World* (Leiden: Brill, 1969), 5.G, as reprinted in Mary R. Lefkowitz and Maureen B. Fant, *Women's Life in Greece and Rome: A Source Book in Translation*, 3rd ed. (Baltimore: Johns Hopkins University Press, 2005), 158.

65. *CIL* X.810 and X.813, as reprinted in Lefkowitz and Fant, *Women's Life in Greece and Rome*, 159–60.

66. Pleket, *Epigraphica II*, 8, excerps. G, in Lefkowitz and Fant, *Women's Life in Greece and Rome*, 160.

67. Dio Cassius 54.16.1–2 (after Fantham et al., *Women*, 304); see also *Digest* 23.2.44, from the *Lex Julia et Popia*, book 1 (in Lefkowitz and Fant, *Women's Life in Greece and Rome*, 109–10).

68. Sarah Pomeroy, *Goddesses, Whores, Wives, and Slaves: Women in Classical Antiquity* (New York: Schocken, 1975), 203.

When girls entered puberty—about age twelve—they were deemed ready for a husband. Marriages were arranged by fathers. Roman custom and law granted fathers near absolute power over their wives, sons, and daughters.[69] When a girl married, that power passed formally to her new husband—though her right to divorce nullified much of its effect.[70] This practice of "marital subordination" could be effected through a variety of means—cohabitation, or ritually, or by contrived sale of the bride to the groom. Fathers, though, could still intervene in the lives of their daughters where matters of sexuality and honor were concerned. If he caught his daughter in the act of committing adultery, for example, it was his right to kill both her and her lover on the spot.[71]

The success of the marriage was defined by its progeny. Girls began having children as young as they could bear them. If they were lucky, a few might survive, but infant mortality was very high. So was maternal mortality. In the absence of proper obstetrics, a woman was more likely to die in childbirth than by any other cause. It is still one of the leading causes of death among women of maternal age (second only to HIV/AIDS worldwide).[72] So a woman's life course was to bear children, watch most of them die, until, one day, she herself was taken in the pangs of birth.

> Here I lie, a woman named Veturia. My father was Veturius, my husband Fortunatus. I lived for twenty-seven years, and I was married for sixteen years to the same man. After I gave birth to six children, only one of whom is still alive, I died. Titus Fortunatus, a soldier of Legion II Adiutrix, provided the memorial for his wife who was incomparable and showed understanding devotion to him.[73]

As to "devotion," what might that entail? A woman's wifely duties included what you might expect: cooking, hauling water, tending to any surviving children, making and mending clothes. The symbol of respectability for the Roman matron was the distaff used in spinning wool or linen.

---

69. Justinian, *Institutes* 1.9, 11, in Lefkowitz and Fant, *Women's Life in Greece and Rome*, 100.

70. Gaius, *Institutes* 1.108–18, 136–37a, in Lefkowitz and Fant, *Women's Life in Greece and Rome*, 112–14.

71. Justinian, *Digest* 48.5.23–24 (in Lefkowitz and Fant, *Women's Life in Greece and Rome*, 108) and Paulus, *Opinions* 2.26.1 (in Lefkowitz and Fant, *Women's Life in Greece and Rome*, 104).

72. According to the World Health Organization, "Women's Health Fact Sheet #334," last updated September 2013, World Health Organization, http://www.who.int/mediacentre/factsheets/fs334/en/.

73. *CIL* III.3572—a grave inscription.

But not all women enjoyed such domestic bliss. Poor women often worked outside the home in various roles, including manufacturing (e.g., bricks), as shopkeepers, in domestic service (especially those former slaves), and as butchers, hairdressers, fishmongers, wet nurses, cloak sellers, unguent boilers, salt sellers, frankincense merchants, horse tenders, waitresses in taverns and (sometimes simultaneously) prostitutes, and (occasionally) even gladiators.[74]

There were miseries enough for men in the ancient world as well. Life was "nasty, brutish, and short" for everyone, especially the common poor. But there was a real difference between men and women all up and down the class lines. Women in Greece and Rome were simply not free in the same way men were. Under normal circumstances, a woman lived her life under the power and control of a man. A woman was under her father's paternal power (*patria potestas*); or, when married, the power (*manus*, or "hand") of her husband; or, if neither circumstance applied, the authority of an appointed guardian. Boys too had guardians, but only until they reached age twenty-five. Women needed guardians beyond this age, as the jurist Ulpian explains, "on account of the weakness of their sex as well as their ignorance of legal matters."[75] Only the most extraordinary women ever attained any degree of power in the ancient world. Among elites, a woman in Roman times might come to a marriage *sine manus*, that is, not under the power of her husband. But most women lived their lives "under the hand" of a man.

Although it is somewhat late for our purposes, the example of Augustine's mother, Monica, is too revealing to leave aside. The well-known passage is in the *Confessions*, where Augustine describes the virtues of his beloved mother. She served her husband "as if he were her master," he says.

> She learned that an angry husband should not be resisted either in deed or even in word. But when he had calmed down and seemed receptive, she used to give him an explanation of her conduct, if by chance he had been imprudently enraged. Many women, whose husbands were actually more mild-tempered than hers, bore the scars of beatings on their disfigured faces. But when, in conversations with friends, they criticized the behavior of their husbands, my mother gave them a serious warning—though phrased as a humorous remark—about their tongues, advising them that from the moment they had first heard the so-called marriage tablets read aloud, they should think of those tablets as the

---

74. See the wealth of material in Lefkowitz and Fant, *Women's Life in Greece and Rome*, 208–24 (for gladiators: 213–14).

75. Ulpian, *Edict*, Book 11, in Lefkowitz and Fant, *Women's Life in Greece and Rome*, 101.

instruments by which they had been turned into slaves, and that, mindful of their status, they should not be insolent toward their masters.[76]

This, finally, is why a man would say "I thank the gods that I was not born a woman." Western civilization has never quitted this legacy entirely.

WHY THESE THREE, AGAIN

The foreigner, the slave, the woman—why did ancient free men long to dominate these "others" so fiercely? They were afraid of them, for one thing. Greeks feared the Persians; Romans feared the Gauls. They feared invasion, war, and domination. They feared their slaves. How could they not? No society that has ever held slaves did not fear the day when those slaves would turn on their masters, overwhelm them, outnumber them, and tear them limb from limb. And women? Do men fear women? A person so different, and yet so close, so intimate, so inside the castle—perhaps here is the most terrifying thing of all. Men fear what they do not understand. Ancient men were afraid of the foreign other, the slave, the women in the bed next to them, so they did what all men do, have done, will do: they sought to dominate that which they feared. They faced down fear with power.

And that is the second thing really to notice about these three dyads: they involve a differential of power. In considering each of them separately, scholars have missed this. "There is no Jew or Greek," when taken alone, as perhaps the Apostle Paul did, sounds like the utopian dream of one great and universal human family, in which all *cultural* differences are ignored in favor of our common humanity. But in our creed it stands together with "free and slave" and "male and female." It is a Jewish inversion of the cliché that thanks Fortune that I, a man, was not born a foreigner, a slave, or a woman. This has little to do with universal humanity and everything to do with power. A foreigner has no standing in Rome. Though it must have been rare, and contextual, in certain places and times it was indeed better to be a Jew than a Greek. Among Jews, Jewish slaves were treated as indentured servants; Greek slaves were just chattel. "There is no male and female" has sometimes been treated in relation to ancient notions of primordial androgyny—the idea that the original human being was neither male nor female, but both, androgynous. This mythology did in fact find its way into earliest Christianity, as we shall see, but "I thank God I was born

76. Augustine, *Conf* 9.9.

a man and not a woman" was not primarily about primordial androgyny. It was about power and status.

The followers of Jesus who created this elegant manifesto were trying to see themselves and others in a new way. That ancient cliché, "I thank God that I was not born a foreigner, a slave, or a woman," crystallized for them a problem, a theory of identity they had learned to reject. It is the banal theory that says, quite simply, "At least I'm better than somebody." A native is better than a foreigner. A master is better than a slave. A man is better than a woman. Why? Men of privilege, like Aristotle, have been creating rational answers to this question for centuries. But really, it is all about the fear of difference and the power to assuage that fear through domination. Whoever composed this baptismal creed had the extraordinary wisdom to see through this pretense. There is another identity, another way to lay claim to human worth: "You are all children of God."

CHAPTER 3

⌘

Children of God

"For you are all children ('sons') of God through the Spirit." That is how our ancient credo begins. But isn't it a universal claim of Christians everywhere that Jesus is the Son of God, the *only* Son of God? "I believe in God the Father, maker of heaven and earth, and in Jesus Christ, his only begotten Son, our Lord." That is how the Apostles' Creed begins. But long before Christians made this a central tenet of Christian faith, the followers of Jesus believed something else: that Jesus had taught them to see themselves as "sons" or "children of God."

BECOMING "SONS OF GOD"

One of the oldest shards of tradition associated with Jesus of Nazareth is the Sermon on the Mount in chapters 5 through 7 of the Gospel of Matthew. A shorter, older version of this sermon occurs in Luke 6:20–49. The things that occur in both of these sermons are the most interesting, historically speaking, for they probably derive from an earlier gospel used by the authors of Matthew and Luke, the lost gospel scholars commonly refer to as "Q." For those unfamiliar with Q, a quick paragraph of explanation is in order.

Students of Matthew, Mark, and Luke generally agree that these three gospels are related intertextually. Moreover, most agree that the pattern of their intimate relationship is as follows: Mark was written first, and then, about a generation later, Matthew and Luke were written by authors who knew and made use of Mark, though independently of one another. This is called the hypothesis of Markan priority, and it accounts for most of the close literary parallels between all three of these "synoptic" gospels. But Markan priority leaves unexplained a series of equally close literary parallels that exist between Matthew and Luke only—no Markan precursor. The authors of Matthew and Luke, then, must have used a second source in addition to Mark. That second source is what everyone refers to as "Q." Why "Q"? This missing gospel source was discovered first by German scholars in the nineteenth century, who began referring to it simply as "the source"—in German, *die Quelle*. In English-speaking lands *die Quelle* became simply "Q." Q, then, is a lost gospel source used by the authors of Matthew and Luke in the composition of their gospels.[1] And Q, it turns out, had a sermon too, upon which Matthew's author based his Sermon on the Mount and Luke's his Sermon on the Plain. This ancient Q sermon, so far as we can reconstruct it, is the oldest known summary of the teachings of Jesus.[2] In that very early sermon, there was the following (familiar) tradition. I'll quote it to you as scholars of the Society of Biblical Literature's International Q Project think it would have appeared in Q:

> Love your enemies, and pray for those who persecute you, so that you may become sons of your Father, for he raises his sun on the bad and the good alike, and rains on the just and the unjust.
>
> Q 6:27–28, 35[3]

That bare-bones reconstruction of this tradition has always struck me as somewhat spare. Still, one can get a pretty good idea of what these early followers of Jesus were thinking. God treats everyone, friend and

---

1. For a thorough explanation of the Q hypothesis and its implications, see John Kloppenborg Verbin, *Excavating Q: The History and Setting of the Sayings Gospel* (Minneapolis: Fortress, 2000), or Stephen J. Patterson, *The Lost Way: How Two Forgotten Gospels Are Rewriting the Story of Christian Origins* (San Francisco: HarperOne, 2014).

2. For the Sermon on the Mount as an early summary (*epitome*) of the preaching of Jesus, see Hans-Dieter Betz, "The Sermon on the Mount (Matt. 5:3-7:27): Its Literary Genre and Function," *Journal of Religion* 59 (1979): 285–97; reprinted in Betz, *Essays on the Sermon on the Mount* (Philadelphia: Fortress, 1985), 1–16. What Betz argues for the Sermon on the Mount is true, *mutatis mutandis*, for the Q sermon as well.

3. As reconstructed from Matt 5:44–45 and Luke 6:27–28, 35. My translations of Q are based on the reconstruction of Q created by the Society of Biblical Literature International Q Project; see James M. Robinson, Paul Hoffmann, and John S. Kloppenborg, eds., Milton Moreland, managing ed., *The Sayings Gospel Q in Greek and English, with Parallels from the Gospels of Mark and Thomas* (Minneapolis: Fortress Press, 2002); the translations are my own, as published in *The Lost Way* (see note 1, earlier).

foe alike, with the same graciousness and generosity. People should do this too—act like God acts and become a "son of God." Like father, like son. Here is how the author of the Gospel of Luke waxed eloquent in drawing out the idea:

> But I say to you who are listening, love your enemies, do good to those who hate you, bless those who curse you and pray for those who persecute you. To anyone who strikes you on the cheek, offer the other one also, and from the one who takes your coat, do not withhold your shirt. Give to everyone who begs from you, and from anyone who takes your things, do not ask for them back. Treat others as you would have people treat you. If you love those who love you, what credit is that to you? Even sinners love those who love them. And if you do good to those who do good to you, what credit is that to you? For even sinners do the same. And if you lend to those from whom you expect a return, what credit is that to you? Even sinners lend to sinners expecting to get something in return. No, love your enemies, do good, and lend expecting nothing in return, and your reward will be great and you will be called sons of the Most High, for he is kind to the ungrateful and the selfish. Be merciful, just as your Father is merciful.
>
> Luke 6:27–36

Now we can see just what was implied by this idea. These followers of Jesus were trying to be like God, to imitate God. God is merciful and kind to everyone. They could see this for themselves: God causes it to rain on the good and the bad alike. Be like that, they thought. Perform random acts of goodness. In that way they could become like God. They could become the "sons of God." So says Jesus, according to Luke, Matthew, and that earlier source from which they drew, Q.

In this early period the practice of referring to the Jesus people as "the sons of God" must have been very common. This is suggested by several passages in the letters of Paul. For example, in a letter to the community Paul helped to found at Philippi, a Roman colony in ancient Macedonia, he offered this advice:

> Do all things without complaining and questioning, that you may be blameless and innocent, children of God, without blemish in the midst of a crooked and perverse generation, among whom you shine as lights in the world.
>
> Phil 2:14–15

In this case, I have rendered the phrase "children of God," because Paul's language uses the more diminutive form, *tekna theou*, literally "children of God." Across a range of early Christian texts both "children of God" and "sons of God" are used synonymously to refer to the followers of Jesus.[4]

That people might be thought of as the children of God was a common enough idea in the ancient world. "From thee was our begetting," intones Cleanthes's ancient Hymn to Zeus, "ours alone of all that live and move upon the earth the lot to bear God's likeness. . . . Save, we pray, thy children from this boundless misery."[5] Among Stoics, like Cleanthes, all of humanity could claim a kinship because all were ultimately children of God. But if we are all children of God, should we not act like it? Epictetus famously explored the question: if you take seriously the idea that God is your father, then faithfulness to God, self-respect, and wisdom in navigating the world will be its fruit. But most people don't, and they are miserable.[6] Or they are arrogant. How can you treat your slave like an animal if you know that your slaves too are children of God, he asks? But I have a bill of sale, you say. His answer: you ought to be ashamed!

> Do you see to where you bend your gaze, that it is to the earth, to the pit, to these wretched laws of ours, the laws of the dead, and not to the laws of the gods that you look.[7]

Jews too believed that the children of Israel were the children of God, and pondered what this should mean.[8] The Talmud reconstructs a debate among the rabbis: who is the true child of God? You are children of God when you behave like God's children; when you don't, you are not, says Rabbi Judah. No, says Rabbi Meir, in both cases you are still children of God—just ungrateful children! Even to those in whom there is no faith, only corruption or foolishness, even where it is said, you are not my people, "it shall be said unto them, 'You are sons of the living God.'"[9] And so the debate went—who is a true child of God, and what makes one so? The followers of Jesus were part of this debate, but they were in no wise unsure of their status. They were children of God: they were made children of God by nothing less than the spirit of God's son. In fact, Paul thought that it was

---

4. Son(s) of God: Matt 5:9, 45; Luke 6:35; 20:36; 2 Cor 6:18 ("sons and daughters"); 1 Thess 5:5 ("sons of light"); Rev 21:7; children of God: John 1:12; 11:52; Rom 8:16–17; 9:8; Gal 4:6; Eph 5:1, 8; 1 John 3:1–2, 10; 5:2; cf. Acts 17:28: God's "offspring" (*genos*); Heb 2:10–18 (*huioi, paidia*).

5. Stobaeus, *Anth* 1.1.12, in F. C. Grant, *Hellenistic Religions* (New York: Liberal Arts Press, 1953), 152, 154.

6. Epictetus, *Disc* 1.3.1–6.

7. Epictetus, *Disc* 1.13.5.

8. Ex 4:22; Deut 14:1; Isa 1:2; Jer 3:22; 31:9, 20; Jub 1:24–25; etc.

9. *b. Qidd.* 36a.

God's Spirit that made people in his communities cry out "Abba! Father!" Back, then, to Paul.

WHEN WE CRY "ABBA"

The Epistle to the Romans is unique among Paul's letters. First, it was a letter written to strangers. Unlike the other places to which he wrote, Paul had never actually been to Rome. He wrote to the Jesus followers in Rome because he was hatching plans to travel further west, into what is now Spain. Paul's plan was apparently to visit Rome, present himself as a kind of ambassador of the Jesus movement, stay a while with the Jesus followers there, raise funds for his travels, and then move on with their blessing.[10] The problem was that Paul did not know whether or not they would agree with his point of view. It may be hard to believe now, but in his own day and time, Paul was not universally admired among the followers of Jesus. In fact, his letters reveal quite the opposite. Almost no one, it seems, agreed with him. So Paul wrote the Epistle to the Romans, as it is known today, to explain his various ideas and to win these strangers over to his novel claims. To do this, he had to show how his ideas were actually consistent with what he thought they believed. One of the hardest things he had to sell them—he guessed—was the idea that Gentiles could join in following the Jewish messiah without observing the Jewish Law. They too could become children of God. Unfortunately, his argument for this is complex and often hard to follow. We will pick it up in chapter 7 of the letter.

At this point in the letter, Paul is arguing that as long as people are living life oriented to the material world, the Law will do them no good. Simple human desire makes people flout the Law. You may want to observe the Law, says Paul, but sin takes root in the flesh and the only law you end up obeying is the law of sin.[11] In other words, as a rule, people generally end up doing things they know they shouldn't, drawn to them by simple desire—for food, sex, the next shiny object, and so forth. Now, the solution to this problem, he says (in chapter 8 of Romans), is rooted in an *idea* and an *experience* they all share. The *idea* is actually Platonic—that we are not simply flesh, but spirit too. And the Spirit (let's capitalize it now) is a gift from God.[12] That is the idea, and it was a fairly common one in antiquity.

---

10. See Rom 15:22–29. For a discussion of the purpose of Romans, see Robert Jewett, *Romans, A Commentary*, Hermeneia (Minneapolis: Fortress, 2007), 42–46.

11. See Rom 7:7–25.

12. See Rom 8:9, for example.

In fact, it must have been a common enough idea among early followers of Jesus that Paul could assume that the Roman branch of the Jesus movement would follow what he was saying and more or less embrace it.

The *experience* was the spiritual ecstasy they had been seeing in their gatherings and celebrations. This included speaking in tongues, prophecy, visions of the risen Jesus, and so forth—also very common among the early communities of Jesus's followers.[13] Even Paul himself claims to have had such experiences.[14] Paul, like everyone else, took them to be signs, visitations of the Spirit of God. So Paul goes on with his argument: "You are not in the flesh," he says, "you are of the Spirit, if, in fact, the Spirit of God dwells in you" (Rom 8:9). Notice how he now identifies their spirits with the Spirit of God. Again, this was not an unusual way to think about this Platonic notion—it is all just one spirit: the divine Spirit that is God is present piecemeal also in individuals. So finally, he says, by the power of the Spirit of God dwelling in them, they "will put to death the deeds of the body" (Rom 8:12). That is how they will serve God, he says, by the power of the Spirit, not the Law. This, of course, is Paul's real point. But he then goes on to drive this point home—and this is where his words become interesting to us. He says, "All who are led by the Spirit are sons of God (*huioi tou theou*)" (Rom 8:14). Paul next says something that may explain why he believed this, referring to actual ecstatic experiences they had been having. He says,

> When we cry out, "Abba! Father!" it is the Spirit itself witnessing to the fact that we are children of God (*tekna theou*), and if we are children, then we are heirs, heirs of God and fellow heirs with Christ (provided that we suffer with him in order that we might be glorified with him).
>
> Rom 8:15–16

If it is a little hard to believe that Paul actually means this, note that he repeats a very similar claim in Galatians 4:6–7. When the Galatian believers cry out "Abba," he says, this is "the spirit of God's son," sent into them to make them "sons" of God by adoption. He means just what he says. Anyone who is possessed by the spirit—"of God" or "of God's son"—becomes a "son" or "child of God," a "fellow heir with Christ." Of course,

---

13. The Pauline statement of this phenomenon is in 1 Cor 12 and 14; the opening chapters of the Acts of the Apostles offers a fictionalized memory of the early, spirit-filled years of the church; visions and prophecy are everywhere in early Christian literature; see David E. Aune, *Prophecy in Early Christianity and the Ancient Mediterranean World* (Grand Rapids, MI: Eerdmans, 1983).

14. See 1 Cor 14:18.

Paul thought that to be a child, or son of God, meant suffering like Christ. To become a son of God you had to become like *the* son of God, and Paul's take on Jesus was all wrapped up in his suffering and martyrdom. But not everyone would have focused the idea in just this way. The Galileans who created the Q sermon thought the key thing was to become kind and forgiving. For them, *the* son of God was a teacher, so the sons of God would naturally embody his teaching. But Paul reveals something more about this idea that may have had broad resonance through the Jesus movement: that experiences of spiritual enthusiasm were correlated with the claim of being a child of God. It was apparently common for people in these communities to cry out "Abba! Father!" when lost in spiritual ecstasy. Who could say that but a true child of God?[15]

BORN OF GOD

This idea that the followers of Jesus could become sons or children of God, like Jesus, persisted for a long time in early Christianity. It still turns up almost fifty years later in the Gospel of John. This is surprising, because among the biblical gospels, we normally consider John to have the "highest Christology." That is, John's author speaks about Jesus in more highly mythological terms than in any other New Testament gospel. It is in John that one finds the roots of the idea, expressed in the Apostles' Creed, that Jesus is the one and only Son of God. And yet, even here the followers of Jesus are elevated too: by identifying with him they can become "children of God."

This is what John claims in the opening lines of the gospel, in what is normally called the Prologue to the Gospel of John (John 1:1–18). It is here, in fact, that we find some of the most highly concentrated mythological content in the gospel. Statements like "In the beginning was the Word, and the Word was with God, and the Word was divine," "The light shines in the darkness and the darkness has not comprehended it," and "The Word became flesh and dwelt among us" seem to cast Jesus in the role of a divine being, hardly human at all. And yet, among these poetically powerful sentences we also find these:

> The true light that enlightens everyone came into the world.
> He was in the world, and the world came into being through him.

---

15. For the ecstatic nature of what Paul is describing, see Jewett, *Romans*, 498–99. The word *krazo*, "to cry out," is commonly associated with ecstatic religious utterance.

Yet, the world did not know him. He came to his own home, and his own people did not accept him. But whoever did accept him—those who believed in his name, who were born neither from blood, nor lust, nor male desire, but from God—he gave to them authority to become children of God.

John 1:9–13

This passage is critical for the author of the Gospel of John. The Prologue casts Jesus in the role of God's eternal companion, sent into the world to awaken a sleeping humanity from its indifferent slumber.[16] In other ancient versions of this mytheme, the messenger is rejected, as is Jesus, the "true light," in John's Prologue. "He came to his own home, and his own people did not accept him" (John 1:11). But ultimately someone does accept him—the sectarians weaving their story into the myth. John's people believed that they alone had received the savior. They "believed in his name," he says. And so they received "authority to become children of God." They, like him, were born "of God."

The myth of God's heaven-sent redeemer was well suited to capturing the basic conviction behind these claims: that Jesus and his followers were alike. In various versions of this mythic story, the divine messenger comes into the world, but people do not accept him/her. They are blind or deaf or half asleep, or more than this, they just do not have what it takes to recognize what is standing before them. The messenger comes from another world, the heavenly world of the spirit. Only people who have come from that world themselves are able to recognize the messenger for who he/she really is, for they too are of the spirit. The author of the Gospel of John plays with this idea in a well-known, even iconic story in chapter 3 of this gospel: the story of Nicodemus.[17]

Nicodemus in this story is a Jewish leader who comes to Jesus to honor him with the title "Rabbi." "Rabbi, we know that you are a teacher who has come from God, for no one can do these signs you do apart from the presence of God" (John 3:2). It seems like he's on the right track—but not for the author of John. "Rabbi," for him, doesn't even begin to touch the significance of Jesus. So he has Jesus rebuff him, saying, "Unless you are born from above, you cannot see the Reign of God" (John 3:3). But Nicodemus

---

16. A long-held thesis about John: for a classic early statement of the idea, see Rudolf Bultmann, "The History of Religions Background of the Prologue to the Gospel of John," in *The Interpretation of John*, ed. and trans. John Ashton (Philadelphia: Fortress, 1986), 18–35 (German original published in 1922); also Wayne Meeks, "The Man from Heaven in Johannine Sectarianism," *Journal of Biblical Literature* 91 (1972): 44–72 (reprinted in Ashton, *Interpretation of John*, 141–73).
17. See John 3:1–15.

seems more than rebuked by what Jesus says. He's confused. This is because John has inserted a clever double entendre into this sentence, a kind of insider joke to be shared with his audience that you can see only if you are reading the sentence in Greek. The words "from above" in this sentence are a translation of the Greek word *anothen*, a polysemic word—that is, a word with two very different and unrelated meanings. It can mean "from above," but it can also mean "again" or "anew." "Again" is what Nicodemus hears. You have to be born "again" to see the reign of God. This is what confuses and flusters Nicodemus. "How can you enter a second time into your mother's womb?" he stammers (John 3:4). But Jesus is talking about the world of the spirit, not the world of the flesh. To be born *anothen* is to be born "from above," to come from the heavenly world of the spirit.[18] Nicodemus is not from that world, so he cannot see God's reign. He can't even understand Jesus when he speaks about it. Jesus says to him, "That which is born of the flesh is flesh, and that which is born of the spirit is spirit." Then, "The wind [or spirit—another double entendre] blows where it will and you hear its sound, but you do not know where it comes from or where it goes. But anyone born of the spirit does know." Nicodemus just says, "What?" (John 3:6–9). In this well-known passage, John uses the myth of God's divine messenger, and a lot of verbal misdirection, to create solidarity with his audience. If Nicodemus doesn't know what he is talking about, John's audience most certainly does.[19] They, like Jesus, are born from above.

So what is he talking about? As in the Prologue, John here uses the mytheme of God's divine messenger to interpret Jesus in the lives of his audience. When Nicodemus is baffled by the idea of being born *anothen* (again?/from above?), Jesus answers him like this: "Truly, truly I say to you, unless you are born of water and the spirit, you cannot enter the Reign of God" (John 3:5). That makes it fairly clear, at least to John's insiders. To be born *anothen* is to be baptized. This is what makes one a child of God, born from above, a spirit person, able to hear the spirit, see the spirit, to know where it comes from and where it is going. This is what John meant in the Prologue: "to those who believed in his name, who were born neither from blood, nor lust, nor male desire, but from God—he gave to them authority to become children of God" (John 1:12). The baptized are all children of God.

The author of the Gospel of John probably also wrote the First Epistle of John, a pseudonymous letter/essay attributed, like the gospel, to a close companion of Jesus. But the text actually comes from the end of the first

---

18. See John 3:31–36, where John resolves the wordplay very clearly.
19. See Meeks, "The Man from Heaven" for this point.

century, perhaps ten to fifteen years after the Gospel of John. It contains a less intense, less desperate version of his message. In the gospel, it is shear blind faith that characterizes the life of the children of God. Many students of the Gospel of John believe that John's community was then at the point of dissolution, and therefore, somewhat desperate. You either believe or you don't. Decide![20] But a generation later, things had settled down. Now it is not mere blind faith that makes them the children of God, but something more—love. "Beloved, let us love one another, for love is from God. Everyone who loves is born of God and knows God" (1 John 4:7). The whole letter is structured more or less around this theme. The children of God are characterized by love. This is what makes them like the Son of God.

> See what love the Father has given us, that we should be called children of God—and so we are. The reason why the world does not know us is that it did not know him. Beloved, we are now children of God; it is not yet clear what we shall be. We know that whenever he appears, we shall be like him, so we shall see him as he is.
>
> 1 John 3:1–3

The person who wrote this letter and the people who read it were mostly the same people who heard and sang the words of the Prologue to the Gospel of John. They believed they would recognize Jesus whenever he returned to them because they were like him. Jesus was the Son of God; they now are children of God. But nobody else knows this about them, just as nobody knew that Jesus was the Son of God. In this sentiment one can still feel something of the sectarian vibe most specialists think forms the backdrop to the Johannine literature. It is as though the writer and his audience are all in on a secret. They know the truth about Jesus and the truth about themselves. They are special. They are children of God. But in this later generation their sectarianism had taken on very strong elements of moral responsibility. "Do not be astonished, brothers and sisters, that the world hates you. We know that we have passed from death to life because we love our brother or sister" (1 John 3:14). Then, "But whoever has the world's goods and sees his brother or sister in need, yet closes their heart to them, how does the love of God dwell in them? Children, let us not love in word or speech, but in actions and in truth" (1 John 3:17–18).

20. See esp. J. Louis Martyn, *History and Theology in the Fourth Gospel*, 3rd ed., The New Testament Library (Louisville and London: Westminster John Knox Press, 2003).

SONS OF THE LIVING FATHER

In another early Christian gospel it is not faith or love that makes one a child of God, but wisdom and knowledge of the reign of God within. The Gospel of Thomas is a wisdom gospel.[21] It is premised on the idea that seeking wisdom and insight is life's highest calling. "Seek and you will find," says Jesus in the opening strains of this gospel (Thom 2:1). What are you to seek? The reign of God within you. Here is more of the opening salvo from the Gospel of Thomas:

> Jesus said, "If those who lead you say to you, 'Behold, the kingdom is in the sky,' the birds of the sky will precede you.' If they say to you, 'It is in the sea,' then the fish will precede you. Rather, the kingdom is inside you and outside you. When you come to know yourselves you will be known and you will realize that you are sons of the Living Father. But if it happens that you never come to know yourselves, then you exist in poverty, and you are the poverty."
>
> Thom 3:1–5

Know thyself—the ancient Delphic Maxim. The Gospel of Thomas represents a branch of earliest Christianity that was rooted in Hellenistic Judaism of the sort to be found, say, in Egypt or far to the east in ancient Edessa. These Jews were intrigued by Platonic philosophy and enjoined it heartily as part of the Platonic renaissance that was sweeping the ancient academies of the time.[22] Here, for example, is how Philo of Alexandria, a Jew steeped in this tradition, once articulated it:

> Know thyself and the parts of which thou dost consist, what each is and for what it was made and how it was meant to work, and Who it is that, all invisible,

---

21. So, originally, James M. Robinson, "LOGOI SOPHŌN: On the Gattung of Q," in James M. Robinson and Helmut Koester, *Trajectories Through Early Christianity* (Philadelphia: Fortress Press, 1971), 77–113; also Stevan Davies, *The Gospel of Thomas and Christian Wisdom* (New York: Seabury, 1983); and Thomas Zöckler, *Jesu Lehren im Thomasevangelium*, Nag Hammadi and Manichaean Studies 47 (Leiden: Brill, 1999).

22. See Stephen J. Patterson, "Jesus Meets Plato: The Theology of the Gospel of Thomas and Middle Platonism," in *Das Thomasevangelium, Entstehung – Rezeption – Theologie*, ed. J. Frey et al., Beihefte zur Zeitschrift für die neutestamentliche Wissenschaft 157 (Berlin: de Gruyter, 2008), 181–205; reprinted in Patterson, *The Gospel of Thomas and Christian Origins: Essays on the Fifth Gospel*, Nag Hammadi and Manichaean Studies 84 (Leiden and Boston: Brill, 2013), 33–60.

invisibly sets the puppets in motion and pulls their strings, whether it be the Mind that is in thee or the Mind of the universe.[23]

Notice the very Platonic way that Philo, a Jew, speaks of God's presence and activity in the world. God is the Mind of the Universe, and each person bears a piece of that divine Mind within him- or herself. It is through this piece of God, the Mind of God dwelling within, that God makes an impression on the world, influences it, governs it, "pulls the strings." This is all very Platonic—straight out of the *Timaeus*. Of course, the older, more traditional Jewish way of speaking about this intimate relationship between God and humanity was with the language of "sonship," as we have seen. Recall, for example, that rabbinic opinion we saw earlier: "When the Israelites do the will of God they are called sons, when they do not do God's will they are not called sons."[24] Philo would have agreed. Those who "do what is pleasing to nature and what is good are sons of God," he says.[25] And this is the language the Gospel of Thomas uses—"know thyself, that you are a child ('son') of God." This was a very Jewish way of articulating a very Middle Platonic maxim to answer a question of central importance to the Jesus movement: what did Jesus mean by the reign of God? It had to do with the way one acts in the world. For Platonists, leading a life responsive to God meant listening to the Mind of God guiding you from within. Translated into the language of the Jesus movement, this meant seeking the reign of God within and finding that you are a child of God, intimately connected to the One who rules the universe. This is the beginning of wisdom.

But what then? Once you seek, find, become self-aware, and understand who you truly are, a child of God, what comes next? There is, of course, the living out of this vision. Be in the world as God would have you be. "Blessed are those who go hungry, that the belly of the one in wont will be filled" (Thom 68). "Blessed is the one who has struggled and found life" (Thom 58). "Observe the Living One while you live" (Thom 59). But in the Platonic tradition there is always more. "Become passersby" (Thom 42). This world is but a place of temporary sojourn for the Platonist. It is a mere shadow of the real world, the heavenly world of the one true God. Every Platonist eventually turns from this world to that one, to the

23. *On Flight*, 46.
24. *b. Qidd.* 36a.
25. *Special Laws* 1.318.

world that exists above, in the heavens, in the Mind of God. The deeper that Thomas Christians were drawn into the world of Plato, the more they focused there as well. As in the Gospel of John, the children of God are finally not of this world. They come from the realm of the Father, and to that realm they are destined to return. Consider this passage in the virtual center of the Gospel of Thomas:

> Jesus said, "If they say to you, 'Where do you come from?' say to them, "We have come from the light, the place where the light came into being by itself, established itself, and appeared in their image.' If they say to you, 'Is it you?' say 'We are his children, the elect of the living Father.' If they ask you, 'What is the sign of your Father within you?' say, 'It is movement and rest.'"
>
> Thom 50:1–3

There is the myth of the divine messenger in a nutshell. The children of God have come from the place above, the place of light, and the messenger, Jesus, tells them that they are destined to return there again. But the cosmos was not made to allow just anyone to fly up to God whenever they pleased. Many ancients believed that the heavens above were structured like a series of spheres, and that each of the spheres was governed by one of the wandering stars—the planets—each with a name familiar still: Mercury, Mars, Venus, Saturn, Jupiter, and the really big ones, Helios (the sun) and Luna (the moon). Some systems had 7 spheres; some had 3; other more speculative ones might have 70 or 360. In any event, Thomas saying 50 is a flight plan, a catechism revealing a series of passwords to recite as you travel up and out and home.[26] The guardians of the spheres will expect you to know the answers to a series of questions. One will ask, "Where do you come from?" Another, "Is it you?" Another, "What is the sign, the evidence, that you are who you say you are?" When the time comes, it will be important to know, above all, that you are "children of the living Father."

---

26. Most interpreters have understood this as the soul's final journey home after death, but it is also possible that it refers to mystical experiences of the soul during one's lifetime—see April DeConick, *Seek to See Him: Ascent and Vision Mysticism in the Gospel of Thomas*, Supplements to Vigiliae Christianae 33 (Leiden: Brill, 1996), 50–63. For the present exegesis and interpretation see Stephen J. Patterson, "Motion and Rest: The Platonic Origins of a Mysterious Concept," in *Scribal Practices and Social Structures Among Jesus Adherents: Essays in Honour of John S. Kloppenborg*, ed. William E. Arnal et al., Bibliotheca Ephemeridum Theologicarum Lovaniensium 285 (Leuven, Paris, and Bristol: Peeters, 2016), 251–61.

BAPTISM AND THE CHILDREN OF GOD

So "son of God" was not a title reserved initially for Jesus. The followers of Jesus were also "sons" or "children of God." They were children of God in the same way that Jesus was *the* Son of God—God was their father. They were "born of God," in the words of John. But why associate these claims with baptism? Why, in John, are those who are born "from above" said to have been born "*from water* and the spirit?" Why does our creed declare that "you," the baptized, "are all children (sons) of God?" It is because in earliest Christianity the ritual of baptism was apparently associated with becoming, or being, children of God. This seems to have been true right from the beginning, when the followers first began to baptize one another in the way John had baptized their hero and leader, Jesus.

One way to see this is in the story that the followers of Jesus first began to tell about John's baptism of Jesus in the Jordan. One of the oddities in the history of Christian baptism is the fact that, in spite of this story, we do not have a very clear picture of how Christian baptism actually originated. The gospels tell of how Jesus was baptized, but they never depict Jesus baptizing anyone else.[27] The *baptizer* was John, to whom Jesus himself apparently went to be baptized. So the history of this key ritual in Christendom begins with John the Baptist, leaps over Jesus himself, and somehow lands in the emergent communities of the Jesus movement. The story of how, exactly, that happened would be more involved than we would find useful to tell here.[28] But the story of Jesus's baptism by John can nonetheless tell us something important about how Jesus's followers understood baptism

27. The Gospel of John mentions that Jesus baptized (see John 3:22, 26; 4:1), but then, oddly, in an editorial aside, denies that he did (see John 4:2).

28. Some recent good attempts to tell the story include Hans-Dieter Betz, "Transferring a Ritual: Paul's Interpretation of Baptism in Romans 6," in *Paul in His Hellenistic Context*, ed. Troels Engberg-Pedersen (Minneapolis: Fortress, 1995), 84–118; reprinted in Betz, *Paulinische Studien. Gesammelte Aufsäzte III* (Tübingen: Mohr Siebeck, 1994), 258–62; Adela Yarbro Collins, "The Origin of Christian Baptism," in *Cosmology and Eschatology in Jewish and Christian Apocalypticism*, Supplements to the Journal for the Study of Judaism 50 (Leiden: Brill, 1996), 218–38; Michael Labahn, "Kreative Erinnerung als nachosterliche Nachschöpfung. Der Ursprung der christliche Taufe," in *Ablution, Initiation, and Baptism: Late Antiquity, Early Judaism, and Early Christianity/Waschungen, Initiation und Taufe: Spätantike, Frühes Judentum und Frües Christentum*, ed. David Hellholm et al., 3 vols., Beihefte zur Zeitschrift für die neutestamentliche Wissenschaft 176 I, II, III (Berlin: De Gruyter, 2010), vol. I: 337–76. For my own effort to tell this story in a new way, see Stephen J. Patterson, "From John to Apollos to Paul: How the Baptism of John Entered the Jesus Movement," in *Christian Origins and the Establishment of the Early Jesus Movement*, ed. Stanley Porter and Andrew Pitts; Early Christianity in Its Hellenistic Context 4 (Leiden: Brill, 2017).

in those early years of the Jesus movement and why they thought that
through baptism they could become children of God.

The story is best known from the Gospel of Mark. Matthew and Luke
also have it, but Mark's was a generation earlier and served, in part, as the
model for those later iterations. So here is Mark's version:

> Now in those days Jesus came from Nazareth of Galilee and was baptized by
> John in the Jordan. And when he came up out of the water, immediately he saw
> the heavens opened and the spirit descending upon him like a dove. And a voice
> came from heaven, "You are my beloved Son; with you I am well pleased."
>
> Mark 1:9–11

This is, by all accounts, a fairly important story in the Gospel of Mark: it
is the moment when Jesus is unveiled as the son of God. Mark bookends
the acclamation, "You are my beloved Son," with similar words in chapter 9,
verse 7: "This is my beloved Son; listen to him," probably trying to underscore that point. But where does the basic story come from? Did someone
just remember the event and report it? Or did Mark the evangelist create
it for dramatic effect?

It is probably not someone's memory of the time when Jesus was actually baptized. I think that Jesus was actually baptized by John the
Baptist—though not everyone does (and with good reason).[29] But the elements of this story reveal it to be a fictive re-creation of that event, not
an actual memory of it. Many people went out to be baptized by John.
Why would anyone have noticed Jesus in particular? What about the dove?
Wouldn't people have noticed that? Jesus sees the dove, but no one else
does.[30] What about the voice from the sky? A voice is just a voice unless the
omniscient author tells us that it belongs to God.[31] In other words, this is
someone's idea of what the baptism of Jesus should look like—*would* have
looked like—if anyone had been there to notice the unveiling of the Son of
God at that moment.

Did the author of Mark create it? Perhaps—especially the several details
and nuances in Mark's version. But scholars have noticed that Matthew
and Luke share a few details and particulars that do not occur in Mark. This
often signals that those later evangelists had another version of the story
to look at in addition to Mark's, namely, a version from that lost gospel Q,

---

29. See, e.g., Clare K. Rothschild, *Baptist Traditions and Q*, Wissenschaftliche
Untersuchungen Zum Neuen Testament 190 (Tübingen: Mohr Siebeck, 2005), 13.

30. See Mark 1:10b.

31. See Mark 1:11.

from which they also drew, you'll recall, the Sermon on the Mount/Plain (see the discussion earlier). If it is in fact true that Q also had a similar story about John's baptism of Jesus,[32] then we must assume that a story about Jesus's baptism was circulating very early in the Jesus movement, before either Mark or Q wrote it down. How early? Mark is dated to around 70 CE, but Q is usually dated earlier, sometimes much earlier.[33] That means a version of this story was probably already circulating in the oral traditions of the Jesus movement at about the same time Paul was insisting in his letters that the Spirit of God could make people cry out "Abba, Father," thus identifying them as sons, or children, of God.

If this story about John's baptism of Jesus comes from oral tradition, we need to say a few more things about it. In a cultural milieu in which writing is rare and orality common, things like this story only survive because they have a certain usefulness in the communities in which they functioned. If no one uses them, they simply die out. The older form critics would call this usefulness the story's "Sitz im Leben," or "setting in life," meaning the typical situation in the life of a community in which a story would have been useful. Rudolf Bultmann pegged this story as a "biographical legend," which eventually took on the function of a "cult legend," that is, a story told and retold to remind people of why they do the peculiar things they do.[34] Why do we baptize thus? Thus it was in the beginning, when John baptized Jesus in the Jordan River.

Now, Bultmann thought that the form of the story and its details must have come from the particulars of early Christian baptismal practice. That is, after all, how a cult legend functions. To explain the details of some cultic practice, the details in the cult legend have to match those practical details pretty closely, and we should suppose this to be the case here as well. Baptism in the early Jesus movement, then, included ritual washing

32. Scholars have generally been divided on this issue. The International Q Project prints the remnants of a Q version of the story (*The Sayings Gospel Q*, 78–79), but among its leadership, at least John Kloppenborg thought it unlikely. It is clear, however, that Q began with an account of John baptizing in the Jordan and of Jesus being tempted in the wilderness. In Mark, these stories bracket the story of Jesus's baptism, and it would be difficult to imagine why Q would have these stories and not the story they bracket. If you bring John the Baptist onto the scene, he is probably there to baptize someone. So I would infer that Q probably did have the story of Jesus's baptism.

33. The dating of Q is a notoriously thorny problem among students of this document. Most assume that it predates the Jewish War in 66–70 CE, when Mark is usually dated. But how much earlier? Absent any clear historical markers, educated guesses go as early as the 30s CE to the 60s, just before the Jewish War. For a discussion of the issues and proposals, see Kloppenborg Verbin, *Excavating Q*, 80–87.

34. Rudolf Bultmann, *History of the Synoptic Tradition*, rev. ed., trans. John Marsh (Oxford: Blackwell, 1963), 247, 252.

and the imparting of the spirit. And the acclamation "This is my beloved son"? This must reflect something like what Paul is referring to when he writes about the spirit causing the one possessed of it to cry out "Abba, Father," thus signifying that he or she was a child of God. In the Gospel of Mark, this acclamation refers only to Jesus. But in the cult legend, this element of the story would have functioned to explain why all who were baptized were thought to possess the Holy Spirit and become children of God. Baptism, they believed, was the moment when the followers of Jesus were, like Jesus himself, imbued with the spirit and unveiled as sons, or children, of God.[35] That must be why our earliest baptismal creed begins as it does, with the words "For you are all sons of God in the Spirit."

But not everyone thought that Jesus became God's son when John baptized him in the Jordan. Some believed that he became God's son when he was raised from the dead. Paul held this view.[36] So was there an interpretation of baptism that synced up with this notion, that through baptism one could pass, like Jesus, through the crucible of death and return once again to life? Indeed there was. Paul knew such a tradition, referring to it at least once very explicitly. He says in Romans 6:

> Do you not know that all of us who have been baptized into Christ Jesus have been baptized into his death? We have been buried with him through baptism unto death, in order that just as Christ was raised from the dead by the glory of the Father, we too might walk in newness of life.
>
> Rom 6:1–4

Where did this come from? Some think Paul created it himself,[37] others that it too predated Paul's entry into the Jesus movement.[38] In any event, here was another baptismal tradition in which recipients could participate in the event by which Jesus came to be seen as the son of God: his death and resurrection. Just as Jesus had passed through death to life and become truly the son of God, so now his followers could join in that journey, ritually, and become children of God.

---

35. Collins, *Gospel of Mark*, 147.

36. See Rom 1:3–4.

37. See Jewett, *Romans*, 396–98; earlier, Rudolf Schnackenburg, *Baptism in the Thought of St. Paul: A Study in Pauline Theology*, trans. G. R. Beasley-Murray (Oxford: Blackwell/ New York: Herder & Herder, 1964), 33–34, as well as many other scholars.

38. See Rudolf Bultmann, *Theology of the New Testament*, 2 vols., trans. Kendrick Grobel (New York: Charles Scribner's Sons, 1951, 1955), vol. I: 140–41; Ernst Käsemann, *Commentary on Romans*, trans. G. W. Bromiley (Grand Rapids, MI: Eerdmans, 1980), 166–67.

And what about those who believed, like the author of the Gospel of John, that Jesus was the Son of God because he had come down from heaven, the realm of the spirit, and had returned there again? Was there an understanding of baptism that asserted that the believer too was just such a child of God, born from above, a creature more at home in the world of the spirit than here on Earth? Is that not what the author of the Gospel of John meant when he has Jesus explain to poor Nicodemus that being born "from above" means being born "of water and the spirit" (John 3:5)? That must have been what baptism meant in early Johannine Christianity. Baptism was the moment when the baptized claimed their heavenly origin and declared their intention to return there again.

And there were other views of Jesus, who he was and what he meant, and other ideas about baptism that reflect them. In two of Paul's letters we learn that there were some in the Jesus movement who believed that Jesus was a new Adam, born into the world to do what the first Adam had tried and failed to do: obey God. By his obedience, Jesus, the new Adam, could heal the rift that had come between God and humanity since the beginning of time.[39] What was the baptismal tradition that went along with that idea? This one is a little harder to spot, but many students of the Gospel of Thomas believe that there is a remnant of it in saying 37 of that gospel. It reads as follows:

> His disciples said, "When will you appear to us and when will we see you?"
>
> Jesus said, "When you undress without being ashamed and take your clothes (and) put them under your feet like little children and trample them, then [you] will see the son of the Living One, and you will not be afraid."
>
> Thom 37

The baptismal significance of this saying was first noticed by the great historian of religion Jonathan Z. Smith, who argued that it probably came from an early Christian baptismal liturgy.[40] What caught his attention was the phrase "When you undress without being ashamed." In the story of Adam and Eve, recall, after they eat of the tree of knowledge they become aware of their nakedness and are *ashamed*. Smith wondered if this phrase could be a reference to Genesis. That might seem a little far-fetched, but Smith also had in mind a little-known Syrian Christian baptismal tradition that focused precisely here, on this moment in the story of Genesis.

---

39. See Rom 5:12–21 and 1 Cor 15:42–50, esp. 45; discussion: Robin Scroggs, *The Last Adam: A Study in Pauline Anthropology* (Philadelphia: Fortress, 1966).

40. Jonathan Z. Smith, "The Garments of Shame," *History of Religions* 5 (1966): 217–38.

His source for this tradition was Theodore of Mopsuestia (350–428 CE), a bishop of Antioch in the early fifth century. Here is what Theodore says about the meaning of disrobing as one approaches the baptismal waters:

> As in the beginning, when Adam was naked and in nothing ashamed of himself, but after having broken the commandment and become mortal, he found himself in need of an outer covering—so you also, who are ready to draw near to the gift of holy baptism, that through it you may be born afresh and become symbolically immortal, rightly remove your clothing, which indicates your mortality.[41]

Imagining the body as a mortal suit of clothes covering the immortal soul was an idea relatively common among those who indulged in Platonic philosophy, like our Thomas Christians did. That is why in this tradition the clothing of Adam signals his mortality, while the disrobing of the initiate signals his or her immortality. In this telling of the primordial story, Adam and Eve become truly mortal when they are clothed in "garments of skins" provided by God.[42] These "garments of skins" were not clothes given to cover their naked bodies, but mortal bodies given to cover their naked souls.[43] When, in this tradition, the initiates disrobed, they symbolically shed their bodies of mortal flesh and resumed the immortal state Adam and Eve once enjoyed before the fall.

Baptism, then, was a powerful thing. John's ritual of washing in the Jordan caught on among the followers of Jesus, who began to think of themselves as children of God. The same spirit that descended on Jesus had now descended on them. They had passed through death to life. They were the children of God who had come from the world above and would return there again. They had been restored to the glory that once belonged to Adam. So when they first gave verse to the ritual of baptism and began to interpret it for themselves, it should not surprise us that they began with the acclamation: you are all children ("sons") of God. And what did this mean? It could have meant many things. But for the author of this first credo, it meant that among them there would be no Jew or Greek, no slave or free, no male and female, for they were all one. This, notice, is a little different. This acclamation doesn't pass through Jesus, the first son of God, whom the baptized now emulate. It goes directly to the baptized, stating

41. A. Mingana, *Commentary of Theodore of Mopsuestia on the Lord's Prayer and the Sacraments of Baptism and the Eucharist*, Woodbrooke Studies 4 (Cambridge, MA: Heffer and Sons, 1933), 53, after Smith, "Garments of Shame," 227.

42. See Gen 3:21.

43. See, e.g., Philo's interpretation of this phrase in *QG* 1.53.

who they are and how they are to be in the world. Baptism was the moment when they affirmed for themselves: there is no Jew or Greek, no slave or free, no male and female. These distinctions—race, class, and gender—are not real, and their divisive effects are not legitimate. In baptism they made their declaration of solidarity, one with another, in spite of the differences normally used to mark and measure the human community: "You are all one." Did anyone ever take this utopian vision of solidarity seriously? Did anyone ever try to build communities in which race, class, and gender would not be used to exclude, rank, or denigrate the other? Yes, briefly.

CHAPTER 4

༄

There Is No Jew or Greek

The consular year of Aulus Vitellius and Lucius Vipstanus Poplicola, or the seventh year of the emperor Claudius, or 48 CE, by our reckoning, would have found Paul the Apostle in the ancient city of Antioch. What was he doing there? He was trying to get Jews and Greeks to sit together for a meal and it was proving to be more difficult than you might imagine.

Antioch was one of the largest cities in the eastern half of the Roman Empire, and one of the most diverse.[1] In addition to the various local Syrian tribes and Cilicians who made their way to the great city and settled in its skirts, there were many and sundry Greeks: the descendants of Athenians, Cretans, Cypriots, Argives, and, of course, Macedonians, whose ancestors founded the city in 300 BCE. The Macedonian kings who followed in the wake of Alexander the Great were all former generals in Alexander's army. They, like him, were conquerors and colonizers. Seleucus Nicanor, who colonized this corner of Syria, founded Antioch to settle the troops who had fought with him in the campaign

---

1. On ancient Antioch see Glanville Downey, *A History of Antioch in Syria from Seleucus to the Arab Conquest* (Princeton, NJ: Princeton University Press, 1961); more recently see also the essays on the history on Antioch in Christine Kondoleon's volume celebrating the several magnificent mosaics excavated in Antakya in the 1930s: *Antioch: The Lost City* (Princeton, NJ: Princeton University Press, 2000); and Magnus Zetterholm, *The Formation of Christianity in Antioch: A Social Scientific Approach to the Separation Between Judaism and Christianity*, Routledge Early Church Monographs (London: Routledge, 2003), esp. chapter 2 ("The Setting: Antioch on the Orontes").

to conquer this region—today, the little piece of Turkey that juts down along the eastern shore of the Mediterranean Sea, just west of Aleppo in Syria. He named it after his father, Antiochus, a close friend of Alexander's father, Philip of Macedon. Today, its Turkish residents call it *Antakya*, just as the Greeks who founded it did more than two thousand years ago: *Antiochia*. For centuries Antioch was the capitol of the Seleucid Empire, which stretched from the west coast of Asia Minor to the Euphrates River in the east and south to Judea. As Rome moved east, the old Seleucid realm gradually crumbled until Rome, finally, made Antioch the capitol of its own province of Syria. As a city, Antioch was second only to Alexandria as a center for trade and culture. Politically it was unrivaled as the home base of the Roman legate, who commanded the three (and later four) Roman legions that patrolled the region. The Roman East was the Wild Wild West, and Rome worried always about an invasion from its rival, the Parthian Empire, which crouched just beyond the Arabian desert in the land where the Tigris and the Euphrates meet.

Jews had lived in Antioch since its founding. The Jewish historian Josephus tells us that many Jews fought alongside Seleucus's Macedonian troops in the Syrian campaign and were, consequently, rewarded with a place alongside others in Antioch.[2] Like other ethnic groups in this new city, the Jews carved out their own political enclave—a kind of "city within the city."[3] There they governed themselves and lived according to their ancestral customs for generations. The Jewish quarter in Antioch would have made up one of the largest Jewish communities in the Hellenistic Jewish diaspora.

When Paul came to Antioch some three hundred years later, it was still the second city of the Roman East, a large multicultural metropolis. As Paul worked the region of Syria and Cilicia for more than a decade, he probably used Antioch as his home base, lodging with fellow Jews in the Jewish quarter when he was there.[4] That is why he was there in 48 CE.

2. Josephus, *Ant* 12.119.

3. See Josephus, *Ag Ap* 2.38–39.

4. Paul says he wandered the region of Syria and Cilicia between his first visit to Jerusalem (about 35 CE) and his second (about 48 CE)—see Gal 1:18–2:1, following a conventional chronology of Paul's itinerant activity. No particular detail in the complex matter of the Pauline chronology is presupposed here, save that Paul would have been in the region of Syria and Cilicia in the late 30s and early 40s; for details see Rainer Riesner, *Paul's Early Period: Chronology, Mission Strategy, Theology*, trans. Doug Stott (Grand Rapids, MI: Eerdmans, 1998), chapter 1: "Status of Scholarship: A Survey."

PAUL AMONG JEWS AND GREEKS

But Paul himself had grown up in another city, Tarsus, not far from Antioch.[5] Antioch was the capital of Syria, and Tarsus the capital of neighboring Cilicia. It too had a multicultural makeup and Paul would have grown up there as a Jew living among Gentiles. Paul was a self-described Pharisee in those earlier years,[6] which does not mean what one normally assumes it does—nit-picking Jewish zealots who lived strictly by the Law and hated all things Gentile. To the contrary, the Pharisees were the innovators, the liberals of their day, not the conservatives.[7] Pharisees developed an entire system of adaptive Torah interpretation designed to enable them to live viably among Gentiles, while still keeping their ancient covenant with God. So when Paul became part of the Jesus movement, he likely brought with him an interest in how Jews and Gentiles might live amicably together. God called him, he says, to spread the good news about Jesus among the Gentiles.[8] For Paul, this meant bringing Gentiles into the (Jewish) Jesus movement on equal terms. Not much came of it, though. Paul talks of wandering around the region of Damascus for three years, and then another ten years (at least) around Syria and Cilicia, but with no apparent success.[9] There are no churches on the "churches of Paul" tour in eastern Turkey, Syria, Jordan, or Lebanon. The church in Antioch itself would later develop sympathies for Paul,[10] but not when Paul was there. In fact, Paul's time in Antioch ended in disaster.

The story of Paul in Antioch is one that Paul tells on himself in the Epistle to the Galatians 2:11–14.[11] The context is already familiar from chapter 1. Paul had founded a Christ community in Galatia (after his time in Antioch) on the premise that Gentiles could be a part of it without being circumcised. But alas, others had come to Galatia after Paul had moved on and insisted that circumcision was necessary after all. When he learned of it, Paul shot off the angry letter we know today as Galatians in an effort to

5. Acts 21:39; 22:3.
6. Phil 3:5.
7. See Pamela Eisenbaum, *Paul Was Not a Christian* (San Francisco: HarperOne, 2009), 116–49.
8. See Gal 1:16.
9. Gal 1:17, 21.
10. Ignatius, the bishop of Antioch in the late first and early second centuries, writes generally from a Pauline perspective; see, e.g., the classic essay by Rudolf Bultmann, "Ignatius and Paul," in *Existence and Faith: Shorter Writings of Rudolf Bultmann*, ed. Schubert Ogden (New York: Meridian, 1960), 267–77.
11. For a general discussion of the issues and scholarship on the Antioch incident, see Zetterholm, *Christianity in Antioch*, 129–66.

dissuade anyone from taking this new demand to heart—not that many would have! It is hard to imagine Gentiles gleefully lining up to be circumcised. Indeed, changing the rules like this would have driven most of the Gentiles away, which was Paul's real concern. He was, after all, the apostle to the Gentiles. To win Gentiles to the movement, Paul had lowered the bar. Circumcision would not be required of them. It seems to have worked. There were, at least at one time, mixed Jewish–Gentile Christ communities in Galatia.

We don't know exactly when Paul came up with this idea of lowering the bar. It probably did not come to him immediately. This may be why the apostle to the Gentiles did not have much success in those early years. But when Paul went to parlay with the leaders of the Jesus movement in Jerusalem in the late 40s CE, he says he brought with him an uncircumcised Greek named Titus.[12] Titus appears to have been a kind of demonstration project. Here was a Jesus follower who was not Jewish. Could he be part of the association without being circumcised? There was a debate, apparently, and perhaps even some kind of scuffle, but in the end, Paul says, Titus was not forced to submit to circumcision. Instead, they reached an agreement: Paul would be the apostle to the uncircumcised, while Peter and the others focused on the circumcised. Paul claims that James, Peter, and John—the Jerusalem "pillars"—all agreed. Everyone shook hands on it and Paul went back to his home base in Antioch. I think it a reasonable guess that this whole kerfuffle signals the beginning of Paul's new approach to bringing Gentiles to the Jesus movement. Back in Jerusalem, however, there still must have been significant opposition. Someone, after all, had wanted to circumcise Titus.

THE ANTIOCH AFFAIR

That is where things stood when the so-called Antioch affair took place. Back in Antioch, Paul apparently took up his new role as "apostle to the uncircumcised." But if the Jerusalem folk had imagined Paul would concentrate just on Gentiles, they were mistaken. In Antioch he actually had something else in mind. What if Jews and Greeks were to sit at a table *together*? Table fellowship. How hard could that be? Surely Jews and Greeks must have dined together on many occasions before. There was no prohibition against it. Torah-observant Jews would have needed to stipulate a kosher

---

12. Paul tells the following story in Gal 2:1–10.

menu, but that would not have posed an insurmountable problem. Jews can cook. Lamb works for everyone. And so Jews and Greeks began to eat together. Now, at some point, Peter, who had been part of the meeting in Jerusalem, came to Antioch.[13] Apparently, the mixed table fellowship there did not trouble him, for as Paul indicates, he joined right in.[14] So the apostle to the uncircumcised and the apostle to the circumcised were sitting down to eat with circumcised and uncircumcised at a common table. A real kum-ba-yah moment. What could be better? Then all hell broke loose.

What happened next is pretty clear. We just don't know exactly why it happened. The episode is brief and can easily be recalled in full from Paul's Galatian letter:

> But when Cephas [Peter] came to Antioch, I opposed him to his face, because he stood condemned. For, before certain people from James arrived, he ate with the Gentiles. But when they came, he withdrew and separated himself in fear of the circumcision party. And along with him the rest of the Jews also became hypocrites, so that even Barnabas was carried away by their hypocrisy. But when I saw that they were not straightforward about the truth of the gospel, I said to Cephas in front of everyone, "If you, a Jew, live like a Gentile and not like a Jew, how can you insist that Gentiles live like Jews."
>
> Gal 2:11–14

So at some point another group of Jesus followers came to Antioch from Jerusalem. Paul calls them "certain people from James" (Gal 2:12a), referring to another of the "pillars" he had met in Jerusalem before, James, the brother of Jesus. In the same breath he also calls them "the circumcision party" (Gal 2:12b), which must mean that they had been among those who advocated circumcision for Gentiles like Titus. They must have objected to Paul's experiment with mixed table fellowship, for Peter (here called by his original name, Cephas) now withdrew from table fellowship with the Gentiles, as did Paul's friend, Barnabas. The problem might have been that they were eating nonkosher food—"If you, a Jew, live like a Gentile" (2:14b)—but that cannot have been the whole problem. Again, the menu could easily have been made kosher. And Paul does not call the new arrivals "the kosher party," but "the circumcision party." So the people from James must have insisted that Peter and the other Jews not sit at table with the uncircumcised Greeks. But why? It turns out that there was a history here.

13. See Gal 2:11.
14. See Gal 2:12.

In the 40s in Antioch the Jews and the Greeks—the circumcised and the uncircumcised—did not like each other, and with good reason. That history, so crucial to understanding what really happened at Antioch, begins, however, in another city. We learn about it not from Paul, but from his contemporary, Philo Judaeus—Philo of Alexandria, whom we have met before.[15]

JEWS AND GREEKS IN THE ROMAN EAST

Philo was, like Paul, a Jew at home in a Greek world. When Paul was growing up Jewish in the Greek city of Tarsus, Philo was growing up in Alexandria, the greatest Greek city in the Roman East. Like Antioch, Alexandria was founded in the days of Alexander the Great. It had been the capital of the ancient Ptolemaic Empire, founded by Alexander's friend and former bodyguard, Ptolemy. When Alexander died, Ptolemy inherited Egypt and its crown jewel of a city, Alexandria. They called him "Soter"—"the Savior." Jews must have arrived in that city fairly soon thereafter. Some say Alexander himself invited them to settle there;[16] another source says that they were brought there originally as prisoners of war.[17] In any event, they were soon employed by Ptolemy and his successors as garrison troops in certain key areas around his empire,[18] including Alexandria, where they were allotted section "delta" of the city.[19] There they structured their lives around the ancient customs that had marked them as a people from the days of Moses.

As in Antioch, the Jewish enclave in Alexandria was a city within a city. Over the years it prospered politically, economically, and culturally alongside other civic enclaves. Alexandria was, though, primarily a Greek city, and Greeks made up the majority of its inhabitants. Its kings and queens—a long list of Ptolemies and Cleopatras—were descendants of Alexander's Greek successors. When Rome conquered the last great Ptolemaic leader, Cleopatra VII, and made Alexandria the capital of its Egyptian province,

15. We met Philo as a religious figure in chapter 3. Now we encounter him as a key political figure in his Jewish community in Alexandria. An older, highly regarded study of Philo from this standpoint is that of E. R. Goodenough, *The Politics of Philo Judaeus* (New Haven, CT: Yale University Press, 1938).

16. Josephus, *Ag Ap* 2.36–37, 42; *Wars* 2.487.

17. *The Letter of Aristeas* 12.

18. See Sandra Gambetti, *The Alexandrian Riots of 38 CE and the Persecution of the Jews: A Historical Reconstruction*, Supplements to the Journal for the Study of Judaism 135 (Leiden: Brill, 2009), 23–34.

19. Josephus, *Wars* 2.488 and 495.

all this changed. Alexandria was now ruled by a Roman prefect. The Greek *boule*, or assembly—the heart of the Greek city—was disbanded.[20] But while Greek fortunes sank, the Jewish situation in Alexandria remained relatively unchanged. Their rights were enshrined on two *stelae* erected in the time of Caesar Augustus, on which were inscribed their rights and privileges.[21] Still, disputes began to surface. Who was a citizen and who was not? Who could be taxed and how much? What rights remained for Greeks, for Jews? Resentments began to fester. In an ancient text known as the Acts of the Alexandrian Martyrs we get a feel for the Greek side of things. In each of these popular tales the plot is always the same: a Greek is reprimanded for an offense against a Jew, who happens to enjoy the good favor of the emperor.[22]

This was the Alexandria into which Philo Judaeus was born in the early part of the first century CE. Philo was thoroughly at home in Alexandria. His native tongue was Greek. His family was a prosperous one, and powerful. One of his nephews was married to a Herodian—the Jewish royal family.[23] Another assimilated completely to Roman society and rose to become the Roman procurator of Judea under the emperor Claudius,[24] and later the prefect of Egypt under Nero.[25] Philo himself was the intellectual of the family. His wealth would have allowed him the leisure to pursue his studies at the Museum of Alexandria, the Harvard of the ancient world, with its famed Royal Library. People came from all over the Roman Empire and beyond to study there. But Philo was by any measure a star. He read philosophy, especially Plato, and became one of the leading lights of the Platonic renaissance known as "Middle Platonism." He held Plato in one hand and a Torah (in Greek) in the other and set out to show that Plato was right—because he agreed with Moses. He wrote prolifically and left behind enough philosophy to fill ten volumes of the Loeb Classical Library. But when Philo was in his golden years, his world suddenly imploded.

The year was 37 CE, the first in the reign of Gaius Julius Caesar Augustus Germanicus—or, as he is remembered today, simply Caligula—the same Caligula whose excesses of cruelty and salaciousness were portrayed in

---

20. As mentioned in Papyrus London 1912—see Gambetti, *The Alexandrian Riots*, 57.

21. As mentioned by Josephus, *Ant* 4.188 and *Ag Ap* 2.37—see Gambetti, *The Alexandrian Riots*, 59.

22. Herbert Musurillo, *The Acts of the Pagan Martyrs: Acta Alexandrorum* (Oxford: Clarendon, 1954).

23. Marcus Julius Alexander, whose marriage is mentioned by Josephus in *Ant* 19.277.

24. This was Tiberius Julius Alexander mentioned by Josephus in *Ant* 20.100.

25. Josephus, *Wars* 2.309.

Gore Vidal's 1979 shock film by the same name (stilled banned in Canada). Historians today tend to discount the depth of Gaius Caligula's actual depravity, but still, he had his friends and his enemies and it was better to be his friend than his enemy. One of his enemies was Aulus Avilius Flaccus, who had been appointed prefect over the Roman province of Egypt in 31 CE by Gaius's predecessor, Tiberius. Flaccus was, even by Philo's reckoning, a decent ruler.[26] But Gaius hated him. The reason was not petty. Flaccus had been among those who laid conspiracy charges against Gaius's mother,[27] for which she was flogged so harshly that she lost an eye. She later died in prison of starvation.[28] So when Tiberius died and Gaius became emperor, Flaccus sensed that his fortunes were about to change. It was only a question of when.

Among Gaius's friends was Herod Agrippa, a young Jewish aristocrat.[29] He was in many respects a perfect match for Gaius Caligula. In the biblical book of Acts he is remembered as the Jewish king who executed James, the brother of Jesus, and arrested Peter.[30] But for most of his life he was a ne'er-do-well playboy. He grew up not in Jerusalem, but in Rome, in the imperial household alongside the emperor's own son, Drusus. There he grew accustomed to a lifestyle well beyond his means. He spent his youth fleeing unpaid debts and intemperate political miscues. Later, he got to know Gaius in Tiberius's entourage on the Isle of Capri and they became fast friends. But when Agrippa casually mentioned one day how nice it would be if Tiberius were to kick off so that his friend Gaius could take over, Tiberius threw him into prison. That is where he was when Tiberius did die some months later. Gaius, now the emperor, freed his prescient friend and appointed him king over the small realm once ruled by Agrippa's uncle, Herod Philip—the area today known as Banias in northern Galilee. So Agrippa soon set sail for Judea. But he did not go directly there. Rather than making for the closer ports of Antioch, Ptolemais, or Caesarea Maritima, he sailed instead for Alexandria, where he arrived under the cover of darkness and entered the city in secret with a retinue of well-armed bodyguards.[31] Flaccus was alarmed. In his account of these events, Philo says that Agrippa was only taking the fastest route to Judea, and as for all the secrecy, he simply did

26. Philo, *Flaccus* 108.
27. Philo, *Flaccus* 9.
28. Suetonius, *Lives* 3.53.1–2.
29. The principal account of Herod Agrippa's illustrious career is in Josephus, *Ant*, books 18 and 19—esp. 18.143ff. For the present discussion, see Martin Goodman, *Rome and Jerusalem: The Clash of Civilizations* (New York: Random House, 2007), 76–85.
30. Acts 12:1–5.
31. Philo, *Flaccus* 25–27.

not want to make a fuss.[32] But Flaccus probably did not trust Caligula's playboy friend. He was there precisely to make a fuss.

So when three prominent Greeks approached Flaccus and offered to protect him from whatever Caligula might have sent Agrippa to do, he was interested. All he had to do was deliver the Jews into the hands of the Greeks.[33] Flaccus agreed. But why? Why would Flaccus turn to the Greeks for protection against Agrippa, and why did the Greeks demand that he throw the Jews under the bus as part of the bargain? The answer to these questions, so critical to our story, requires a little more history.

THE JEWS IN EGYPT

The Jewish presence in Egypt was not limited to the Jewish quarter in Alexandria. Over the years, the Ptolemaic queens and kings had created many Jewish enclaves around their empire, giving them the right of settlement in exchange for their loyalty and military support. The oldest went back to the first Ptolemy, who invited the Jewish warrior-priest Ezechias to come to Egypt with his followers and settle somewhere in the empire— exactly where is unclear.[34] We do know that a Jewish fortress was located at Pelusium, a critical defensive post near the mouth of the Nile,[35] and another somewhere in the western delta region.[36] Another was placed on the Ptolemies' western frontier in Cyrene.[37] The most famous, though, was at Leontopolis, known for the Jewish temple Onias IV built there on the model of the Jerusalem temple itself.[38] Onias was a refugee from the Jewish conflict with Antiochus IV Epiphanes, a Syrian king of the Seleucid line, which rivaled the Ptolemies for dominance in the Mediterranean East from the death of Alexander to the Roman conquest. The purpose of the colony at Leontopolis was probably to defend an important Nile crossing against Seleucid incursions. But Leontopolis soon became strategically important in the internal politics of Egypt itself.

The first time this happened was upon the death of Ptolemy VI in 145 BCE. His widow, Cleopatra II, favored her son as the next king, but the

---

32. Philo, *Flaccus* 28.
33. Philo, *Flaccus* 18–23.
34. Josephus, *Ag Ap* 1.186–89.
35. Josephus, *Wars* 1.175.
36. Josephus, *Wars* 1.191; *Ant* 14.133.
37. Josephus, *Ag Ap* 2.44.
38. Mentioned by Josephus several times: *Ant* 12.387ff.; 13.62ff.; 20.236; *Wars* 1.33; 7.422ff.

Alexandrian Greeks favored her brother-in-law. In the ensuing conflict, Cleopatra turned to the Jew, Onias, for support.[39] With his troops behind her, she was able to face down her Alexandrian foes, force a compromise, and ultimately stay on the throne. The Jews of Leontopolis also supported Cleopatra III against the Alexandrians in a similar dispute in 116 BCE.[40] A pattern was developing. Fifty years later a similar situation arose, but by now Rome had extended its influence into the region. Ptolemy XII Auletes was crowned in 76 BCE, but the Alexandrians thought that he was too much in the pocket of the Romans. In 58 BCE, he was finally driven from power. Three years later he returned to Egypt to reclaim his throne, now, however, with the famous Roman general Gabinius at his side. When they came to the Nile crossing at Pelusium, guarded by the Jewish fortress, there was a standoff. But a member of the Jewish royal family in Gabinius's company intervened and convinced the Jews to let Gabinius pass unhindered. Auletes was restored to the throne and his rebellious daughter, whom the Alexandrians had made their queen, was executed.[41]

The most famous of these incidents, though, involved the infamous tryst between Julius Caesar and Cleopatra VII, the last queen of Egypt. The circumstances were as follows: Cleopatra was feuding with her brother and coregent, Ptolemy XIII. Caesar favored Cleopatra, the Alexandrians Ptolemy. When Caesar arrived in Alexandria and settled the dispute in favor of Cleopatra, the Alexandrians laid siege to the palace, where Caesar and Cleopatra holed up and cavorted through the winter.[42] When, at last, a Roman rescue party arrived, in their company were a thousand Jewish warriors, led by Antipater, the same Jewish prince who had helped Gabinius a few years before. Antipater now persuaded the Jewish garrison at Leontopolis to join their campaign and together they crushed the Alexandrians and placed Cleopatra on the throne.[43] This was the real beginning of Roman rule in Alexandria. Since that time, Greeks in Alexandria had seen their power and fortunes wane. Alexandria was no longer a Greek city, but a Roman one. Where they had once been lords, the Greeks were now tenants. They became in their own eyes martyrs to a glorious past now swept away by Roman rule. And the Jews, their ancient allies, had sided with Rome.

39. Josephus, *Ag Ap* 2.49–56.
40. Josephus, *Ant* 18.284–87.
41. Cassius Dio, *Rom Hist* 39.58; Josephus, *Wars* 1.175.
42. Cassius Dio, *Rom Hist* 42.34–44.
43. Josephus, *Wars* 1.187–94; *Ant* 14.127–39.

That is how things stood in 37 CE when a Jewish king, raised in the imperial household in Rome, arrived under the cover of night with an armed guard. Why was he there? Flaccus must have thought he had come to depose him. The Greeks must have assumed so too. That is how the Greeks and Flaccus found common cause. Flaccus feared what was about to happen. The Greeks resented it: another Jewish emissary sent to do Rome's bidding and depose a governor they had adopted as their own.

THE FIRST POGROM

And so it began. First, the Greek mob hounded and vilified Agrippa.[44] Philo does not say so, but they must have driven him from the city and sent him ingloriously on his way to Judea. Next they turned on the Jewish community itself. Philo reports that they began by setting up imperial images in Jewish synagogues and prayer halls—a calculated show of loyalty in the wake of their having driven off an imperial envoy.[45] When this met with Jewish protest, Flaccus rescinded the political rights that guaranteed the Jews self-governance and freedom to worship as they pleased.[46] Again, the Jews protested. Now Flaccus began to restrict the movement of Jews around the city. Normally, Philo says, the Jews had inhabited two of the five districts of Alexandria. Flaccus ordered them now to squeeze into a small part of just one of these areas. The Jewish homes, synagogues, and businesses left behind were looted or destroyed. Food and water were cut off from the ghetto.[47] Hunger and starvation began to set in. In desperation, individuals now ventured out in search of food.[48] But as they entered the markets, mobs of Greeks attacked them, as Philo so thoroughly recalls:

> Poor wretches, they were immediately seized by those who wielded the weapon of mob rule, stabbed and dragged through the whole city, trampled on, and so completely mangled that not a piece of them was left to be properly buried. . . . Any Jews who appeared anywhere they stoned or beat with clubs . . . and some threw away these slower acting weapons and took up the most efficient ones, fire and steel, and killed many by the sword, while not a few were done away with by fire. Indeed, whole families, husbands with their wives, babies with their

44. Philo, *Flaccus* 33–40.
45. Philo, *Flaccus* 41–43.
46. Philo, *Flaccus* 53.
47. Philo, *Flaccus* 55–57.
48. Philo, *Flaccus* 62–64; see the similar account in *Embassy* 124–31.

parents, were burned in the heart of the city. . . . And when they lacked proper fire wood, they collected brushwood and did them in with smoke rather than fire, thus inventing a more pitiable and drawn out death for the wretched victims, whose bodies lay half burned and contorted, a painful and heart-rending sight. . . . Many, while still alive, were dragged by the feet tied at the ankle while people lept on them and pounded them to pieces . . . dragging them through just about every lane of the city until the corpses, their skin, flesh, and muscles, battered by the unevenness and roughness of the ground . . . till nothing was left.[49]

Philo goes on like this at length with accounts of scourgings, crucifixions, and various forms of torture—he clearly wanted to leave a complete record of what happened. But our partial account paints a clear enough picture. Many have called this the first pogrom. News of its atrocities traveled far and wide and surely would have soon washed up onto the banks of the Orontes, where Paul the Apostle was just beginning his mission to the Gentiles. What might he have thought about it? What did his fellow Jews think about it? Could the same thing happen in Antioch? How strong were the ties that knit these complex multicultural cities together? Would Greeks there turn on their Jewish neighbors too? Surely not.

The ethnic violence in Alexandria came to an end later that year, in the fall of 38, during the Jewish celebration of Succoth, when Gaius sent a centurion with a company of soldiers to arrest Flaccus. He entered the city under cover of darkness, as Agrippa had done a few months before, and took Flaccus by surprise as he dined at the house of a friend.[50]

GAIUS AND THE JEWISH QUESTION

When the new prefect, Vitrasius Pollio, arrived in Alexandria in 39 CE, he quickly put things in order. Rome relied on Egyptian wheat much in the same way Americans rely on Middle Eastern oil today. Trouble in Alexandria was completely unacceptable. Peace in Egypt meant grain for Rome. So two delegations, one Greek, the other Jewish, were summoned to Rome to settle the matter before Gaius himself. Apion, a well-known Greek antagonist of the Jews, led the Greeks.[51] Philo led the Jewish delegation.[52] Our source for most of what transpired is Philo's own work, *The Embassy to Gaius*.

---

49. Philo, *Flaccus* 65–71 (Colson, trans., LCL, 10 vols. [Cambridge, MA: Harvard University Press, 1937]).
50. Philo, *Flaccus* 104–15.
51. Josephus, *Ant* 18.259.
52. Philo, *Embassy* 370.

Philo and his colleagues must have had high hopes as they departed for Rome. After all, the emperor had befriended Agrippa, whom the Greeks had mistreated while he was in Alexandria on an errand from Gaius! But this was Gaius *Caligula*. By the time the delegations arrived in Rome (probably in the summer of 39 CE), Gaius was already descending into the megalomania that would eventually be his downfall just a year and a half later. What happened next comes to us in two different versions. Philo himself says the Jews were kept cooling their heels for weeks, and when they finally did get a hearing, they had to make their case while tagging along on a tour of some country estates Gaius wished to remodel, following him from room to room as he made architectural suggestions.[53] Josephus tells of a more formal hearing in which both sides were to speak. But when it came time for Philo to make his case, Gaius cut him off in a rage.[54] One way or the other, the gist of what happened was this: the Greeks played heavily on Gaius's vanity and convinced him that the real issue was the Jews' refusal to honor the emperor as he wished to be honored. Everyone else had set up altars and dedicated temples to Gaius and worshipped him as a god, but the Jews would not. What could Philo say? It was true. When the Greeks had tried to place images of the emperor in their synagogues and prayer halls, they had resisted. Philo's protest, that they had their rights, was brushed aside. The Jews never really got a hearing. In Josephus's version, Philo, unphased, calmly assured his delegation that God would intervene. But in his own account, Philo recalls being quite shaken:

> How cruel that the fate of all Jews everywhere should rest precariously on us five envoys. For if he should decide in favor of our enemies, what other city will keep tranquil or refrain from attacking its fellow inhabitants, what house of prayer will be left unscathed, what kind of civic rights will not be upset for those whose lot is cast under the ancient institutions of the Jews. Water-logged by such considerations, we were dragged down and submerged into the depths.[55]

As news of these goings-on spread throughout the empire, Jews everywhere must have begun to worry. Paul, Peter, James, and the rest of the Jewish Jesus movement would not have been exempt. They were a minority, especially when they traveled beyond the walls of Jerusalem or out of the Jewish enclaves of Galilee. Things were beginning to fall apart and uncertainty filled the air. Paul must have worried. As a Jew moving through

---

53. Philo, *Embassy* 349–67.
54. Josephus, *Ant* 18.257–60.
55. Philo, *Embassy* 371–72 (Colson, trans.).

the Greek cities of the Roman East, these once-familiar surroundings must have begun to feel different to him. Clouds were gathering.

THE TROUBLE SPREADS

Jewish fears soon turned out to be well founded. When Gaius learned from the Alexandrians that the Jews had refused to honor his image as a god, he hatched a plan to test the entire Jewish people. Were they loyal to him or not? Gaius was about to send a new imperial legate out to Antioch, Publius Petronius.[56] Josephus tells us that Gaius gave him the following instructions: when Petronius arrived in Antioch, he was to put together a large expeditionary force, proceed south to Judea, and place an image of Gaius in the Jerusalem temple to be worshipped as a god. Petronius did as instructed. When he arrived, he mobilized two legions and marched as far as the coastal city of Ptolemais. But as he encamped there, Josephus reports that thousands of Jewish petitioners descended on him and warned that there would be resistance. Petronius was alarmed. He did not want to risk provoking a Jewish war, but if he failed in his mission, Gaius would surely ask for his life. So Petronius took his inner circle and traveled inland to the Galilean town of Tiberias to assess the mood. What he found there was profound. Tens of thousands had gathered, says Josephus, each vowing they would rather risk war with Rome than violate their ancestral Law. When Petronius called their bluff, they lay face down, bared their necks, and vowed their willingness to die rather than allow Petronius to proceed. For forty days they persisted in their nonviolent protest. Finally, Petronius relented, returned to Antioch, and wrote to Gaius, advising him to give up on the scheme. Then he waited.

Had Petronius known that Gaius's Jewish friend, Agrippa, had already made his way back to Rome with a scheme of his own to turn Gaius from his folly, he might have saved himself some anxious days. But he did not. Instead he simply had to wait. What happened next is not reported by Josephus. Perhaps he did not know about these events, or perhaps he simply passed over them as out of sync with his own purposes. In any event, we know of them only from the Byzantine historian, Johannes Malalas, whose history of Antioch is the primary source for most of what we know about this city during the period in question.[57] According to Malalas, massive

56. The following account comes from Josephus, *Ant* 18:261ff. He also mentions the incident in *Wars* 2.184–87. Philo's account is in *Embassy* 188 and 207–8.

57. The *Chronicle* of Johannes Malalas is not well known among biblical scholars. For a relatively new critical edition of the Greek text of Malalas's *Chronicle*, see Johannes

Jewish–Greek rioting broke out in Antioch "in the third year of Gaius," referring the reign of Gaius Caligula.[58] The third year of Gaius would have been 40 CE. Following the disastrous events at Tiberias, Petronius would have been passing the time waiting for his fate to arrive by messenger from Rome. One day he was attending the great circus of Antioch, watching the games that were renowned there. Malalas says that the ruckus began when the anti-Gaius circus faction, the Blues, began to chant that the days of the long-dominant pro-Gaius faction, the Greens, were numbered. Petronius must have been alarmed. Soon the entire city was engulfed in rioting. But it wasn't just the circus factions that began to brawl. In fact, the very existence of Blue and Green circus factions in the first century is doubtful and Malalas is merely using them to cover his ignorance of how the thing actually began.[59] In any event, here is what Malalas says happened next:

> There followed a great faction riot and disaster fell upon the city. For the Greeks
> of the city set upon the Jews there in a faction brawl, killing many Jews and
> burning their synagogues. When a priest of the Jews in Palestine named Phineas
> heard this, he collected a large number of Jews and Galileans who were citizens.
> With about 30,000 of these he moved quickly from the city of Tiberias to the
> city of Antioch and killed many there, for he made a single unexpected attack
> with armed men. Then Phineas broke off the attack and returned to Tiberias.[60]

Thurn, *Ioannis Malalae Chronographia*, Corpus Fontium Historiae Byzantinae 35 (Series Berolinensis) (Berlin: De Gruyter, 2000). A good translation—though based on a Greek text antedating Thurn's new critical edition—is Elizabeth Jeffreys et al., *The Chronicle of John Malalas*, Byzantina Australiensia 4 (Melbourne: Australian Association for Byzantine Studies, 1986). An assessment of Malalas's reliability as a source is offered by Glanville Downey, *A History of Antioch in Syria from Seleucus to the Arab Conquest* (Princeton, NJ: Princeton University Press, 1961), 37ff. The insight that Malalas's description of events in book 10 of *The Chronicle* correspond roughly to the incident with Petronius comes from Karl Kraeling, "The Jewish Community in Antioch," *Journal of Biblical Literature* 51 (1932): 148–49. Kraeling simply conflates the events; in what follows I will suggest another way to understand the sources.

58. *Chronicle* 10; for the basic historicity of Malalas's account—not necessarily in all details—see Downey, *History of Antioch*, 93; Kraeling, "The Jewish Community in Antioch," 148; and Wayne Meeks and Robert L. Wilken, *Jews and Christians in Antioch in the First Four Centuries of the Common Era*, Society of Biblical Literature: Sources for Biblical Study 13 (Missoula: Scholars Press, 1978), 4. Zetterholm (*Christianity in Antioch*, 114–17) offers the most thorough discussion of the events in relation to Paul's time in Antioch, but does not draw any conclusions about how they might help us understand the Antioch affair.

59. Kraeling, "The Jewish Community in Antioch," 148. The Blue and Green circus factions were a factor of Malalas's time, but not before the fourth century CE: see Alan Cameron, *Circus Factions: Blues and Greens at Rome and Byzantium* (Oxford: Clarendon, 1976), 198–200.

60. *Chronicle* 10.20 (Jeffreys et al., trans.).

These events are eerily close to the riots Philo experienced in Alexandria two years before. In fact, the situations were quite parallel. A local governor, in this case, Petronius, had fallen out with Gaius and needed a way to re-establish his credibility with the emperor. After being forced to back down in the face of Jewish opposition at Tiberias, perhaps he saw this as his chance to demonstrate his *bona fides* with Gaius. Or perhaps just waiting for the death sentence he knew was sure to come, he had begun to resent how the Jews and their religious scruples and gotten him into trouble. In any event, Petronius must have decided that if the Greeks wanted to slaughter Jews and burn their synagogues, he would not interfere. But this ill-conceived plan backfired. When word of the riots reached Tiberias, the Jews there must have thought Petronius had betrayed them. So Phineas and his volunteers marched to Antioch and ravaged the city, leaving many dead and the city in chaos. Petronius now had a second black mark on his record. Malalas says Gaius was furious. All Petronius could do was fetch Phineas up from Tiberias, execute him, and stick his head on a pike outside the city as a warning against further violence.[61] Paul would have seen it as he came and went from that devastated city. Its desiccated remnants might even have still been there to greet "the circumcision party" when it arrived from Jerusalem eight years later.

There is a brief, but interesting, epilogue to this story. When Gaius received word of the Jewish resistance and how Petronius had backed down, he did indeed send a letter to Petronius directing him to do the right thing and fall on his sword. He was to become an example to anyone who should dare flout the commands of the emperor. But within days of this dispatch, Gaius Caligula was himself killed by rivals in Rome. In the melee that followed, Claudius became emperor—according to Josephus, with a lot of encouragement from Agrippa. As it happened, word of these developments reached Antioch *before* Caligula's letter, so Petronius was spared. Instead, he became a hero for having resisted Caligula's madness.[62] Still, Antioch lay smoldering, a city now divided into hostile camps, one Greek, one Jewish. What to do? The answer came from the new emperor, Claudius, in the form of an edict issued originally to Alexandria, but sent also at the request of Agrippa to Antioch as well, which ordered Jews and Greeks to lay down their arms and return to their corners.[63] Everything was to return

---

61. Malalas, *Chronicle* 10.20.

62. Josephus, *Ant* 18.302–9.

63. Papyrus London 1912, Claudius's "Letter to the Alexandrians" (originally published by H. Idris Bell in *Jews and Christians in Egypt* [London: Oxford University Press, 1924]). That this is probably the letter to which Josephus refers in *Ant* 19.279 is argued by Kraeling, "The Jewish Community in Antioch," 149; Zetterholm (*Christianity in Antioch*, 116) assumes this too.

to the *status quo ante*. Greeks and Jews each had their rights, and everyone was to be respected.

But as Petronius set about to rebuild the city, the legacy of Gaius Caligula's brief reign lay heavy over the Jews. How tenuous their position had proven to be. After living in these great cities for centuries as equals, they could now see that the Greeks who surrounded them did not see them as equals, but as enemies. Going forward, life for Jews in Antioch and the surrounding cities and towns of Syria would be quite different. Our sources are silent about the next thirty years, but when we next hear about Jews in Syria, Josephus tells us that they "passed their days in blood, their nights, yet more dreadful, in terror."[64] The occasion was another rebellion in the Jewish homeland, the great Judean War of 66 to 70 CE, when the Jews tried to throw off Roman rule. The rebellion ended in disaster. Jerusalem was sacked, the Jewish Temple destroyed, and thousands of Jews killed or sold into slavery. Greeks thought that surely now Roman authorities would support their efforts to rid their cities and towns of Jews. But they did not. As in the days of Petronius, the Romans intervened and played the role of referee. War in Judea did not mean they expected to war with Jews all over the empire. So Jews and Greeks carried on as before, in fear and loathing and mutual contempt. And all of this, we should note, was not at all loathsome to the Romans. Over the years, they had become quite adept at playing Jews and Greeks against one another—in Antioch, Alexandria, or anywhere the technique of "divide and conquer" could give them a critical advantage in ruling so diverse an empire.

NO JEW OR GREEK

By now the significance of Paul's ill-fated experiment with mixed Jewish and Greek table fellowship in Antioch must be obvious. In a city torn by ethnic strife, Paul found in the Jesus movement a framework or an ideology, or perhaps just the courage, to reach across ethnic boundaries hardened through political strife and violence. Scholars of the history of Jews in the Roman Empire have worked hard to get this right, so I do not want to casually misspeak here. The relationship between Jews and Greeks in the Roman Empire was complex.[65] And the question of Jews

64. Josephus, *Wars* 2.463.
65. On the complex relationship between Jews and Gentiles, especially Romans, see Goodman, *Rome and Jerusalem*; earlier, Martin Hengel, *Judaism and Hellenism: Studies*

and Gentiles—including Romans—was even more complex and varie-
gated. Agrippa had grown up in the imperial household, he was Gaius's
friend, and Claudius later made him king of the Jews. Jewish customs
had become so widespread among Gentiles in the Roman Empire that
by Josephus's day, he could boast that there wasn't a city on Earth in
which the Jewish Sabbath was not observed by both Jews and Gentiles.[66]
Romans, Greeks, Jews—they all mixed freely in the cities of the Roman
Empire, and usually without recorded incident. But in the years of Gaius
Caligula, in Alexandria and in Antioch, this was not so. When Paul was
working the region around Antioch all through the 40s CE, he worked as a
sheep among wolves. In those days it might have been a very remarkable
thing for the wolves to invite the sheep to dinner. What did it mean for the
sheep to invite the wolves? And when the envoys from James arrived and
were alarmed—who could blame them? Hadn't the head of Phineas been
stuck on a pike outside the city gates?

And yet, this was the world in which the author of our baptismal
creed lived, and in which he or she decided that "in the Spirit" Jew and
Greek simply did not exist. Of all the aspects of the creed, it was this that
appealed most to Paul. He bought into it totally. This is probably why he
quoted the creed in Galatians in the first place. He had become a true
believer: "in Christ Jesus there is no Jew or Greek," he wrote (Gal 3:28). In
Antioch, in Syria, where Paul wandered and preached a message he called
the *euangelion*—"the good news"—the world was divided into Jews and
Greeks. Paul believed that these enemies could become friends. I believe
this is what Paul meant when he told the pillars of the Jesus movement
in Jerusalem that he would be the apostle to the uncircumcised. Titus,
the uncircumcised Greek, was there to show that this might be possible
even from the Greek side. When they left Jerusalem for Antioch, their
purpose was to construct a new community in which fierce enemies could
sit together at a common table and form new bonds of friendship and
reconciliation. When Peter came to Antioch and saw for himself what
was possible, he was moved to join in. For a moment, the apostle to the
circumcised and the apostle to the uncircumcised joined forces to bring
the circumcised and the uncircumcised together around a common table.
Peace in the valley.

in *Their Encounter During the Hellenistic Period*, trans. John Bowden (Philadelphia: Fortress Press, 1974), and Victor Tcherikover, *Hellenistic Civilization and the Jews*, trans. S.
Applebaum (Philadelphia: Jewish Publication Society of America, 1959).

66. *Ag Ap* 2.282.

A NEW PAUL

This is not the Paul most people think they know. Could Paul have been interested in something so prosaic and yet so high-minded as forming communities of reconciliation by reaching across fiercely guarded ethnic boundaries? If so, this surely must have been a mere sideline for him, something he squeezed in between starting a new religion and formulating doctrine that would be parsed through the centuries for its eternal verities. Actually, no. Paul had no interest in starting a new religion. He was Jewish and remained a Jew, worshipping the God of his ancestors his entire life. If you had asked Paul what he believed, he would have said, "The Lord is our God, the Lord is one." The letters he wrote were not theological treatises, but rhetorical efforts to address particular issues in the communities he founded. And chief among those issues was the inclusion of Gentiles. This is true especially for Galatians and Romans, the two letters theologians have mined again and again for doctrinal insights, including original sin, predestination, and justification by faith. But all of the passages upon which these ideas are based were originally arguments in Paul's fight to include Gentiles. Justification by faith was not Paul's answer to the question of how sinners can be saved, but a rationale for why Gentiles can be included in the Jesus movement without observing the Law, in particular, the custom of circumcision.

This understanding of Paul is generally known as the "New Paul," and it is widely embraced by scholars of the New Testament today. It stems from a Lutheran theologian who was, at various points in his long and distinguished career, the dean of Harvard's Divinity School and the bishop of Stockholm. Krister Stendahl published his insights in a 1963 essay entitled "The Apostle Paul and the Introspective Conscience of the West."[67] Later he expanded his thoughts in a small volume of lectures called *Paul Among Jews and Gentiles*, published in 1976.[68] Stendahl argued that the church, and especially the Lutheran church, had been misreading Paul for generations. Perhaps only a Lutheran of such standing as Stendahl could have had the credibility to point out that Paul's doctrine of justification by faith was actually not the answer to Martin Luther's question, "How can I, miserable sinner though I am, be saved?" Justification by faith was Paul's answer to his own question, "How can Gentiles be included in the promises of God?"

---

67. Published originally in the *Harvard Theological Review* 56 (1963): 199–215.
68. Krister Stendahl, *Paul Among Jews and Gentiles* (Philadelphia: Fortress Press, 1976). More recent statements on *The New Paul* include John Gager, *Reinventing Paul* (Oxford and New York: Oxford University Press, 2000) and Pamela Eisenbaum, *Paul Was Not a Christian* (see note 7, earlier).

After Stendahl, scholars of Paul have attempted to place the apostle more and more precisely in his own context, to sense what his own questions were, his own priorities. This is what I have been doing in this chapter. Why would Paul, a Jew, be interested in reaching out to Gentiles? Why would he have been interested in a baptismal creed and ceremony in which people vowed to set aside the distinction between Jew and Greek? A close look at Jewish–Greek relations in the Roman East in the years when Paul was active there tells a very clear story. Jews and Greeks were locked in a culture war that often looked like *war* war. The Jesus movement taught that you should love your enemies, pray for those who persecute you, turn the other cheek. Paul, it appears, had a dramatic and transformative religious experience—I will avoid the word "conversion" to limit confusion—in which he became convinced that the spirit of the person who had said these things, Jesus of Nazareth, lived on and had come to inhabit him, to direct him, to control him. From then on, in Paul's own words, "It is no longer I who live, but Christ who lives in me" (Gal 2:20). Paul's course was set. He would devote himself entirely to creating communities in which Jews and Gentiles would gather and mix without distinction until the new empire, the Kingdom of God of which Jesus had spoken, would come, and with it, a new community in which there would be "no Jew or Greek." That was his purpose. It was not to create a new religion and stock it with a new set of theological ideas intended to last the ages. Paul's gospel was the very simple and humane insight that it was God's will that love should someday conquer violence and hatred. It was a gospel with profound relevance for a place like Antioch in the 40s CE.

But of course, if there was peace in the valley for a brief moment in Antioch, it did not last. Jewish–Greek relations went downhill from there. Even within the Jesus movement, Jews and Gentiles could not see eye to eye. Paul's efforts to include Gentiles, though, did bear fruit and eventually Gentile Christians outnumbered Jewish Christians so greatly that "Jewish Christianity" came to be seen as an aberration, a heresy. Ironically, Christianity did become a new religion and Paul became, in the eyes of the church, its chief architect. Paul's words, once uttered in defense of an integrated community, were repurposed to explain why Christianity was superior Judaism. How did that happen?

NO LONGER JEW

Exactly how or when the Jesus movement ceased to be a part of Judaism and became a new religion attractive mostly to non-Jews is still something of a mystery. It did not happen in a single moment, but gradually, over time.[69] But if you ask about the role played by Paul and his letters, the story probably begins with Marcion.

Marcion of Sinope was a prominent Christian leader, active in the first half of the second century.[70] Today he is remembered as an early heretic, but that would be twenty/twenty hindsight. In the late first and early second centuries there were, as yet, no heretics. Early Christianity was a soup of ideas swirling through communities in the midst of much labored social formation. Marcion was simply a very powerful and influential early Christian teacher and organizer.

Marcion was a Greek, who had little interest in being part of a Jewish community. After the great Jewish rebellion in 66 to 70 CE, the Roman East saw a series of Jewish uprisings, culminating in the Bar Kokhba rebellion, which broke out in 132, when Marcion was in his forties and about to move to Rome. In 135 the emperor Hadrian crushed Simon bar Kokhba and his followers and sacked Jerusalem a second time. This time, though, the Romans leveled the temple mount and constructed a new Roman city on the remains, calling it Aelia Capitolina. Jews were banned from the new city—the beginning of a long diaspora that would last until the founding of the modern state of Israel. Practicing the Jewish religion became an act of sedition. In that environment, non-Jews, like Marcion, wanted nothing to do with Jews. But Marcion was born into a Christian family in Asia Minor. He could not avoid the question of his own roots. Was Christianity a form of Judaism, or something new entirely? Marcion was one of the first—perhaps *the* first—to claim that Christianity was a completely new religion. He found justification for this view in Paul and in the Jewish scriptures, what we think of today as the Old Testament.

While other Christians saw in the Old Testament myriad veiled references to Jesus Christ, Marcion read it literally. He thought the Old Testament was talking about what it *is* talking about: the creation, a covenant with God, the Law, prophets railing against injustice, and so forth. He concluded that the God of the Law and the prophets was not a God wholly good, but good only in the way human beings are good—sometimes good. He is a God whose presence in the world brings both happiness and suffering. He is a just God, but not the God of pure love. He is the creator

69. The issue has been reframed as a much more gradual process especially by Daniel Boyarin in *Borderlines: The Partition of Judeo-Christianity* (Philadelphia: University of Pennsylvania, 2004).

70. A recent introduction to Marcion is Judith Lieu's *Marcion and the Making of a Heretic: God and Scripture in the Second Century* (Cambridge and New York: Cambridge University Press, 2015).

of the world we know and can see, not unlike the creator, or *Demiurgos*, posited by Plato in the *Timeaus*. Genesis, he argued, speaks of this God, the creator God. But Marcion believed that there is another God, the "unknown God," who stands outside of creation, unsullied and un-implicated by it. Again, the notion was a common Platonic one, much in ascendancy in the intellectual world of which Marcion was a part. This is the Platonic God who is wholly Good, pure Truth, whose Mind fills the universe and holds all the perfect Ideas of which our world is but an imperfect imitation. This, according to Marcion, is the God who sent Jesus Christ into the world. Jesus's original Jewish followers misunderstood him and thought he was the Jewish messiah sent to save his people and establish the kingdom of God on Earth. But in fact he was a messenger from the unknown God, sent to tell anyone who has ears to hear about the realm beyond and to offer salvation and rescue from this imperfect world below. Marcion believed that Paul was another intervention, a second revelation of the unknown God and his intentions. All who have faith in this God of pure love and goodness will be saved from the present world of sorrow and perdition. He believed that this was the gospel of which Paul spoke. The Old Testament knew only the God of the Law. Christianity was all about the gospel. Law versus gospel. Marcion created this trope still common today, especially among Protestant Christians. I encounter it just about every time I introduce the Bible to a new class of college students: the Old Testament is all about wrath; the New Testament is all about love. The illusion doesn't last long once we begin to read the actual texts.

In Marcion, all of Paul's arguments about the Law now found a new context. The old question of whether Gentiles could participate in the Jesus movement without observing the Law was now moot. The church, once a kind of Jewish synagogue, was becoming a Gentile communal association. The new question was how Gentile Christianity should regard its Jewish roots. Now Paul's words about the Law, especially in Galatians and Romans, could be read, not as arguments for including Gentiles, but as arguments against being Jewish. For example, when Paul writes in Galatians that "we have believed in Christ Jesus, in order to be justified by the faith of Christ and not by works of the Law,"[71] it was no longer to make the point that Gentiles could be justified by faith, but that no one could be justified by observing the Jewish Law. Did Marcion misread Paul? As we have seen, Paul often disparages the Law in the course of his arguments. "For all who rely on works of the Law are under a curse . . . "; "It is clear that no one is

---

71. Gal 2:16.

justified before God by the Law . . . "; "Christ redeemed us from the curse of the Law . . ." (Gal 3:10–14, etc.). But Paul was writing those things to Gentiles to convince them that they should pay no heed to Jews who say they must submit to circumcision. This was how Paul bridged the gap be-tween Jews and Greeks—he set aside circumcision. But that original con-text was lost on Marcion. Paul's letters to the Galatians and Romans were for him no longer simply rhetorical arguments designed to win a debate over circumcision. Paul wrote occasional letters; Marcion read them as scripture.

That is how Christians read them today, as scripture. No one today cares about circumcision. No one today questions whether Gentiles can be included in Christian churches. But, like Marcion, Christians through the ages have asked about Judaism. If Jesus was Jewish, then what could be wrong with Judaism? Why are we Christians Christian and not Jewish? And Marcion's answer is still widely assumed today: Jesus and Paul revealed a whole new religion. If one reads the gospels and Paul very selectively, it is not hard to sustain that idea. That is what Marcion did. He created his own gospel, based on the Gospel According to Luke, and his own corpus of Pauline letters, purged of anything that seemed to endorse Jewish ideas or the Old Testament.[72] This was, so far as we know, the first attempt at a Christian scriptural canon. Upon it, Marcion founded a new church.

Marcion's church spread throughout the Roman Empire and lasted for three centuries before it died out under the weight of imperial Christianity in the period after Constantine. His idea that there are two gods in heaven was vilified as heresy. And the ascetical rigor Marcion required of his true followers lacked broad appeal. But the idea that Christianity and Judaism were two different religions, and that Paul had articulated the difference, had very broad appeal. This much seems to have been imprinted even on Marcion's opponents. The architect of the more enduring form of Marcion's position was the author of the biblical Acts of the Apostles. Many scholars today argue that Acts was actually composed to counter Marcion's ideas.[73] And that appears to be true, at least in part. No one could read Acts and conclude that the first disciples had misunderstood Jesus, while Paul got him right. Instead, in Acts, Peter and Paul are of one accord in proclaiming Jesus as the messiah sent from the one true God. And when Paul speaks

---

72. For a reconstruction of Marcion's *Euangelion* (a gospel based on Luke) and *Apostolikon* (a heavily edited collection of Paul's letters) see Jason BeDuhn, *The First Testament: Marcion's Scriptural Canon* (Salem, OR: Polebridge Press, 2013).

73. See, e.g., Joseph Tyson, *Marcion and Luke-Acts: A Defining Struggle* (Columbia: University of South Carolina Press, 2006).

of "the unknown God" on the Aereopagus in Athens, he is the "God who made the world and everything in it,"[74] not Marcion's Platonic God who is entirely removed from creation. And like most other Christians of that era, the author of Acts was a dedicated student of the Jewish scriptures in Greek and explained the connection between Christianity and its Jewish roots by interpreting its scriptures as prophesy foretelling Jesus's arrival and the birth of Christianity. All of this would have been a direct affront to Marcion's followers.

But this opponent of Marcionite Christianity shared Marcion's idea that the Christian church represents a decisive break from Christianity's Jewish past. The whole trajectory of Acts' narrative of Christian beginnings is an arc that bends inexorably from Jerusalem to Rome. It begins in Jerusalem, with Peter rising to explain to the Jews exactly what has just happened in the brief career of Jesus of Nazareth:

> Men of Israel, why do you wonder at this . . . ? The God of Abraham and of Isaac and of Jacob, the God of the Fathers, glorified his servant Jesus, whom you delivered up and denied in the presence of Pilate, when he had decided to release him. But you denied the holy and righteous one and asked for a murderer to be granted to you and killed the author of life, whom God raised from the dead. To this we are witnesses.
>
> Acts 3:12–15

The same message is delivered again in Acts, chapter 7, by Stephen, a "Hellenist," and the first Christian martyr:

> You stiff-necked people, uncircumcised in heart and ears, you always resist the Holy Spirit. As your fathers did, so do you. Which of the prophets did your fathers not persecute? And they killed those who announced beforehand the coming of the Righteous One, whom you have now betrayed and murdered, you who received the Law as delivered by angels and did not keep it.
>
> Acts 7:51–53

And so the theme of Acts is set: Jesus came to his own people, the Jews, but they rejected him. Now Peter and the first apostles fan out through the Gentile world and begin to spread the gospel. Paul soon joins them. As he comes to each new town to preach the good news, a repeating pattern is soon established. Paul goes to the synagogue first, but meets with little

74. Acts 17:24.

success. Then he turns to the Gentiles, who receive his words gladly. This is Marcion light. The author of Acts wants his audience to know that the new religion is grounded in an ancient and sacred tradition. But the heirs to that tradition are not the Jews. The true heirs are the Gentile Christians who now follow Jesus, Peter, and Paul. As the narrative unfolds, the reader follows Paul finally to Rome, the center of the Gentile world. And there at the end of the story, Paul makes one last speech. It is delivered to leaders of the Jewish community in Rome. To them he makes his case that Jesus is the Christ, based on the Law of Moses and the prophets. But most of them remain unconvinced. Paul then says,

> The Holy Spirit was right in saying to your fathers through Isaiah the prophet, "Go to this people and say, You shall indeed hear and never understand, and you shall indeed see and never perceive. For this people's heart has grown dull and their ears are heavy of hearing and their eyes they have closed, lest they should perceive with their eyes and hear with their ears and understand with their heart and turn for me to heal them." *Let it be known to you then that this salvation from God has been sent to the Gentiles; they will listen* (emphasis mine).
>
> Acts 28:25b–28

And that is the end of the story (literally). Acts is the official, canonical account of the origins of Christianity. Jesus was Jewish. But the Jewish people rejected him. The apostles, Peter and Paul, took the message to the Gentiles, who received it gladly. If you forget about Paul's original context and about the credo that inspired him to create communities in which Jew and Greek could be reconciled, it is not hard to read Paul's letters as the backstory to Acts. The author of Acts probably knew Paul's letters, at least some of them. But he did not know Paul's context. Nor did he share Paul's vision. When he read Paul's letters, he did not think, with Paul, "No longer Jew or Greek." He simply thought, "No longer Jew."

And so Paul's experiment with mixed communities of Jews and Greeks was forgotten. His simple humane insight that love can conquer hatred and division was washed over and replaced with a more abstract interpretation of his arguments. If this seems a little starry-eyed and quaint, I understand. And even now I will hasten to add that Paul has indeed inspired Christians to hate Jews through the centuries. But if Paul's intentions count for anything, you have to say that this long, sad history of Christian anti-Judaism based on Paul is one of the greatest intellectual failures of Western civilization.

And it is based on one of the great human failings that plagues all of us in all times and in all places: the fear of difference and what we do not understand. Greeks, for Paul, were the foreign other, who despised his own tribe and thus could be hated with a clear conscience. His attempt to create communities that were mixed of Jews and Greeks was not about creating a church that was no longer Jewish. It was about creating a church that would not endorse the Jewish hatred of Greeks, even when history and circumstances might well justify that and worse. Paul could not have imagined the intricate schemes people of the modern world would one day conjure up to justify racism in all its multifarious forms. He had a simpler case before him: they hate us and we hate them. He could easily have endorsed his side of that ethnic divide. But he listened instead to a creed first introduced to him by fellow Jews involved in the Jesus movement: "there is no Jew or Greek." That made all the difference to Paul. But it made very little difference to those who came after. His efforts instead led to a Gentile church that hated Jews. The irony is as bitter as it is tragic. "Being in Christ" never again meant "there is no us and them." It would instead become yet one more reason to claim that we are us and they are them.

CHAPTER 5

⌒⌝⌒

There Is No Slave or Free

In the year 61 CE, corpses began to wash up on the shores of Briton, left behind by an ebbing red tide. What could it mean? Soon corpses would be everywhere. But the newly appointed Roman legate, Suetonius Paulinus, wasn't there to see the signs. He was busy on the Isle of Mona slaughtering Druids and refugees from Roman Briton who sheltered with them there, when the bad news arrived from the main island across the Menai Straights. Some weeks before, the Icenian king Prasutagus had died, bequeathing his kingdom to his daughters and to the Roman emperor. What he hoped would be the scaffolding of a new alliance and a peaceful incorporation of his realm into the larger Roman Empire apparently sent a much different message to the Roman legionaries in residence. While Suetonius was busy on Mona, they had commenced to pillage the Iceni capital at Camulodunum (Colchester) and dispossess its chieftains of their estates. The daughters of Prasutagus were raped, and Prasutagus's wife, Queen Boudicca, was publically flogged. His former subjects were now "captives and slaves." That, at least, was how Tacitus phrased it in his summary of great events for that year in book 14 of his *Annals*.[1]

But these Roman legionaries did not know the Britons very well.[2] Boudicca was not simply a queen. She was a warrior, for "It was customary . . . with Britons to fight under female captaincy."[3] She rallied the tribes

1. Tacitus, *Annals* 14.31.
2. On Boudicca, see Donald R. Dudley and Graham Webster, *The Rebellion of Boudicca* (London: Routledge and Kegan Paul, 1962).
3. Tacitus, *Annals* 14.35.

and quickly overwhelmed the Roman garrison at Colchester. When the procurator Catus Decianus sent two hundred troops to put down the rebellion, the Britons drove them to refuge in the Temple of Claudius, besieged them for two days, then overwhelmed them with numbers and massacred them in the sacred precinct. Now the Romans sent in the Ninth Legion, which the Britons quickly routed, "slaughtering the infantry to a man."[4] Alarmed, Suetonius made a swift retreat from Mona and evacuated the Roman garrison in London, leaving behind more than seventy thousand Roman civilians to die at the hand of Boudicca, who took no prisoners. He then gathered the Fourteenth Legion and parts of the Twentieth and prepared a counterattack. Boudicca now mounted her chariot and, with her daughters riding beside her, rode from clan to clan delivering her message. They had whipped her like a slave and raped her daughters. She would avenge these wrongs or perish while trying. We women will die in battle, she said; you men can live as slaves if you want.[5]

The revolt of the Iceni was soon over. The Romans, far advanced in the arts of war, quickly wiped them out. Tacitus put the body count at eighty thousand—not counting the pack animals, which they piled together with the Iceni dead. But Boudicca was not taken alive. Tacitus says that she poisoned herself. She had rather die than become a slave. But slaves were taken that day, thousands likely. War was Rome's chief source of slaves. Slavery was a rebel's reprieve from death. The Roman jurist Florentinus explains: "Slaves (Latin: *servi*) are so called because commanders generally sell the people they capture and thereby save (Latin: *servare*) them instead of killing them."[6] His etymologies are bogus, no doubt, but he knew well how war and slavery worked. He adds, "The word for property in slaves (*mancipia*) is derived from the fact that they are captured from the enemy by force of arms (*manu capiantur*)"[7]—more bogus word play based on facts that were nonetheless true. So, as bodies were being piled high outside of London, more bodies were being rounded up as booty to be sent back to Rome and sold. The manifest for those ships transporting them back to Italy would have listed them as just that—"bodies." That is how Romans referred to slaves when speaking of them impersonally or officially.[8] The most valuable booty of Roman warfare was the bodies.

---

4. Tacitus, *Annals* 14.32.

5. Tacitus, *Annals* 14.35.

6. Justinian's *Digest* 1.5.4, in Thomas Wiedemann, *Greek and Roman Slavery: A Sourcebook* (Baltimore: Johns Hopkins University Press, 1981), 15.

7. Justinian's *Digest* 1.5.4, in Wiedemann, *Greek and Roman Slavery*, 15.

8. This salient detail is stressed by Jennifer Glancy, *Slavery in Early Christianity* (Minneapolis: Fortress Press, 2006), esp. 9–38.

Tacitus includes just one other major story in his *Annals* for the year 61. The city prefect of Rome, Pedanius Secundus, was murdered by one of his slaves.[9] Tacitus does not say how he did it, and he is unsure of the motive. He gives two possible backstories. One is that Pedanius insisted on sex with the slave, who had, however, fallen in love with another and no longer wished to tolerate his master's sexual peccadillos. The second is that Pedanius had agreed to manumit (free) the slave for a set price—a common practice once a male slave had reached the age of thirty. But Pedanius had reneged, changing the price or the terms. The terms varied widely in such transactions. A "freedman" was not normally really free after manumission, but had to agree to provide certain continuing services to the master—now patron—after the slave had paid the price of manumission. In any event, Pedanius may have changed things up at the last minute. One way or the other, Pedanius was apparently the kind of person a slave could hate for any number of reasons. But the Senate did not recognize this as just cause for murder, so his slave was convicted and condemned to death.

Now, Roman custom stipulated that when a slave murdered his or her master, all the slaves of the household also had to be executed. After all, how could they have not known something was afoot? Pedanius, a former consul, was rich and owned about four hundred "bodies." Naturally, they had to be executed too. However, before the slaughter could commence, a popular uprising gave everyone pause. Protesters surrounded the Senate house and demanded they be spared. How could anyone tolerate such a senseless waste of human life? That was how the slaves and former slaves who crowded the streets of imperial Rome would have thought about it. But senators, who had many slave bodies of their own, saw things differently. From their deliberations, Tacitus reports the argument of a certain Gaius Cassius. It went like this: There was a time when we knew our slaves, born on our estates, under our own roofs. But now they come from far-off places with customs unlike our own, with different religious practices, or none at all. He was thinking, perhaps, of the Iceni. "You will never coerce such a medley of humanity except by terror."[10] The Senate agreed. And so Nero ordered troops to push back the crowd and line the road so that the four hundred condemned slaves could be marched unhindered to their deaths.

I do not know why Tacitus chose to focus his remarks for the year 61 on these two events. But I chose to open this chapter with them because they help us a little with our perspective on slavery in the ancient world.

9. Tacitus, *Annals* 14.42–45.
10. Tacitus, *Annals* 14.45.

In the first episode, a woman becomes a warrior and leads her people in a desperate fight to avoid enslavement. In the second, the brutalities of Rome's everyday, legal treatment of slaves helps us understand what that fight and struggle were all about. Rome's wars of imperial expansion were in part driven by the expendability of slaves in the economy of the Roman Empire. Manufacturing, mining, agriculture—all were accomplished on a large scale with slave labor. Large households were run by slaves; brothels were staffed with slaves. Roughly a third of the population of Rome was enslaved. It was a slave society.[11] This was a reality that had not changed in the Mediterranean world for centuries. Every ancient society we know about was made economically viable through the enslavement of large numbers of people. Boudicca probably owned slaves of her own. About a decade after the sacking of Boudicca's London, Titus would snuff out a similar rebellion among the Jews by sacking the city of Jerusalem and selling its inhabitants into slavery. As we have seen, Jews too owned slaves. Slavery was a given, it was ubiquitous, and it was large scale. But the givenness of slavery did not mean that people did not see its cruelties and offer resistance to it.

RESISTANCE

The First Servile War (134–132 BCE) broke out in the Roman province of Sicily over the simple issue of excessive cruelty.[12] Diodorus Siculus called it the greatest civil conflict in the history of Rome.[13] Like all slaves, the slaves of Sicily endured such brutal practices as branding and manacling, but a slumping economy left them lacking even basic necessities like food and clothing. They turned to a slave prophet of the Great Mother goddess named Eunous (the "Good Mind"), who prophesied about a new kingdom in which slaves would break free and rule themselves. When the revolt broke

---

11. On the role of war in the acquisition of slaves, see Sandra Joshel, *Slavery in the Roman World*, Cambridge Introduction to Roman Civilization (Cambridge and New York: Cambridge University Press, 2010), 54–56; on the occupations of slaves, see 161–214.

12. Livy 32.26.4. The main primary sources for the First and Second Servile Wars are the recovered books of Diodorus Siculus's *Biblioteca historica*, which survive intact only in part. The lost books pertaining to the revolts are preserved by the medieval historians Photius and Constantine Porphyrogenitus. All of the relevant excerpts are collected by Wiedemann in *Greek and Roman Slavery*, 198–215. On slave rebellions generally see K. R. Bradley, *Slavery and Rebellion in the Roman World, 140–70 BC* (Bloomington: Indiana University Press, 1989).

13. Diodorus Siculus 34.2, in Wiedemann, *Greek and Roman Slavery*, 200.

out, slaves from all over Sicily—as many as two hundred thousand—rallied to Eunous and proclaimed him king. Soon they controlled the entire island. Meanwhile, smaller local revolts inspired by the Sicilians erupted in many other places, including Attica, Delos, and Rome itself. Eunous's slave kingdom on Sicily lasted three years before Roman troops finally recaptured the island and executed its slave king. The Second Servile War broke out on Sicily a generation later (104–101 BCE), and then the Third (73–71 BCE), this one on the Italian mainland. This last is the most famous of these revolts. This is the one that was led by Spartacus, the gladiator.[14] Many, if not most, gladiators were slaves, forced to fight in exhibition matches for the entertainment of others. In 73 BCE, Spartacus and about seventy other gladiators broke out of their slave prison cum training facility at Capua and started a rebellion just a few days' march from Rome itself. Eventually more than seventy thousand slaves rallied to Spartacus on the slopes of Mt. Vesuvius, where they fortified themselves and began raiding the countryside. It took two years and ten Roman legions to put down the rebellion. When it was over, the Romans crucified six thousand of the rebels, lining the Appian Way from Rome to Capua with the crosses. As Sandra Joshel points out, that's a crucified slave body about every hundred feet stretching along this main thoroughfare for more than a hundred miles.[15] The impression created lasted a very long time.

NORMAL

All of this is to say that one can imagine a wide range of ideas about slavery among those who lived in its ever-present shadow. There were those who saw it for what it was and rebelled. That the person who coined our ancient credo could imagine a community in which there was "no slave or free" is not incredible, though it is perhaps extraordinary. Centuries would pass before enough people began to think those unthinkable thoughts to turn the tide against slavery and finally bring it to an end. Slavery was an assumed part of Western civilization for at least three millennia. We have been free of it for about a century and a half—and we are not truly free of it even now. So it is just as conceivable that most people—even most followers of Jesus— would scarcely have given "no slave or free" a second thought. And that is

---

14. The primary texts are Plutarch's *Life of Crassus*, chapters 8–11, and Appian's *Roman History*, book 14. Wiedemann collects the relevant excerpts in *Greek and Roman Slavery*, 215–23.
15. Joshel, *Slavery*, 63.

in fact what happened. After the credo itself, there is little evidence that anyone in the early Christian church thought there was anything wrong with slavery. To the contrary, many believed that slavery was part of God's plan. That is the view that prevailed among Christians until a more secular ethics began to challenge it at the dawn of the modern age.

For most of that time Christians assumed they had good and sound warrant for this view. As we have seen, the Jewish law, while placing certain restrictions on slavery—when Hebrew slaves are involved—did not criticize, let alone outlaw slavery. This was a kinder, gentler form of slavery perhaps—but then everyone thinks their slavery is humane, unlike slavery among barbarians, say. And when it came to the enslavement of non-Jewish others, Jews in antiquity were just like everyone else. If American Christians living below the Mason-Dixon before 1860 wondered what the Bible said about holding slaves, they had only to consult Leviticus for a very clear answer:

> As for the male and female slaves whom you may have, it is from the nations around you that you may acquire male and female slaves. You may also acquire them from among the aliens residing with you, and from their families that are with you, who have been born into your land; and they may be your property. You may keep them as a possession for your children after you, for them to inherit as property.
>
> Lev 25:44–46

This could not be clearer. God has given to us the alien to possess as a slave. This was divine law as much for Jews in the first century as it was for Christians in the nineteenth. Most of those who followed Jesus were Jews and thus regarded Leviticus as Torah. Why would they question the practice of holding slaves? Like Greeks, Romans, Cypriots, Egyptians, Syrians—like everyone in virtually every culture that grew up around the Mediterranean Sea—they simply assumed the reality and normalcy of slavery.

JESUS

Did Jesus himself ever question the holding of slaves?[16] There is no evidence in the gospels that he ever did. Why is this? Slaves were part of the landscape in which Jesus conjured up his vision for the new Empire of

---

16. For a discussion, see Glancy, *Slavery in Early Christianity*, 102–29.

God, and slaves occasionally appear in the stories and parables he used to depict it. For example, Jesus's Parable of the Tenants[17] includes the slaves of an absentee landlord, who go to collect the rent from a tenant-run vineyard, only to be abused by the tenants and turned away. In another story, the Parable of the Entrusted Money,[18] three slaves are given money to invest while their master is away. When the master returns, the slaves are each rewarded or punished based on their relative success or failure in the financial markets. In these stories, slaves appear as stock characters; their enslavement is not made the issue. So perhaps it just never occurred to Jesus that slavery itself could succumb to his utopian imaginings. As Orlando Patterson has argued, the power of slavery has always resided precisely in its assumed normalcy.[19] No one ever thinks to question it. Perhaps. But if tens of thousands of slaves could imagine a slave-free society vividly enough to join in rebellion in Sicily, Italy, Delos, Athens, and many other places, it would be at least a little disappointing if the most inhumane aspect of ancient society somehow escaped the notice of Jesus of Nazareth.

But there may be another problem. The gospels in which the stories of Jesus survive were written many years after the fact by men who were literate and probably of a different social class from Jesus himself. This sometimes makes a difference. Here is an example. In the Gospel of Mark, chapter 13, there is an apocalyptic prediction about the Jewish War placed on the lips of Jesus, speaking to his disciples. This Markan apocalypse ends with the following parable:

> Take care, watch, for you do not know when the time will come. It is like when a man goes on a journey, when he leaves home and puts his slaves in charge, each with his own work, and commands the doorkeeper to keep watch. Watch therefore, for you do not know when the master of the house will return—in the evening, or at midnight, or at daybreak, or in the morning—lest he come and find you asleep. So what I say to you I say to everyone: Watch!
>
> Mark 13:33–37

Nothing remarkable here. Slaves are simply part of the story, a necessary element in the plot. But the author of the Gospel of Matthew also knew this story. Most scholars believe that he knew it, in fact, from Mark,

---

17. Found in Mark 12:1–11, Matt 21:33–43, Luke 20:9–18, and the Gospel of Thomas, saying 65.

18. Found in Matt 25:14–28 and Luke 19:12–24, a parable originally appearing in Q.

19. Orlando Patterson, *Slavery as Social Death* (Cambridge, MA: Harvard University Press, 1982).

which he used as a source. In Matthew's version, a master goes away, leaving a slave in charge of the household, in particular, the food. Blessed is that slave, says Jesus, who treats everyone well and makes sure all have enough food. So far, so good. But look what happens when the story takes a more sinister turn, when the slave hoards the food and beats his fellow slaves:

> The master of that slave will come on a day when he does not expect him and at a time he does not know, *and he will cut him to pieces* and put him with the hypocrites, where people shall weep and gnash their teeth.
>
> Matt 24:50–51

That's harsh, even by ancient standards. If this gruesome scene came from the imagination of Jesus, we would just have to swallow hard and adjust our expectations. But alas, it did not. It came from the anonymous author who wrote the Gospel of Matthew roughly fifty years after the death of Jesus.[20] I mention this story in particular because it is sometimes cited as an example—the example, really—of how callous Jesus could be to the plight of slaves.

If Jesus did not in fact imagine God as a ruthless master who dismembers disobedient and scurrilous slaves, how *did* he think about slaves? At least one scholar has argued that Jesus would have been very sympathetic to the plight of slaves, for he was himself a slave, born to a woman who was a slave. Winsome Munro, one of the most creative minds in biblical scholarship until her death in 1994, contended that the Jesus tradition is so full of references to slaves that Jesus must certainly have been a slave.[21] But few have agreed with her. Some of her slaves look more like day laborers, tenant farmers, or perhaps indentured servants. And of the authentic parables of Jesus, only one actually focuses on slaves (the Parable of the Entrusted Money, mentioned earlier). There is really nothing in the record that indicates Jesus or his mother were slaves, though as a "carpenter" (more accurately, "common laborer") he would have been among the poorest of the

---

20. Most scholars of the New Testament agree that Mark served as the source for both Luke and Matthew, written about a generation later. This is known as the "hypothesis of Markan priority" and it serves as the basis for most scholarship on these gospels today. In this case it indicates that Matthew first read the story in Mark and then rewrote it for his own gospel, adding the trailing episode and its scene of dismemberment. The scene, then, comes from Matthew, not Mark or any other earlier source, let alone Jesus himself. For an explanation of Markan priority, see Raymond Brown, *Introduction to the New Testament*, Anchor Bible Reference Library (New York: Doubleday, 1993), 111–16.

21. Winsom Munro, *Jesus, Born of a Slave* (Lewiston, NY: Mellon, 1998).

poor. There was no union shop in the ancient world. He would have known slaves, feared enslavement, and on bad days when work was scarce perhaps even envied a slave for the three squares a day and the roof over head that came with being valued property: "Foxes have holes, birds their nests, but the Son of Man has no place to lay his head and rest" (Luke 9:58//Matt 8:20 [= Q]).

If Jesus was not a slave, he must have known many. His world was heavily populated with slaves and former slaves. He would have encountered them, for example, in the sex trade. Most brothels made use of female slave bodies to satisfy their clients.[22] There is one story in the Gospel of Luke in which Jesus befriends a prostitute, or "courtesan."[23] In the Gospel of Matthew Jesus is remembered as saying to religious authorities, "tax collectors and prostitutes go into the kingdom of God before you."[24] And in a well-known scene in the Gospel of Mark, Jesus even uses the metaphor of slavery to describe the mutual devotion he expects his followers to show one another: "anyone who would be first among you must be a slave to all."[25] But this all falls well short of any real critique of slavery. In fact, the only clear evidence for a voice of protest raised against slavery in the first century of Christian literature is the second dyad in our little creed: "There is no slave or free." Someone—a Jew, a baptizer, a follower of John the Baptist and/or Jesus—dared to say what very few people in the ancient world managed to say, boldly, clearly, fearlessly: there should be no slave or free. We know this, of course, because Paul, at least, dared to repeat it. But did he really believe it?

PAUL AND SLAVERY

Howard Thurmon's grandmother hated the Apostle Paul. The great African American theologian, activist, and spiritual teacher was raised by his grandmother in Florida in the early twentieth century. She had been born into slavery and worked on a plantation near Madison, Florida, until the Civil

22. For the common use of slaves as prostitutes, see Thomas McGinn, *The Economy of Prostitution in the Roman World: A Study of Social History and the Brothel* (Ann Arbor: University of Michigan Press, 2010), 55–77.

23. See Luke 7:36–50. The woman in this story is not, by the way, Mary Magdalene, who is never referred to as a prostitute in the Bible. The idea that she was a prostitute comes from Pope Gregory the Great, who conflated other passages with this story to infer that this unnamed woman was in fact Mary.

24. Matt 21:31.

25. Mark 10:44; see also Matt 20:27.

War. She still had vivid memories of how religion was used to reinforce the "peculiar institution" of the Old South. As a boy it was Thurman's task to read to her, for she could neither read nor write. Often he would read to her from the Bible. She asked him to read from the Psalms, often the Prophets, and always from the gospels, but never from the letters of Paul, save the occasional recitation of 1 Corinthians 13, the "Love Chapter." Thurman never questioned her choices as a boy, but later, while on a visit home from college, he summoned the courage to ask her why she had never wanted to hear from the letters of Paul. Thurman recalls her answer:

> During the days of slavery the master's minister would occasionally hold serv-
> ices for the slaves. Old Man McGhee was so mean that he would not let a Negro
> minister preach to his slaves. Always the white minister used as his text some-
> thing from Paul. At least three or four times a year he used the text: "Slaves be
> obedient to them that are your masters . . . , as unto Christ." Then he would go on
> to show how it was God's will that we were slaves and how, if we were good and
> happy slaves, God would bless us. I promised my maker that if I ever learned to
> read and if freedom ever came, I would not read that part of the Bible.[26]

The passage Thurman's grandmother is referring to is notorious: Ephesians 6:5–9:

> Slaves be obedient to those who are your earthly masters, with fear and trem-
> bling, in singleness of heart, as to Christ; not in the way of eye-service, as
> people-pleasers, but as slaves of Christ, doing the will of God from the heart,
> offering service with a good will as to the Lord and not people, knowing that
> whatever good anyone does, they will receive the same again from the Lord,
> whether they are slave or free.

The same words—almost verbatim—occur in Colossians 3:22–25. In 1 Timothy 6:1 Paul says, "Let all who are under the yoke of slavery regard their masters as worthy of all honor, so that the name of God and the teaching may not be blasphemed." And in Titus 2:9, again: "Let slaves be submissive to their masters and give satisfaction in every respect." No wonder Howard Thurman's grandmother did not like Paul.

But Paul did not actually write any of these things. The problem with understanding Paul today is that not everything ascribed to him in the New

---

26. Howard Thurmon, *Jesus and the Disinherited* (Boston: Beacon Press, 1976 [orig. 1946]), 30–31.

Testament was written by him. Paul inspired a following that for many years after his death continued to produce letters in his name. Among them are Colossians, Ephesians, and 2 Thessalonians (usually called the "Deutero-Pauline Epistles") and 1 Timothy, 2 Timothy, and Titus (usually called the "Pastoral Epistles"). Scholars have for years referred to these letters as "pseudepigraphical" and opined that writing falsely in the name of one's teacher was a common thing in antiquity, a kind of school exercise. But recently Bart Ehrman has shown that "pseudepigraphy" in antiquity was regarded as forgery no less than it is today.[27] He argues that we should just call these letters what they are: forgeries. Regardless of what we agree to call them, critical scholars do agree that Paul did not write them.[28] Their language is different, their theology is different, and their views on a variety of social matters are different. In the years after Paul's death, followers of Paul created letters to commandeer the great apostle's authority to speak to issues of great importance to them in their own time. One of those issues was slavery. But how or why did slavery become an issue for the followers of Paul? To answer this question, we had better go back to Paul himself and what he actually said about slavery.

THE REAL PAUL AND SLAVERY

Slavery was an issue for Paul because our little creed made it an issue for him. Anyone who embraced baptism in this early period had to come to terms with the idea that "in the Spirit . . . there is no slave or free." In the plainest terms, it should have meant that in the communities associated with Jesus the most basic class distinction in antiquity should not count for anything. But what would that mean in *practical* terms? Would these nascent Christians manumit, that is, buy the freedom of their brothers and sisters who were enslaved? Probably not, at least not normally. It would have been too expensive to be practical. The manumission of just a handful of slaves would have emptied their coffers very quickly. Would they, then,

27. Bart Ehrman, *Forged: Writing in the Name of God—Why the Bible's Authors Are Not Who We Think They Are* (New York: HarperOne, 2011) and *Forgery and Counterforgery: The Use of Literary Deceit in Christian Polemics* (Oxford and New York: Oxford University Press, 2012).
28. Most critical introductions to the New Testament offer the straightforward evidence of this conclusion: their language and usage is different from Paul's, their manner of argumentation and formal features are different, and the situation and organization of the Pauline churches they presuppose cannot be squared with what is apparent from the authentic letters. For a standard, uncontroversial treatment of the issue, see Brown, *Introduction,* 662–68.

have facilitated the escape of their enslaved brothers and sisters, like the Underground Railroad? Again, not very practical. There were no free states in the ancient world to harbor escaped slaves and their abettors. Moreover, as we'll learn in just a moment, some members of the fellowship would have themselves owned slaves, and they did not free them as a condition of their association with an early Christian community. The issue of runaway slaves would have split these communities, as bewildered slaveholders looked upon those who had helped their slaves escape as betrayers, and antislave activists regarded their slaveholding brothers and sisters as inhumane. This could only end in arrest and execution for the activists, whose activities would have been known to the slaveholders and reported on.

All of this will explain, perhaps, why Paul's words on slavery are few, and when he does speak, he is incredibly unclear. He is so opaque, in fact, that scholars still argue over what it was he was actually saying. There are only two such instances, and each is a study in diplomatic obfuscation.

One is the Pauline letter known as 1 Corinthians. This is the letter in which Paul engages the followers of Apollos, who brought baptism to the communities Paul had founded in Corinth, and with it ideas about a new freedom and identity in the Spirit imparted through baptism. Paul's words on slavery occur in chapter 7 of this letter. The context is this: someone in the communities at Corinth had written to Paul and asked about the necessity of asceticism. Some members of the community had adopted the position—and the slogan—that "It is good for a man not to touch a woman" (1 Cor 7:1). Others, however, were leading more or less normal lives of love, courtship, and marriage. So, should followers of Jesus abstain from sex, or should they get married and have sex like everyone else? Paul's answer is at first very simple. He was himself an ascetic and did not have a family. He says, "I wish that all were as I myself am" (1 Cor 7:7). He realizes, though, that this is not so. Some have the discipline and self-control necessary for the life of celibacy, but some do not. Those who don't, he says, should get married and have sex—not to procreate, by the way, but primarily to recreate (see 7:2–5). Men and women should give to their partners their conjugal rights, he says. Asceticism isn't for everyone.

That would have been enough, probably, but Paul decides to forge on through the issue in all its complexity. Pretty quickly he lands in a thicket of conditions and contingencies requiring daisy chain explanations. Are you already married? What if you are just engaged? How about if you are married to an unbeliever? To cut himself out of the weeds, Paul finally says, "Just . . . , to each as the Lord has apportioned; as God has called each, let them so live" (1 Cor 7:17), or more simply, "Let each remain in the state in which he or she was called" (7:20). Remain as you are. No one needs to change his or her status. Again, that would have been enough. But even as he is laying down this principle, he begins to think of examples. The examples, it turns out, seem to reflect our little creed. If you are circumcised, stay circumcised; if not, don't go to the trouble, he says (1 Cor 7:18–20). That is the question raised by the first dyad in our creed: "no Jew or Greek." "What if you were a slave when called?" (7:21). That is the question raised by the second dyad: "no slave or free." The third dyad, "no male and female," is probably behind the whole question of celibacy and marriage. At least one scholar has therefore proposed that chapter 7 of 1 Corinthians actually represents Paul's best thinking on the creed and its practical implications.[29] So what does he actually say about "no slave or free"?

The honest answer to that question is, "It's not clear." It truly isn't. The verses in question are 1 Corinthians 7:21–23, which are as confusing as anything in the Bible. The problem begins with verse 21. Here Paul says, "Were you a slave when called? Never mind." Never mind what? Never mind what he just said in verse 20 about remaining as you are? Or never mind the fact that you are a slave? Paul does not say. He continues, "But if you are able to become free, instead *make use*." That is a literal translation, but it doesn't make much sense. "Make use" is a literal rendering of a Greek word, *chra'omai*, a word that can mean a lot of things. It can mean, for example, "be of service." Is that Paul's meaning? If so, then we might render the sentence something like "if you are able to become free, instead be of service." That is how the sentence was sometimes translated in the antebellum American South. But the word can also mean "make use of X," where you plug in the "X" (make use of that hammer, make use of your imagination, make use of the stove). The problem is, Paul does not supply "X" in this sentence. So make use of what? In nineteenth-century slaveholding America, scholars would sometimes finish the sentence something like this: "make use of *your present situation*." But their abolitionist opponents would finish it differently: "make use of *the opportunity*." That would seem to make more sense to a slave. If you are able to become free, make use of the opportunity. But Paul's communities also had slaveholders. What would have made more sense to them? In verse 22, Paul seems to throw them a bone: "For anyone who was called in the Lord as a slave, is a freedman of the Lord. And anyone who was free when called, is a slave of Christ." Ah . . . slave, free, free, slave, who cares? It's all a state of mind— we're all slaves; we're all free. That was, in fact, a common take on slavery

29. S. Scott Bartchy, *First-Century Slavery and the Interpretation of 1 Corinthians 7:21*, Society of Biblical Literature: Dissertation Studies (Atlanta: Scholars Press, 1973), 162–65.

among Stoic philosophers, with whom Paul was well familiar.[30] But then, in verse 23, Paul flirts with clarity in the other direction: "You were bought with a price. Do not become slaves of people." That gave ammunition to the abolitionists and their antislavery interpretation.[31]

So what *did* Paul mean? It really isn't clear. The question, then, is not what Paul meant to say, but why he said it in a way that was so unclear. Why can scholars read this sentence two thousand years later and seriously, competently, propose two diametrically opposed positions for the apostle? The answer is that Paul was truly ambiguous on this matter. Was this on purpose, or was he simply fumbling with a volatile topic? Slavery was the third rail of ancient society. To question its legitimacy was to risk breaking the spell. Why did slaves not wake in the night, rise up, and simply slaughter their masters as they slept? Why, as they caravanned across the desert, did slaves not turn on their drivers, bury them in the sand, and walk away? Who would know? For centuries, Western civilization lived under that same spell. Everyone—even slaves—believed in slavery. Did Paul know this, and consciously avoid saying the unspeakable? Or was he too under the spell and just couldn't find the words to point clearly to a new way of thinking?

WHAT ABOUT ONESIMUS?

The second place Paul discusses slavery should offer, one might think, a clearer picture. This is the letter known as "Philemon" in the Bible. This is a very brief, authentic letter of Paul, written to a certain Philemon about one of his slaves, Onesimus. But there is very little about this short letter that is clear. Paul wrote the letter while imprisoned somewhere—we don't know where. He wrote it to a person named Philemon—probably, for two others are also named in the letter's salutation. One of these two corecipients, Archippus, and the subject of the letter, Onesimus, are mentioned in the letter to the Colossians,[32] so many scholars assume that they all lived

---

30. E.g., Horace, *Satires* 2.7.75–94, and several examples offered by Wiedemann, *Greek and Roman Slavery*, 224–51. Wiedemann thinks Paul such a good example of this view that he lumps Stoics and Christians together under "The True Freedom of the Spirit."

31. J. Albert Harrill offers a discussion of pro- and antislavery interpretations of the slave passages in Paul in the great nineteenth-century debates about slavery in the American South in his book *Slaves in the New Testament: Literary, Social, and Moral Dimensions* (Minneapolis: Fortress Press, 2006), 165–92.

32. See Col 4:17 (Archippus) and 4:14 (Onesimus).

in Colossae. But Colossians is probably not an authentic letter of Paul, so these may simply be the forger's artful efforts to create verisimilitude. They all might have lived somewhere else for all we know. None of this really matters much, however. The letter is a letter of Paul. In it he discusses with the recipient the fate of Onesimus, a slave, whom Paul is sending back to Philemon. Surely here we will find something more useful to our efforts to understand how Paul felt about slaves and slavery. But alas, the letter is almost as confusing and opaque as 1 Corinthians 7:21–23.

Most readers of this letter assume that Paul is writing to Philemon about his runaway slave, Onesimus, and that Paul is saying in a very polite and nonconfrontational way that Philemon should free him. But over the years, scholars reading this letter very closely have noted how unclear and unstated these circumstances actually are.[33] The letter is very short, so you might pause five minutes now to read it and see for yourself how well this scenario holds up.

Was Onesimus a runaway slave? The slave part seems secure from verse 16, which speaks of Onesimus as a slave. He also has a slavish name. Onesimus means "useful." Was he a runaway? Verse 11 is usually taken as evidence for this: "Formerly he was useless to you." Onesimus apparently wasn't a very good slave for Philemon, but was he a runaway? Verse 15 is another piece of the evidence: "Perhaps this is why he was separated from you for a time, in order that you might have him back." This seems like a diplomatic way of referring to the fact that Onesimus ran away. He didn't really "run away." He "was separated" from you. Note Paul's use of the passive voice, as if no one actually did anything. It just happened. Finally, scholars usually read verse 18 as part of this scenario: "If he has wronged you at all, or owes you anything, charge it to my account." Did Onesimus then steal something from Philemon, or defraud him somehow? If so, was Onesimus on the run from an angry master when Paul first met him? Did he flee to Paul for help, believing for some reason that Paul might help him? In this case we would call him a "truant" slave,[34] rather than a runaway.

But some see the situation quite differently. One scholar thinks that Onesimus was probably sent to Paul to serve him while he was in prison.[35]

33. For various contemporary alternative understandings of Paul's letter to Philemon, see Carolyn Osiek, *Philippians, Philemon*, Abingdon New Testament Commentaries (Nashville: Abingdon, 2000), 126–31, and Demetrius Williams, "'No Longer a Slave': Reading the Interpretation History of Paul's Epistle to Philemon," in *Onesimus Our Brother: Reading Religion, Race, and Culture in Philemon*, ed. Matthew Johnson et al. (Minneapolis: Fortress Press, 2012), 11–46.

34. Peter Lampe makes the distinction in "Keine 'Sklavenflucht' des Onesimus," *Zeitschrift für neutestamentliche Wissenschaft* 76 (1985): 137.

35. Sara Winter, "Paul's Letter to Philemon," *New Testament Studies* 33 (1987): 1–15.

Paul is sending him home, but perhaps belatedly. Another argues that Onesimus had been apprenticed to Paul,[36] and another that Onesimus was not a slave at all, but Philemon's estranged brother.[37] As for me, I think the more common view makes the most sense, but the terseness of the letter and its vagaries do not necessitate it. As with 1 Corinthians 7, Paul seems reluctant to speak clearly when it comes to slaves and their masters.

This is especially evident when we try to understand just what it is Paul is asking Philemon to do. In verses 8 and 9 he says something like this: "While I am bold enough to command you to do your duty, I would rather appeal to you out of love—and I am an old man and in prison for Jesus Christ." One can easily see the problem: Paul does not actually say what he wants Philemon to do. Do your duty—literally, "what is required." But what *is* required? If Onesimus is a truant slave, Philemon's duty would be to punish him—though not as badly as if he were a runaway. Slaveholders had wide latitude in punishing disobedience, from scourging or other forms of torture to summary execution. But from the rest of the letter it is obvious that this is not what Paul wants. He loves Onesimus like a son. He is Paul's "own heart" in verse 12. Paul later says in verse 17, "Receive him as you would receive me." Paul has subtly made Onesimus *his* slave now, his surrogate body.[38] Anything Philemon now does to Onesimus, he will be doing to Paul. So perhaps leniency is what he wants.

Does he want Philemon to *free* Onesimus? If he does, he does not say so. In verses 13 and 14 it seems that he might even want Philemon to lend Onesimus to him, or perhaps give him the slave so that Onesimus might serve him. If Onesimus was on loan or apprenticed to Paul, this would make sense. What he does say in verse 16 is that Philemon should take Onesimus back "no longer a slave, but as more than a slave, a beloved brother." But does he mean this literally? Perhaps he means that Onesimus is no longer just a slave, but now *also* a brother. That could mean Philemon does not actually need to free Onesimus, but simply treat him a little differently, better. But then Paul says Onesimus is to be seen as a brother "both in the flesh and in the Lord." "In the Lord" means that he is talking about brotherhood metaphorically. But "in the flesh" means he is talking about something more real. Real brothers do not own one another. Or does he only mean to imply that real brothers don't scourge one another?

36. Harrill, *Slaves in the New Testament*, 14–16.

37. Allan Callahan, "Paul's Epistle to Philemon: Toward an Alternative Argumentum," *Harvard Theological Review* 86 (1994): 357–76.

38. For discussion of the principle, see Glancy, *Slavery in Early Christianity*, 15–16.

As much as we might like Paul's letter to Philemon to say something clear about "the Bible's view of slavery," it does not. Like 1 Corinthians 7, it only reveals how skittish Paul is when discussing matters where slavery is involved. Slavery was the hidden land mine in Roman social discourse. Paul did not directly challenge it and could scarcely even discuss it without dissembling before our very eyes.

SLAVE RESISTANCE AMONG THE *CHRISTIANI*

So did anyone ever take the words "no slave or free" seriously enough to actually act on it, clearly, boldly? Perhaps. Early in the second century the bishop of Antioch was being taken to Rome, where he was to be executed. His name was Ignatius. Beyond that, we know little about him. We also do not know why he had been arrested by the Roman authorities in Antioch, or when, exactly, he was eventually killed in Rome. But this mysterious person left behind a collection of letters that are a treasure trove for students of Christianity in the late first and early second centuries.[39] Today these letters—seven in number—are included in a collection of early Christian literature known as the "Apostolic Fathers." Most of them were written to early churches in western Asia Minor—modern Turkey. One, however, was written to another bishop, Polycarp of Smyrna. This is the letter that interests us.

Ignatius's letter to Polycarp is filled with good episcopal advice, like "meet more often," "bring your more pestiferous members to heel," and "avoid the dark arts." But in Polycarp 4:3 he writes this advice: "Do not be arrogant towards male and female slaves, but neither let them be haughty; rather, let them serve even more as slaves for the glory of God, that they may receive greater freedom from God." This, more or less, is what we read earlier in the forged letters of Paul. This Stoic view of slavery—endure slavery without complaint to become truly free—was apparently very widespread in the early second-century churches. But then Ignatius goes on to say something that reveals another way of thinking—not his own, but that of slaves who participated in the churches under his authority. He advises Polycarp: "And [slaves] should not long to be free through the common fund, lest they be found slaves of passion" (Polycarp 4:3). Still Stoic, Ignatius. But in the churches there were evidently slaves who expected something more

---

39. For what we do know about Ignatius and his letters, see William R. Schoedel, *Ignatius of Antioch: A Commentary on the Letters of Ignatius of Antioch*, Hermeneia (Philadelphia: Fortress Press, 1985).

than the Stoic ideal of freedom. And if there were slaves who expected it, there must have been instances where churches under Polycarp's watch had pooled resources and spent from the "common fund" to buy the freedom of slaves who were part of their community. These were Christians who took seriously, and literally, the notion that in Christ there were to be no slaves, only free. Were there others?

At about the same time Ignatius was writing letters to the churches of Asia Minor, the Roman governor of Pontus-Bithynia was also writing letters. Pontus-Bithynia was the Roman province in the northern part of Asia Minor lying along the southern shore of the Black Sea. His name was Gaius Plinius Caecilius Secundus, or, as he is known today, Pliny the Younger. Historians also treasure his many surviving letters for many reasons. They tell us much about how Roman administration of the provinces worked. Two of them are valued by volcanologists for their description of the eruption of Mt. Vesuvius. But the best known of his letters is one he wrote to the emperor Trajan about a new group of dissidents on the rise in his jurisdiction, known as Christians.[40] This is the first time that followers of Jesus appear anywhere in non-Christian literature. Pliny was the governor of Pontus-Bithynia from 111 to 113 CE, the last years of his life. So this letter would have been written in that time frame, very close to the letters of Ignatius.

In the letter, Pliny reports to the emperor his actions with respect to certain *Christiani*, whom he has not encountered before. Their activities in his province were apparently extensive enough to disrupt the normal flow of religious life in the pagan temples. That was their chief crime—they refused to participate in the public rites and thereby threatened to disrupt the *Pax Deorum*, the peace of the gods. Some of the accusations against the Christians had been made anonymously, so he proceeded carefully. Anyone found to be under suspicion he questioned and offered them the chance to repent and properly worship the gods. If they did, all was forgiven. But some did not, so he had them executed. The Romans took their religious duties seriously. Near the end of the letter Pliny tells Trajan of extra steps he has taken to be sure he knows the whole story: "I judged it all the more necessary to find out what the truth was by torturing two female slaves who were called deaconesses."[41] The torture of slaves for information about their masters' activities was common among the Romans. They were suspicious of slaves, and worried that resentful slaves might inform falsely

---

40. Pliny the Younger, *Letters* 10.96.
41. Pliny the Younger, *Letters* 10.96.

on their masters if it were too easy. So slave testimony was never regarded as reliable unless it was exacted under torture, which is what Pliny did with these slaves. But what is of chief interest to us is what he says about them—that they are female slaves and they have a title: *ministra*, or "minister." The Latin noun is feminine in form, so translators usually render it "deaconess." But this is in fact the Latin word that is used to translate the Greek word *diakonos*, which in Christian circles was the title of a church official who fell in rank just below the bishop.[42] They were the recognized leaders of their communities. Here was another way of taking seriously the implications of the claim that "there is no slave or free." Were they actually free? Pliny does not think so. He calls them slaves (*ancillae*), and so they probably still were. They may have been slaves, but in church politics they had power and authority. "No slave or free" did not always mean freedom for the enslaved, but it could at least sometimes mean power.

THE PROPHET SLAVE HERMAS

But it sometimes might have meant freedom too. Another text normally included in the collection known as the Apostolic Fathers reveals a perspective on slavery that is perhaps unique in early Christian literature. The Shepherd of Hermas is today little known among Christians, but in the second and third centuries it was as popular a piece of devotional literature as anything in the New Testament itself, and some would have considered it inspired scripture. It was written in Rome roughly at the beginning of the second century. Its author (fictive or real) is Hermas, who—as we learn in the opening lines of the text—was a foundling, that is, an exposed baby found by a slaver and raised as a slave, a common scenario in the world of the Roman Empire.[43] The slaver eventually sold him to a woman named Rhoda, whom he came to love "as a sister."[44] The Shepherd of Hermas is a series of revelations given to Hermas, first by a sweet elderly woman, who is "the church," and then by the "Shepherd," an angel-like figure who protects Hermas and his family. When we meet Hermas through this text, he is by now a freedperson. But like all freedpersons, he was not entirely free and would have still carried the memory of what it meant to be enslaved. And that brings us to a parable included among the many things the shepherd

42. See, e.g., 1 Tim 3:8–13.
43. See Hermas, *Vision* 1.1.1.
44. Hermas, *Vision* 1.1.1.

is said to have revealed to Hermas: the Parable of the Son, the Slave, and the Vineyard.[45]

The premise of this parable is the same trope that lay behind the handful of slave/master parables in the Jesus tradition. The master leaves the slave in charge of something, then returns to find out how the slave has done. But unlike those more typical stories told from the perspective of the slave-holding class, where the unreliable slave is punished—even dismembered—this story ends quite happily for its slave subject. The story begins with a journey and a command. There is an estate holder who has many slaves. On his estate there is a vineyard. It so happens that the master is about to go on a long trip, so he summons one of his slaves and tells him, while I'm gone, build a wall around the vineyard. Do this, and nothing else. If you do this well, I will give you your freedom. So off he goes and the slave gets to work. In due course the slave finishes the wall, but then notices that the vineyard is in pretty rough shape. It needs cultivating. So he sets about to cultivate the vineyard and pull out all the weeds. Alas, when he is finished, the vineyard really starts to produce. About now the master returns home. He sees the wall; he sees the nicely cultivated vineyard producing so well; he is really pleased. So he summons his son, the heir to his estate, together with all his friends, to make a big announcement:

> I promised freedom to this slave if he kept the commandment I gave to him. He did what I commanded and added more good work to the vineyard. He has pleased me greatly. In return for the work he has done, I want to make him joint heir with my son, for when he saw the good to be done, he did not ignore it, but did it.[46]

About now you might expect the trouble to start. The son has just lost half his inheritance to a slave. This can't be good. But no, in a somewhat utopian turn the story continues: "And the son of the owner was pleased with this idea that the slave should become joint heir with him."[47] A happy ending!

That is probably where the original story ended.[48] But the Shepherd of Hermas is a complex work, perhaps with many additions and layering. Someone just could not resist adding yet another happy ending to this

45. Hermas, *Similitude* 5.2.1–11.
46. Hermas, *Similitude* 5.2.7.
47. Hermas, *Similitude* 5.2.8.
48. Carolyn Osiek, *Shepherd of Hermas: A Commentary*, Hermeneia (Minneapolis: Fortress Press, 1996), 171.

story. It goes like this: The owner now throws a great banquet. There is lots of food, so he sends much of it to the slave to enjoy. But instead of keeping it all to himself, he shares his windfall with all the other slaves. Pleased with his largess, the slaves report to the master how generous and kind the slave has been to them. This calls for another gathering of the friends, and the son, to share with them the story of the slave's amazing generosity. Trouble this time? No: "And they were even more pleased that the slave would be joint heir with the son."[49] A double happy ending!

The Shepherd of Hermas does not tell us to take this story literally. It says, in fact, that it has something to do with proper fasting. Go the extra mile. Do not be content with simple fasting, but contribute to the needy as well. Then you will be rewarded, like the slave.[50] Then yet another interpretation is added to the parable, this one a long and convoluted allegory, in which the master is God and the slave the Son of God.[51] Again, the Shepherd of Hermas is a multilayered composition, with many additions, later alterations, and tendentious redactions. But its traditions were originally gathered together under the presumed authority of a freed slave. For those who followed Hermas, the slave was no joke, a stock character who bumbles around and in the end gets a little beating. Their prophet, like the women ministers who led the Christ communities of Pontus-Bithynia, was of the slave class. For them, the new community they were forming meant a happy ending for slaves. The conviction that in the Spirit there would be "no slave or free" had made it possible for them to "cut a path through the wilderness of their despair" and see a future of human freedom and dignity born of generosity and good will.

IN A WORLD . . .

That phrase just quoted comes from Howard Thurmon's journal, entered on the day he first caught sight of Africa from the ship on which he was traveling to Nigeria in 1963. He was on that morning imagining the inner lives of countless slaves who made the "middle passage" in "the deep, heavy darkness of the foul-smelling hole of the ship."[52] The American slave trade was

---

49. Hermas, *Similitude* 5.2.11.
50. Hermas, *Similitude* 5.3.1–9.
51. Hermas, *Similitude* 5.4.1–8.
52. Howard Thurmon, *With Head and Heart: The Autobiography of Howard Thurmon* (New York and London: Harcourt, Brace, Jovanovich, 1979), 193.

not invented from scratch; its rationale was nothing novel. Western civilization was a slaveholding society in its very beginning. Greeks, Romans,
Jews—everyone in antiquity held slaves. Our little credo registers a tiny
protest against that tradition. In the folds of various sources we see that
idea flicker to life, but ever so briefly. It lasted maybe a hundred years, and
then was snuffed out altogether. The desire to conform as closely as possible
to Roman—that is, *common*—social norms was its undoing. In the forged
letters of Paul—Colossians, Ephesians, 1 Timothy, Titus—the authority
of the great apostle became the hand that shut the door on hope for slaves
in the Christian church, and the entire civilization it would one day shape.
Paul himself had wavered. Perhaps if he had been clearer, more courageous,
it would have been more difficult for the church to take this right turn and
make the slave's obedience the will and command of God. Perhaps. But
none of that happened. Instead, "no slave or free" became, along with the
prophet Hermas and the women of Pontus-Bithynia, an obscure footnote
to a forgotten minority report on slavery. It would take centuries, countless years of suffering, and millions of lives before people in the Christian
West would reawaken to the moral challenge of slavery and finally make it
a byword to our history.

But slavery was more than slavery in the ancient world. It was the basic
class distinction. In the Roman system you were either slave or free, and
the difference, the divide was nearly impossible to bridge. Perhaps the
church's ability to absorb and live with this distinction made it possible
to live with many such distinctions. Slavery is no longer a legitimate part
of our world, but radical class division is. For centuries Christendom was
entirely complicit in a class structure that knew both royalty and serfdom.
It was the religious authority by which radical class division could survive
in spite of its harsh cruelties and gross unfairness. Christian Stoicism always said that this is the world as God has ordained it. Learn to live with
it and you'll be happier for it. Christian Socialism came late to the story, in
the Social Gospel of Rauschenbush in America and the Marxist priests and
nuns who gave life to liberation theology in Latin America in the 1960s
and '70s. Today Christianity is of two minds. Pope Benedict XVI rose to
power as the voice of opposition to liberation theology and all things
modern. His successor, the present Pope Francis, is the spiritual and intellectual product of liberation theology that came to flower in Argentina. In
the 2016 American presidential elections, the billionaire Trump chose the
evangelical Christian Mike Pence as his vice presidential running mate and
thereby drew the all-important evangelical voting black to his side. Hillary
Clinton chose Tim Caine, who as a young man spent time among the radical socialist priests of Guatemala serving the poor. Clinton–Caine lost to

Trump–Pence by a nose. Does Christianity endorse the world of the billion-aire and the pauper, or the utopian vision of a world without radical class division?

Christianity's first statement about class was "there is no slave or free." Such radical class distinctions do not, should not, cannot exist. What if that clear and unwavering statement had become the plumb line of for all of subsequent history in the lands that would be shaped by Christian ethics and consciousness? Would that have made a difference? Or was the Stoic position always inevitable? Is it now?

CHAPTER 6

cʌɔ

There Is No Male and Female

There is a room in the Altes Museum in Berlin that shows how profoundly different from us the ancients were in their attitudes about gender, sex, and sexuality. In it there are a dozen or so glass cases containing the oddest collection of sexually explicit *varia*[1]—for example, oil lamps, little round terracotta gems with tiny scenes of people in various poses of salacious copulation. There are oil lamps in the shape of Priapus, the god who always appears with a giant erect phallus, in which the little hole where one lights the oil is located on the very tip of his long, extended member. There are other such Priapus figures as well, not all of them luminary devices, some with animal body parts to go with their bizarre sexual apparatus. One has a male chicken head, with a mane and wattles, as if to anticipate a particular American euphemism for the male anatomy. Most curious, perhaps, are the necklace charms, where the body of the sex god has been reduced to just the penis. One such charm consists of a penis, with legs, which has its own penis extruding from between its legs, and (as if a penis with a penis were not enough) there is a third penis arising out of its anus. This, if you can believe it, was a good-luck charm to be worn around the neck or hung in a shop. There is, if one might prefer it, a version of this charm that comes with angel wings. This is all Roman-era stuff, demonstrating that in spite of the famous prudishness of one such as Caesar Augustus, the Roman male seems to have had a phallic obsession that expressed itself in the broadest of taste.

1. If you do a web search of "phallic art in the Altes Museum in Berlin," a number of images of this material will come up.

Strikingly absent from this display is anything representing the sexuality of the female. This is a male-focused pornography, suggesting a different kind of resonance in the male psyche than that struck by your modern *Playboy* magazine. For these ancients, the male phallus was not primarily a plaything. It was an instrument of power. The erect penis was a symbol of male power. That is why it could be worn as an amulet. That is why one finds it carved into doorposts and displayed on city gates. It is a warning, an apotropaic symbol to ward off evildoers: if you try to mess with us, we will definitely mess with you. Male sexuality was about power first and pleasure second—or perhaps, all about the pleasure and the power together. Love might be a distant third.

But in the center of this room there is a piece of marble statuary executed on a larger, near-life-size scale. It is a second-century Roman copy of a lost Greek original work of unknown provenance.[2] It appears to be a woman resisting the sexual advances of a Satyr. She is seated and, as you face the artwork, she looks every bit the female. But as you stroll clockwise around the sculpture there is a point at which you can see what was mostly hidden in the folds of her fallen *chiton* before: a small set of male genitalia. Surprise! This, it turns out, is the god known by Greeks and Romans as Hermaphroditos/Hermaphroditus. What would it mean to depict a woman with male genitalia?

There were, of course, people in the ancient world who were born with sexually ambiguous genitalia, as there are today. In the classical period such a birth was considered a bad omen and the child was normally killed. But at some point ideas about intersexuality changed and what was once abhorrent became interesting and attractive.[3] The resulting stories reveal two different takes on hermaphroditism as a phenomenon. They are illustrated by two very different depictions of Hermaphroditus, both of which happen to reside today in the Louvre: *Hermaphroditus endormi*[4] and *Hermaphroditus stante*.[5]

---

2. To see images of the sculpture, do a web search of "Satyr and Hermaphroditus in the Altes Museum."

3. To catch the range of interpretations of intersexuality, including the intersexual gods and demigods, see Luc Brisson, *Sexual Ambivalence: Androgyny and Hermaphroditism in Graeco-Roman Antiquity*, trans. Janet Lloyd (Berkeley: University of California Press, 2002); for more on androgyny across many periods and religious traditions, see Mircea Eliade's classic study, *Mephistopheles and the Androgyne: Studies in Religious Myth and Symbol*, trans. J. M. Cohen (New York: Sheed and Ward, 1965).

4. No. D'Inventaire: MA 231; to view an image visit: https://www.photo.rmn.fr/archive/13-555827-2C6NU054FWC9.html.

5. No. D'Inventaire MA 4866; to see an image visit: https://www.photo.rmn.fr/archive/10-504886-2C6NU0Q9VDL4.html.

HERMAPHRODITUS ENDORMI

Hermaphroditus endormi is the more famous of the two works. It is, like the Hermaphroditus in the Altes Museum, a Roman copy of an earlier Greek original, probably from the third to the first centuries BCE. He/she lies prone on a mattress and pillow, exposing his/her very feminine back and derriere to the casual observer. His/her left leg is slightly bent, however, raising the left hip to expose male genitals to anyone curious enough to inspect the sculpture with care. This is what I will call the *amorous* Hermaphroditus. He/she is beautiful, subtle, and often (though not always) revealed as an element of surprise. One version of his/her story is narrated in Ovid's *Metamorphoses* by the daughter of King Minyas, defiant Alcithoe, who dared to spend the feast day of Bacchus telling such tales— for which he, later, turned her into a bat. But before her metamorphosis, Alcithoe told this story about Hermaphroditus:[6]

Hermaphroditus, the son of Hermes and Aphrodite, came wandering one day in the land of the Carians—the region around the ancient city of Halicarnassus, now the modern city of Bodrum in southwestern Turkey. There he came upon a lovely spring-fed pool, home to the water nymph, Salmacis. No sooner had her eyes come to rest on this beautiful creature had Salmacis fallen madly in love with Hermaphroditus. "Marry me," she said. "No," he replied. "Kiss me, at least!" "No." "Just one little kiss?" "No." "Then I'll go away," she said. "Good," said he. And with that, Salmacis disappeared into the forest. Alone at last, the shy Hermaphroditus tried the water. It was cool, and the day was hot. So off came the clothes and in he dived. But alas, Salmacis had not gone, after all. She was, instead, hiding in the nearby bushes. Out she sprang and into the water to have her way with Hermaphroditus. He put up a good fight, but as she wrapped her legs around the lad, the smitten Salmacis sent up a prayer to the gods: "Grant this, O gods, that no day comes to part me from him, or him from me."[7] It worked. The gods heard her plea and granted her wish. There in the pool, the bodies of Salmacis and Hermaphroditus merged into one, her feminine form and his male parts joining to make one hermaphrodite.

In this Ovidian adaptation, the story is offered as an explanation for the strange properties believed to belong to the Pool of Salmacis: to this day, anyone who bathes in that pool becomes effeminate—so says Alcithoe. But one senses behind Ovid's secondary use an earlier tale in which we

6. Ovid, *Metam* 4.285–388.
7. Ovid, *Metam* 4.370–72.

would have learned how the hermaphrodite, Hermaphroditus, came to be—part man (Hermes) and part woman (Aphrodite). The myth must have been a kind of love (or lust) story, in which man and woman are attracted to one another so strongly that the two become one. There are such stories in antiquity, extending back perhaps to the pre-Socratic philosopher Empedocles. The best known, though, is the story told by Aristophanes in Plato's *Symposium*. It goes like this:[8]

In the beginning, when human beings first walked the earth, they were different from how they are today. They were round. And each person had two faces, two sets of legs, two sets of arms, two sets of genitalia, and so forth. Some had two sets of male genitalia, some two sets of female genitalia, and some had one of each. Now, these first humans were very powerful in their fullness and the gods came to fear them. So Zeus took his thunderbolt and, with a blow, divided them all in two. Now each had but two arms and two legs, one face, and one set of genitals. But the division of them was too harsh. They became weak and depressed, each longing for their own missing half. So the gods took pity on them and, with a little anatomical rearranging, made it possible for these halved wholes to connect with others—thus, sex was born. Now their longing could be fulfilled as each cleaved to their other half in sexual union. Those who had previously been part male and part female each desired to cleave to someone of the opposite sex; those who had been male–male experienced male-to-male desire; and those who had been female–female experienced female-to-female desire. And so it is to this day that people seek out an appropriate lover to feel complete and whole.

These mythic stories sprang from a handful of basic questions about human beings, their bodies, and desire. Why are there male bodies and female bodies? And why are people attracted to one another, sexually? And why does desire arise (usually) between people of the opposite gender? And why are people of the same gender sometimes similarly attracted to one another? Once someone noticed that human beings don't, in fact, come in just two varieties, male and female, an answer was born. The hermaphrodite was no longer seen as a bad omen, a monstrosity to be destroyed, but a symbol of original perfection, a reminder of a time when human beings were both male and female. That original account of Empedocles—though difficult now to reconstruct from fragmentary sources—may have gone something like this:[9]

---

8. Plato, *Sym* 189d–192e.

9. Following Dennis R. MacDonald, *There Is No Male and Female: The Fate of a Dominical Saying in Paul and Gnosticism*, Harvard Dissertations in Religion 20 (Philadelphia: Fortress Press, 1987), 25, n. 21.

In the beginning, Love reigned supreme, and the male and the female were united as one. But then Hate intervened, defeated Love, and produced division. Thus was enmity born, two sexes, and two genders. The hermaphrodite is a reminder of that original perfection. Desire is the residue of that original, primordial state of androgyny. Marriage, which in antiquity was simply connubial cohabitation, was a response to the ancient siren call of one's other half, a recapitulation of the whole person, now both male and female. The Ovidian legend of Hermaphroditus was a ribald version of this story, perhaps told as an entertainment at many a wedding banquet. Most of the museums of southwestern Turkey today have a handful of small figurines of Hermaphroditus from the Hellenistic period, just the right size for a wedding gift bearing well wishes for a long and affectionate marriage.

So is this myth of the primordial androgyne behind the third member of our early baptismal creed: "there is no male and female"?

THE TWO SHALL BECOME ONE

Yes and no. Yes, if you realize that this third clause could be peeled off and considered on its own.[10] Consider this saying of Jesus from the now-lost *Gospel of the Egyptians*:

> When Salome asked when the things about which she had inquired would be made known, the Lord said, "When you (pl) trample upon the garment of shame and when the two become one and the male with the female is neither male nor female."[11]

This quotation comes from Clement of Alexandria, whose work, *Stromateis* (or *Miscellanies*), was written in the late second century. But a version of the saying also appears about a century earlier in a work commonly known as *2 Clement*[12] and pieces of it are found in the *Gospel of Thomas*.[13] Dennis MacDonald argues that these various witnesses indicate that there must have been an early saying of Jesus that spoke of "trampling upon the

---

10. Thus, MacDonald, *No Male and Female*, 14–15 and 17–23.
11. *Gospel to the Egyptians*, fragment quoted by Clement of Alexandria, *Strom* 3.13.92 (following the text and translation of William D. Stroker, *Extracanonical Sayings of Jesus*, Society of Biblical Literature: Resources for Biblical Study 18 [Atlanta: Scholars Press, 1989], 12).
12. See 2 Clem 12:2.
13. See sayings 21, 22, and 37.

garment of shame" and "making the two into one" so that there is "no longer male and female."[14] Probably so, but what could it have meant?

The key to understanding this saying lies in the way Jews in the period of Christian origins bought into the myth of the original androgyne. When Jews interested in Plato and Hellenistic philosophy looked for evidence of the original androgyne in their scriptures, they did not have to look very far. In Genesis 1:27 they could already see that when God created Adam in his own image, he created him "both male and female." Again, in Genesis 5:1–2 the Torah states: "When God created Adam, he created him in the likeness of God, male and female he created him." The rabbis read this and some thought immediately of the myth of the primordial androgyne. Some of these ideas are collected in Genesis Rabbah, a compilation of early, learned rabbinical opinion about Genesis:

> R. Jeremiah b. Leazar said: When the Holy One, blessed be He, created Adam, He created him an hermaphrodite, for it is said, "Male and female created He them and called their name Adam (Gen. v, 2). R. Samuel b. Nahman said: When the Lord created Adam He created him double-faced, then he split him and made him of two backs, one back on this side and one back on the other side.[15]

Or, again, in Leviticus Rabbah:

> R. Levi said: When man was created, he was created with two body-fronts, and He sawed him in two, so that two backs resulted, one back for the male and one back for the female.[16]

The "splitting" spoken of here refers to Genesis chapter 2, where God creates woman by removing a rib from Adam's side.[17] A rib? These rabbis simply concluded that "rib" means "side" in this case—God took one of Adam's *sides* and made Eve.[18] So Adam was a primordial androgyne—much like the creatures in Aristophanes's myth. But God split off one of his sides to create the woman, Eve. And desire? Genesis continues: "This is why a man leaves his father and mother and cleaves to his wife, and they become one

---

14. MacDonald, *No Male and Female*, 23.

15. *Gen Rab* 8.1, after the translation of H. Freedman in Freedman and Maurice Simon, *Midrash Rabbah*, 10 vols. (London: Soncino, 1939), vol. 1: 54.

16. *Lev Rab* 14.1, as cited in *Eve and Adam: Jewish, Christian, and Muslim Readings on Genesis and Gender*, ed. Kristen Kvam et al. (Bloomington: Indiana University Press, 1999), 78.

17. See Gen 2:21–22.

18. See Gen Rab 8.1.

flesh" (Gen 2:24). Genesis Rabbah records no comment on this detail, but Philo of Alexandria did not let it pass. So long as Adam was singular, he says, he spent his life learning about nature and other such noble pursuits. But after the woman was created, he looked upon her, and she upon him, and before you know it,

> Love takes over, brings together the divided halves, so to speak, of a single living creature and fits them into one, and creates in each of them a desire for communion with the other for the purpose of creating offspring like themselves.[19]

This is the tale of Aristophanes in a nutshell: the original division of woman from man is the beginning of sexual desire and, ultimately, marriage. This idea would have been current among learned Jews who followed Jesus as well—like the author of the Gospel of Mark, who places the following words on the lips of Jesus in response to the question of whether divorce is permissible:

> But from the beginning of creation, God made them male and female. For this reason a man shall leave his father and mother and be joined to his wife, and the two shall become one. So they are no longer two, but one. What therefore God has joined together, let no one put asunder.
>
> Mark 10:7–9

If the author of Mark saw the existence of gender and the joining of male and female together in marriage as a good thing, ascetics, like Philo, took a rather dim view. He preferred Adam when he was still androgynous, both male and female. The separation only produced desire, and desire "led also to bodily pleasure, which is the beginning of injustice and lawlessness, and for which people bring upon themselves mortality and wretchedness instead of immortality and bliss."[20] The separation of Eve from Adam produced only desire and sex, the source of every evil.

Many Jews, then, would have a distinct understanding of what it meant "to make the two into one," so that there is "no longer male and female." It meant returning to that original state of primordial perfection—androgyny—Adam's state before God used part of him to create woman. But how? How could one return to Adam's original form, both male and female?

---

19. Philo, *On the Creation* 152.
20. Philo, *On the Creation* 152.

THE BRIDAL CHAMBER

One way, now long forgotten, was the ancient Christian ritual known as the "Bridal Chamber." The Bridal Chamber is now something of a mystery.[21] No one has practiced it for centuries, and of the many ancient texts that mention it, none ever actually describes what it entailed. Nonetheless, in the second-century Gospel of Philip it is named as one of the five sacraments established by Christ, alongside baptism, anointing, the Eucharist, and something called "the Redemption."[22] It probably involved men and women being united ritually so as to reconstitute in themselves the original androgyny of Adam. Consider the following intriguing passage from the Gospel of Philip:

> If the woman had not separated from the man, she should not die with the man. His separation became the beginning of death. Because of this, Christ came to repair the separation, which was from the beginning, and again unite the two, and to give life to those who died as a result of the separation, and unite them. But the woman is united to her husband in the Bridal Chamber. Indeed, those who have united in the Bridal Chamber will no longer be separated.[23]

If this is what it meant, what did the Bridal Chamber ritual actually entail? We have only hints, but one text may reveal something of its secrets. This is the second-century Syrian text known as the Acts of Judas Thomas. This Judas Thomas is the same Judas Thomas to whom the Gospel of Thomas is ascribed (which also mentions the Bridal Chamber in passing—in Saying 104). The Acts tell of the exploits of this apostle as he travels about the East spreading the gospel of asceticism and chastity. His adventures take him first to the royal city of Andropolis, where he finds himself invited to the wedding celebration of none other than the king's own daughter. The king would have him bless the marriage by visiting the couple as they enter the bridal chamber to consummate their union. So it is that the bridal chamber becomes the "Bridal Chamber." The elaborate prayers and blessings that then flow from the apostle's

---

21. To explore the discussion, see Risto Uro, "The Bridal Chamber and Other Mysteries: Ritual System and Ritual Transmission in the Valentinian Movement," in *Sacred Marriages: The Divine-Human Sexual Metaphor from Sumer to Early Christianity*, ed. Martti Nissinen and Risto Uro (Winona Lake, IN: Eisenbrauns, 2008), 457–86.
    22. *Gos Phil* 67.27–30.
    23. *Gos Phil* 70.9–22.

mouth may well have been drawn from the Christian ritual itself. For example:

> My Lord and my God, who travels with your servants, who guides and corrects those who believe in You, who is the refuge and rest of the oppressed, the hope of the poor, who ransoms the captives, the physician of souls that lie sick and the savior of all creation. . . . You, Lord, are the one who reveals hidden mysteries and secret words. . . . I ask you, Lord Jesus, and offer you supplication for these young people, that you would do for them the things that will help them and be expedient and profitable for them.[24]

After this prayer, Judas Thomas lays hands on the couple and pro-nounces, "The Lord be with you," and then leaves them. It is hard to avoid the impression that you have just witnessed the essential elements of the Christian ritual of the Bridal Chamber. What happens next suggests this too. The bride and groom are now left alone to consummate the marriage. But alas, Jesus appears to them. He takes his place on the bed before the bride and groom, who are seated in chairs, and begins to instruct them. Don't have sex. Don't have children, "whose end is destruction." Instead,

> if you keep your souls chaste before God, there will come to you living children . . . , and you will be without care, leading a tranquil life without grief and anxiety, looking to receive that incorruptible and true marriage, and you will become groomsmen who enter the Bridal Chamber of immortality and light.[25]

What happens next is nothing. Nothing happens. The bride and groom pass the night together, but they do not have sex. The king finds them the next morning sitting in their chairs, still virgins, but giddy with joy at what they have experienced, convinced that they are now joined as a true hus-band, a true wife.

This is only a guess, of course, but it seems very likely that this entire scene is conjured up as a kind of myth of origins for the ritual of the Bridal Chamber. Judas Thomas, the patron apostle of the East, who was thought to be the brother of Jesus himself, first introduced it in the court of Andropolis. It was, apparently, a kind of celibate or "spiritual marriage," as it is often called, in which men and women took a vow of chastity in a cere-mony constructed on the model of an actual marriage. The ritual effect was to reunite the male and the female and thereby recapture the innocence

24. *Acts Thom* 10.
25. *Acts Thom* 12.

that was lost when God created gender and sexuality, whereupon follow all the cares of the world.

In our twenty-first-century birth-control-enabled sexually liberated world, it is perhaps a little difficult to sense the appeal of such ideas. Sex is a satisfying part of a healthy life. Celibacy is a discipline, a sacrifice. But imagine what a difference celibacy would have made to ancients, especially women.[26] Girls married when they reached puberty—often to much older men—and began to have children immediately. They continued having children as frequently as their bodies would allow until, finally—usually—death came in the form of a complication. To ancient women celibacy made a huge difference. That is why when a group of women asked Paul about celibacy in Corinth, he recommended it: "The unmarried woman and the virgin are concerned for the affairs of the Lord, in order that she might be holy in both body and spirit. But the married woman is concerned about the affairs of the world, how to give pleasure to her husband" (1 Cor 7:34). To live a life free of the sexual demands of a man, free of the perils of childbirth, free to pursue other passions—that is what celibacy meant to ancient women. That is why celibacy played a role among first- and second-century Christians far beyond what anyone today imagines.

But did it work? Could men and women live in "spiritual marriages," abstaining from sex indefinitely? What if one of the partners changed his or her mind? Consider what Paul says in this same context of 1 Corinthians, right after advising men and women to remain celibate:

> If anyone thinks that he is behaving dishonorably with his virgin, if he has reached his prime (sexually) and it just has to be, let him do as he wishes—it is no sin—let them marry. But whoever stands firm in his heart, un-coerced, in control of his own desires, and wishes to keep her has his own virgin, let him do this. So, the one who marries his own virgin does well and the one who does not marry, does better.
>
> 1 Cor 7:36–38

This may be the earliest reference we have to spiritual marriages in early Christianity—though some have doubted it.[27] I think it is, and it reveals

---

26. See esp. Virginia Burrus, *Chastity as Autonomy: Women in the Stories of the Apocryphal Acts*, Studies in Women and Religion (Lewiston, NY: Mellon, 1987).

27. Since the fourth or fifth century, the church has treated 1 Cor 7:36–38 as though it were referring to fathers and daughters. But that defies the plain sense of the text—unless the question is a matter of fathers tempted to incest (unlikely). The two modern options are (1) that Paul is addressing young people who are putting off their marriage, even though they have become engaged, or (2) spiritual marriage. Those who prefer the first find it easier to square with the expression "his own virgin," the possessive pronoun referring to the engagement. Those who prefer the second note that Paul does not mention engagement here. I prefer the second, and assume that the possessive expresses the assumed terms of patriarchal marriage, upon which "spiritual marriage"

a side to spiritual marriage to be considered, especially when the cultural context was still the patriarchal world of Roman antiquity. Note how Paul's remarks are directed here to the man, not to "his virgin." Even in spiritual marriages, it would appear that men still did the owning, and the deciding about how long the whole celibacy thing would last.

TRAMPLING THE GARMENTS OF SHAME

Another common way to express the ideal of "no male and female" was through the ritual of baptism, as the third clause of our *baptismal* creed would imply. Returning to MacDonald's archaic saying of Jesus, we should now notice the first part of it, which goes like this: "*When you trample upon the garment of shame* and when the two become one and the male with the female is neither male nor female."[28] Christian baptism involved removing one's clothing before entering the water to be immersed. This was simply practical. But as the ritual developed, the act of disrobing itself acquired a significance, also derived from the Genesis story. At the end of the story, recall, God addresses the shame of Adam and Eve's nakedness by making for them "garments of skin."[29] As we have seen in chapter 3, for Jews like Philo, looking for Platonic concepts lurking in the Mosaic text, the real meaning of this text was not the literal meaning, that God provided the first humans with clothing (why would God care about something so mundane?). They preferred a metaphorical reading, in which these "garments of skin" were understood to be Adam and Eve's new, gender-specific, flesh-and-blood bodies.[30]

What seems to us a stretch was not so much for Philo. Platonists often spoke of the body as a suit of clothes worn by the soul during its earthly sojourn. At death, the soul sheds this suit of clothes and ascends to heaven where—in some scenarios—it receives a new garment drenched in light. In baptism, then, the act of disrobing came to signify that moment when the believer left behind the old body of sin and mortality—the "garments of shame"—descended into the waters of death and rebirth, and emerged to be clothed in a new, white, baptismal garment, this one signifying the new

was based. For a standard argument for the spiritual marriage position, see John C. Hurd, *The Origin of I Corinthians* (Macon, GA: Mercer University Press, 1983), 169–82. For the engagement position, see Gordon Fee, *The First Epistle to the Corinthians*, NICNT (Grand Rapids, MI: Eerdmans, 1987), 349–55.

28. MacDonald, *No Male and Female*, 23.
29. See Gen 3:21.
30. See, e.g., Philo, *QG* 1.53; also 4.78.

life of the baptized. Paul himself may have been giving voice to this concept when he said that anyone who is baptized is baptized "into Christ's death." In baptism, he says, "our old self was crucified with him so that the sinful body might be destroyed" (Rom 6:6). This is how Dennis MacDonald understands the phrase "trampling upon the garments of shame." In baptism one symbolically leaves the old body behind by disrobing and shows one's contempt for that old life by "trampling upon the garments of shame."[31] In this way, the ritual returned the baptized to that original androgynous state enjoyed by Adam in the garden, where "the two become one and the male with the female is neither male nor female."

But what might this have looked like in practical terms? Did these newly baptized androgynes do anything to mark themselves in their new, ritually acquired state of primordial purity? Sometimes, yes. One very early well-known example worth looking at is in Paul's letter known as 1 Corinthians. Baptism has in fact been the issue that lay behind many of the questions Paul takes up in this letter. One of them is a case of liturgical gender-bending that pops up in 1 Corinthians, chapter 11.

THE PRAYING ANDROGYNES OF CORINTH

1 Corinthians 11:2–16 is without a doubt one of the most misunderstood passages in the Bible. If you go read the passage now, in just about any modern version, you'll come away with the impression that it is all about requiring women to wear veils in worship. Women still wear veils in church in many places today. I remember my own mother and sisters wearing hats to church in the 1960s, each with a little mesh prophylaxis of a veil attached to the front. But the word for veil never actually appears in this text. Paul does speak about women praying and prophesying with their heads *uncovered*, and insists that women should instead *cover* their heads when doing this. Most interpreters just assumed that Paul was talking about veils. But in two essays in the 1980s, Jerome Murphy O'Connor argued successfully that Paul is not referring to veils at all.[32] The covering he refers to is the woman's *hair*. If you read long enough to arrive at verse 15 in this passage, this becomes quite obvious: "if a woman has long hair it is her glory, for her

---

31. MacDonald, *No Male and Female*, 60–62; cf. Jonathan Z. Smith, "The Garments of Shame," *History of Religions* 5 (1966): 217–38.

32. Jerome Murphy O'Connor, "Sex and Logic in 1 Cor. 11:2-16," *Catholic Biblical Quarterly* 42 (1980): 482–500; and "1 Corinthians 11: 2-16 Once Again," *Catholic Biblical Quarterly* 50 (1988): 265–74.

hair is given to her as a covering." In the first century it was customary for women to wear their hair bound up, often in elaborate weaves, so that it really was a covering—a hair hat, so to speak.[33] But the women of Corinth were apparently praying and prophesying with unbound hair. In that context unbound hair might have suggested lack of self-control, even loose morals. So this text is not about veils, but hair.

But as soon as you notice this, you will also notice that Paul seems to be concerned about men's hair as well. Long hair on a man is shameful, he says in verse 14. In fact, scanning back over the entire passage, it is now clear that Paul addresses men and women in more or less equal measure, from start to finish. Verse 4 is about men—who pray and prophesy with something hanging down from their heads (that is literally what the text says in Greek). Presumably, he is talking about the long hair he mentions later in verse 14. Verses 5 and 6 are about women, but verse 7 is about men— how they should not cover their heads. Here he could not be talking about veils, for it was actually quite common for men to pray with a veil covering their heads. That would not have been shameful or disgraceful. He is talking about men growing their hair long and using it like a woman would, as a covering. Verses 8 to 10 are about woman being made from man; verses 11 and 12 are about men now being born of women. Verse 13 is about what is proper for women, verse 14 what is proper for men—and so it goes, back and forth through the entire passage. Paul is not concerned just with the worship practices of the women of Corinth. He is also concerned about the practices of the men as well. So what was the issue?

It would appear that women were praying and prophesying with long, unbound hair ("uncovered"). Men too were growing their hair long and letting it hang down, unbound, also while praying and prophesying. This would have presented a rather unconventional scene, for women generally wore their hair up on their heads, "as a covering," while men generally wore their hair cropped short. Thus, men and women were both praying and prophesying with long, unbound hair, a style that was customary for neither male nor female. Men and women prayed alike and looked alike, blurring the distinction between them. And what was the rationale for this practice? It was probably the creed and its claim that in the spirit "there is no male and female."

Two things indicate this. First, Paul actually mentions the creed a few paragraphs later in the letter, referring to it like this: "For by one spirit

33. Wonderful illustrations of this are to be found in Cynthia Thompson's essay, "Hairstyles, Headcoverings, and St. Paul: Portraits from Roman Corinth," *Biblical Archaeologist* 51 (June 1988): 99–115.

we were all baptized into one body—Jews or Greeks, slaves or free—all were made to drink from the one spirit" (1 Cor 12:13). What's missing here? "Male and female." Paul more than likely omitted the third clause because in Corinth it had led to the transvesting practices reflected in 11:2–16, of which he disapproved. Second, in chapter 11 itself, Paul's argument against the Corinthian gender-benders is derived mostly from Genesis. For example, he says in verse 7 that man is the "image and glory of God," but a woman is the "glory of man." Why? Because "man was not made from woman, but woman from man; neither was man created for woman, but woman for man" (1 Cor 11:8–9). That all comes from Genesis 1–2, of course. He also argues that the sequence of events in Genesis indicates a hierarchy: God is Christ's head, Christ is man's head, and man is woman's head (1 Cor 11:3). It helps that in Greek the word for "head" (*kephale*) is also the word for "source." In Genesis 2, Adam is literally the *source* of Eve, who comes from Adam's side. So why argue on the basis of Genesis? Because the praying androgynes of Corinth based their practices on a Hellenistic Jewish reading of Genesis and the myth of the original androgyne.[34]

So by itself, the notion that "in the Spirit . . . there is no male and female" could, and did, find a lasting resonance in the mythic world and ritual practices of the earliest Christians. In this, they were participating in a broader Jewish theological tradition that regarded the gendered nature of humanity as the source of all our problems, problems that first began when God drew Eve from out of Adam's side. This separation set up a longing, a desire, to be whole once again. In baptism, the Bridal Chamber, spiritual marriages, and the like, early Christians sought to repair this tear in the human fabric, to restore Adam's original perfection in themselves.

If this were the only clause in our creed, we could probably let it go at that. Our credo's third clause is all about turning back the clock to Genesis, to that primordial time when there was not yet "male and female," but only Adam in his original androgynous perfection. But it is not. In the creed, "there is no male and female" stands alongside two other clauses: "no Jew or Greek" and "no slave or free." Moreover, it forms, with them, a response to a well-worn cliché ("I thank God I was not born a Gentile, a slave, or a woman"). Therefore, the meaning of "no male and female" is somehow tied to the meaning of these other clauses as well. Jew or Greek, slave or

---

34. See esp. Wayne Meeks, "The Image of the Androgyne: Some Uses of a Symbol in Earliest Christianity," *History of Religions* 13 (1973–74): 202.

free—these words do not refer to mythic realities in Genesis or Plato. They refer to political and social categories. They express ethnic difference and class ranking. They have to do with power and status. And they are, most important, distinctions that we have seen ancients use most emphatically to define a superior "us" over or against an inferior "them." Therefore, in our creed the statement "no male and female" must also have something to do with power and status and the end of the regime of male dominance.[35] What, then, did those who created the creed think the myth of the original androgyne meant in the real world of men and women, of power and status?

HERMAPHRODITUS STANTE

There is in the Louvre another image of Hermaphroditus, *Hermaphroditus stante*, "the standing Hermaphroditus." Here is a very different image of the original androgyne.[36] Like the sleeping Hermaphroditus, the standing image is primarily female: her head, body, and dress—everything about her offers a typically feminine look, everything except her genitalia. But unlike her dozing cousin, the standing version is not coy about her male attributes. To the contrary, she boldly faces you, dress raised with both hands, to expose an erect penis. And this is not the small, almost dainty penis of the sleeping version. This is the powerful, erect phallus one sees on doorposts and city gates, the symbol of male power and domination seen so commonly throughout the ancient world. Moreover, the power of this phallic image is underscored by the pose of the statue itself—the *anasyrma* pose (the "dress-raised" pose). This shocking gesture is thought to convey the special powers of women to ward off evil-doers.[37] Indeed—especially when the marble flasher exposes not a vagina, but a big erect penis. Surprise! Look what I've got! That would stop anyone in his or her tracks. A woman who has male power—is there any evidence for this idea among the early followers of Jesus?

35. See esp. Elisabeth Schuessler Fiorenza, *In Memory of Her: A Feminist Theological Reconstruction of Christian Origins* (New York: Crossroad, 1983), 217–18.

36. A Google search of "Hermaphroditus stante in the Louvre" will turn up an image of the piece at once.

37. See Ann Suter, "The Anasyrma: Baubo, Medusa, and the Gendering of Obscenity," in *Ancient Obscenities: Their Nature and Use in the Ancient Greek and Roman Worlds*, ed. Dorota Dutsch and Ann Suter (Ann Arbor: University of Michigan Press, 2015), 21–43.

MAKING MARY MALE

The Gospel of Thomas ends with a saying that has been a shocker ever since its publication in the 1950s, especially to women looking for something like a progressive revolution in the newly recovered lost gospels. Saying 114 reads as follows:

> Simon Peter said to them: "Let Mary leave us, for females are not worthy of life."
> Jesus said: "Look, I will guide her along so as to make her male, so that she too may become a living spirit similar to you males. For every woman who makes herself male will enter the kingdom of heaven."

This is a far cry from modern notions of feminine power and equality, but behind it there is a dispute that continues to this day in most of Christendom. The question here is whether or not Mary, a woman, is welcome in the inner circle of the apostles. Is Mary eligible for this role or not?

The identity of the Mary in question is, by the way, not entirely clear. Is this Mary the mother of Jesus, Mary of Magdala, Mary of Bethany (the sister of Martha), or some other Mary (Mary was a very common name among Jews then)? Most scholars assume that this is Mary Magdalene (although Mary of Bethany is a good candidate too), the one Mary who is actually depicted as a disciple of Jesus in Luke 10:38–42. Never mind. The question of which Mary is not important. The salient point is that she is a woman. Could a woman be counted among the apostles? The author of Luke settles the question by telling Mary's sister, Martha, to leave her alone. "She has chosen the good part, which shall not be taken from her" (Luke 10:42).[38] In Thomas the dispute takes on a decidedly more philosophical tone.

In the Gospel of Thomas you always have to be on the lookout for Platonic notions. There are plenty, as we have already seen in our discussion of this gospel in chapter 3. In fact, the Gospel of Thomas is one of the first attempts to integrate Platonism into Christianity—including the idea

---

38. Some have actually argued that Martha has the preferred leadership role in this scene, and Mary is approved for her passive listening (see, e.g., Elisabeth Schuessler Fiorenza, "A Feminist Critical Interpretation for Liberation: Martha and Mary: Luke 10:38-42," *Religion and Intellectual Life* 3 [1986]: 21–35). But this turns on the idea that Martha's "serving" (*diakonia*) is to be understood as "ministry," not the ordinary serving that women did in the home as a matter of course. For a more conventional, and probably more defensible, position see Adela Reinhartz, "From Narrative to History: The Resurrection of Mary and Martha," in *The Feminist Companion to the Hebrew Bible in the New Testament*, ed. Athalya Brenner, Feminist Companion to the Bible 10 (Sheffield, UK: Sheffield Academic, 1996), 197–224.

that human beings have bodies and souls.[39] Now the soul, in Platonism, was always thought of in masculine terms. It helps perhaps to know that those early Platonists actually spoke of the soul more properly as the "mind." A person consists of a mortal body and an immortal *mind*. The Greek word for "mind" is *nous*, a grammatically masculine noun, which may have made it easier to imagine this divine nugget as essentially male. If the divinely imparted, immortal soul—or "mind"—is masculine, then what about women? Do women also have this divine, immortal, rational part of the soul, the *mind*? Aristotle, as we have seen, thought they did not.[40] But Plato himself probably had another view.

The question comes up in a famous passage in Plato's *Republic*, where Socrates and his friends are discussing whether women could be "Guardians," that is, leaders in the ideal republic being imagined in their conversation.[41] Socrates argues, why not? After all, women have the same attributes of the soul that men have. Earlier in the dialogue they had already agreed that Guardians needed to have "the qualities of a philosopher" and "a soul that is full of *thumos*."[42] The Greek word *thumos* is a little hard to capture in one word, but it means something like "courage" and "presence of mind" and "spirit," or "spunk." You find these qualities, he says, in women and in men. It is only a matter, then, of cultivating them, of bringing them out and developing them through education. Women with these gifts could be educated in the same way that similarly gifted men were and thus become perfectly capable Guardians. This only left one embarrassing detail: they had already decided that the best educational program for these Guardians would be gymnastics for the body and music for the soul.[43] No problem with music. But gymnastic training was always done in the nude. Men and women training together in the nude!? That was the sort of proposition that tended to get Socrates into trouble with his fellow Athenians. Nonetheless, convention be damned! If women have the same qualities as men, then with proper education they could become Guardians equal to any man—even if it meant training in the nude.

Saying 114 in the Gospel of Thomas should make a little more sense now, especially if you remember that Jews who were interested in Plato

39. See Stephen J. Patterson, "Jesus Meets Plato: The Theology of the Gospel of Thomas," in *Das Thomasevangelium, Entstehung – Rezeption – Theologie*, ed. J. Frey et al., Beihefte zur Zeitschrift für die neutestamentliche Wissenschaft 157 (Berlin: de Gruyter, 2008), 181–205.

40. See chapter 2.

41. *Rep* 5.451c–457b.

42. See *Rep* 2.375b.

43. *Rep* 2.376e.

sometimes spoke of the divine element, the "mind," as though it were the "spirit" breathed into Adam at creation.[44] This spirit, given to Adam, was the breath of life that made him a true living being.[45] At stake here is Mary's inner nature. Does she have the equipment to become a "living spirit" like the men in Jesus's company? Peter thinks not. That would represent something like an Aristotelian view of things. Women do not have the same divine spirit that men do. But Jesus contradicts him. "I will guide her along," he says. Guidance. Training. With the right education, Mary can become a living spirit, like the men. "For every woman who makes herself male will enter the kingdom of heaven" (Thom 114:3). This grating summation underscores the fact that this is not a modern feminist take on women in leadership. But it is an ancient Platonic one. Women have the same inner makeup as men do. The spirit, the divine element breathed into Adam at the dawn of creation, can reside in women and in men. Mary, it turns out, has the same male power as Peter.

One reason for seeing Mary in this saying as Mary Magdalene is the fact that she was widely believed to have a claim on apostolic status anyway.[46] She was, of course, in the entourage of Jesus. But this was not the decisive thing. Much more important was the idea that Mary Magdalene had been at the tomb and actually encountered the risen Jesus, and even spoke to him. This was critical, for among the earliest followers of Jesus, leadership and status were closely tied to such experiences. When, for example, the Apostle Paul wants to underscore that he was in fact an apostle, equal in status to Peter, James, and the other apostles, he points out that Jesus appeared to him too, the last and "the least" of the apostles—but an apostle nonetheless.[47] In that famous passage in 1 Corinthians 15—where Paul names himself among all those others to whom the risen Jesus had appeared—the apostle does not name Mary Magdalene. But from the gospels themselves, we must infer that this was an omission—whether intentional or not. In every account of the resurrection of Jesus—in Matthew, Mark, Luke, and John—in *all* of them, Mary Magdalene is a central figure. In Mark and Luke, she leads the delegation of women that first discovers the empty tomb.[48] In Matthew, it is Mary Magdalene and "the other Mary"

44. See Gen 2:7; an example of a Platonizing reading of Genesis 1–2 is Philo's *Worse* 83–86.
45. In Hebrew and in Greek the words for "spirit" and "breath" are the same.
46. On Mary of Magdala as an early apostle of Jesus, see esp. Ann Graham Brock, *Mary Magdalene, the First Apostle: The Struggle for Authority*, Harvard Theological Studies 51 (Cambridge, MA: Harvard Divinity School, 2003).
47. See 1 Cor 15:3–11.
48. See Mark 16:1 and Luke 24:10.

(of Bethany?) who first encounter the risen Jesus.[49] The Gospel of John has the most complicated account of the four.[50] In the fourth gospel, Mary discovers the open tomb, but instead of going in, she runs to get Peter and another Johannine character called "the beloved disciple," and they go in and discover that the tomb is empty. But after they leave, Mary stays behind and it is she, then, who actually encounters the risen Jesus lingering around the tomb.[51] By these accounts, if anyone at all has the right to be called an apostle, it is Mary Magdalene![52] Peter doubts her, Paul omits her, and in John she must wait her turn outside the tomb, but there is one gospel in which her role as an apostle stands front and center, the gospel that bears her name.

THE GOSPEL OF MARY

In 1896, the German scholar Carl Reinhardt found an ancient codex for sale in a shop in Cairo. He bought it and brought it home to Berlin, where it came to be known as BG 8502—the Berlin Gnostic Codex. It did have two gnostic tractates in it—the Apocryphon of John and the Sophia of Jesus Christ—works that were later discovered in the famous codices from Nag Hammadi. It also contained a text called the Act of Peter, an otherwise unknown work. The first work in the codex, however, is, for us, the real discovery in 8502: the Gospel of Mary.[53] It occupies the first eighteen pages of the manuscript. Unfortunately, this does not include the beginning of the gospel—a study of the codex reveals that we are missing about six pages from the beginning and several more pages from the middle. Enough of the text survives to see that here was a gospel in which Mary played a leading role. It also reveals that the animosity between Peter and Mary was known well beyond the Thomas circle of Christians.

The surviving text picks up near the end of a complex discourse being delivered by the risen Jesus to his disciples. This scenario, where Jesus returns from the dead to deliver long, extended discourses to his disciples,

---

49. Matt 28:9–10.
50. See John 20:1–18.
51. See John 20:11–18.
52. Thus, esp., Mary Rose D'Angelo, "Reconstructing 'Real' Women from Gospel Literature: The Case of Mary Magdalene," in *Women and Christian Origins*, ed. Ross Kraemer and Mary Rose D'Angelo (New York and Oxford: Oxford University Press, 1999), 105–28.
53. For the text in translation and a discussion, see Karen King, *The Gospel of Mary of Magdala: Jesus and the First Woman Apostle* (Salem, OR: Polebridge Press, 2003).

is common in gospel literature, even though none of these "resurrection discourse" gospels eventually landed in the Christian canon of scripture. In these gospels, Jesus appears to the disciples after his resurrection and delivers a new, important revelation. This, by the way, reflects the same principle presupposed by 1 Corinthians 15:5–7, noted before: the *decisive* encounters with Jesus come after the resurrection, not before. In the Gospel of Mary, most of the new revelation is lost along with the missing pages. The surviving text picks up just before Jesus finishes his discourse and commissions the disciples to "go preach the good news of the kingdom."[54] Then he departs, leaving the disciples to figure things out from there. The disciples, though, are bereft. They're afraid. They can't preach about the kingdom. It will get them into trouble. "If they did not spare him, how will they spare us?" they complain, and they begin to cry.[55] This is where Mary comes in.

In a fragment of this gospel discovered some years after BG 8502,[56] Mary's role begins something like this: "Mary stood and greeted them. She kissed them all tenderly and said, brothers, do not cry, do not be sad or doubtful."[57] But I prefer the version that survives in BG 8502, perhaps because it resonates better with the theme of "making Mary male." There is no kissing in this version. No tenderness. "Stop crying," she says. "Don't chicken out! His grace will be with you all and protect you. Instead, let us praise his greatness, for he has prepared us and made us men."[58] This all runs very much counter to gender type in antiquity. Mary displays the courage, the *thumos*, here, while the men cower and cry. He has made us *men*, says *she*. In the face of danger, it is Mary who steps up and challenges their manhood. Put on your big-boy pants! Get to it! And it works. "She turned their hearts to the good and they began debating the words of the Savior."[59] Then Peter turns to Mary and says, "Sister, we know that the Savior loved you more than all other women. Tell us the words of the Savior that you remember, the things that you know that we don't because we haven't heard them."[60] So far, so good.

54. Gos Mary 4:8.
55. Gos Mary 5:1–3.
56. Papyrus Oxyrhynchus 3525, published in 1983 by P. J. Parsons, in *The Oxyrhynchus Papyri*, vol. 50, *Graeco-Roman Memoirs*, no. 70 (London: Egypt Exploration Society, 1983).
57. Gos Mary 5:4–5.
58. Gos Mary 5:4–8.
59. Gos Mary 5:9–10.
60. Gos Mary 6:1–2.

Then Mary begins to teach them all that Jesus taught her. Unfortunately, not much of this survives either, because several more pages are missing. But the content of this further teaching—a mix of Christianity and Platonism, much like the Gospel of Thomas—is not so important for us. What matters is the reaction. When she finishes, the disciple Andrew starts right in: "Say what you wish about what she has said, but I don't believe that the Savior said these things, for these teachings are truly strange ideas."[61] Then Peter joins him: "So did he speak with a woman privately without our knowing? Are we to turn around and listen to her? Did he choose her over us?" Now Mary starts to cry. "What do you imagine, my brother, Peter? Do you think I have made these things up on my own or that I'm lying about the Savior?"[62] Finally the disciple Levi intervenes:

Peter, you have always been a hot head. Now I see you arguing with this woman as if she were the enemy. If the Savior made her worthy, who are you to reject her? Surely the Savior knew her well. That's why he loved her more than us. Instead, we should be ashamed and clothe ourselves with the perfect man and bring it forth from ourselves, just as he commanded us, and let us preach the good news, laying down no rule or law beyond what the Savior said.[63]

Levi gets the last word. After this, the disciples go out and begin to teach and preach. Mary wins, with Levi's help—but not before we learn that Thomas 114 is not the only evidence of a rift among the disciples. Was Peter the first, or was Mary? In the Gospel of Mary, she is the wisest and most powerful of the disciples. She knows things the others do not. In the Gospel of Mark, she is the first to discover the empty tomb. In Matthew—a gospel otherwise devoted to Peter's authority—she is the first to encounter the risen Jesus. And even in John, while Peter and the beloved disciple vie for the honor of being first to step into the empty tomb, it is still Mary who encounters Jesus in the garden. Mary, it seems, was the first apostle.[64]

61. Gos Mary 10:1–2.
62. Gos Mary 10:5–6.
63. Gos Mary 10:7–13.
64. That Mary was, historically speaking, a prominent disciple of Jesus enjoys widespread consensus today. In addition to D'Angelo's essay and Graham Brock's book, both cited previously, see Carla Ricci, *Mary Magdalene and Many Others: Women Who Followed Jesus*, trans. Paul Burns (Minneapolis: Fortress Press, 1994), 51–161; Esther DeBoer, *Mary Magdalene: Beyond the Myth* (Harrisburg, PA: Trinity Press, 1997), 18–57; and Jane Schaberg, *The Resurrection of Mary Magdalene: Legends, Apocrypha, and the Christian Testament* (New York and London: Continuum, 2002), 204–99, among many other studies.

The church, though, did not embrace her as such. Peter became the pre-eminent figure among the apostles, while Mary became other things. Mary the mother of Jesus became the Virgin Mary, the symbol of female purity and eternal chastity. Mary Magdalene enjoyed a postbiblical career as a whore. Pope Gregory the Great created this tradition in the sixth century by confusing her with a prostitute who appears in Luke 7:36–50. In *The Da Vinci Code*, Dan Brown made her the secret wife of Jesus, the mother of his child, the Holy Grail! Mary could be a prostitute or a girlfriend or a secret wife, but never a disciple, never an apostle. And what of Mary of Bethany, who sat as a disciple at Jesus's feet? Completely forgotten. And these were not the only women who once fell in with Jesus, became his disciples, and went on to teach and preach in his name. There were actually many others.

PAUL'S BOSS: PHOEBE

Even though many assume that the historic patriarchy of the Christian church still prevalent today goes back to its very beginnings, there is a growing body of work to show that this simply is not so. The scholarship of Elisabeth Schuessler Fiorenza, Luise Schotroff, and many others has long been leading to a consensus among historians of Christian origins that women were, in fact, the leaders of many of these early Christian communities.[65] One of the key pieces of evidence in this new consensus is Paul's Epistle to the Romans, chapter 16.

Romans 16 may or may not have been part of Paul's original Epistle to the Romans. There are good arguments for and against it.[66] But most everyone agrees that Paul wrote Romans 16 as a formal statement of

65. Schuessler Fiorenza, *In Memory of Her*; Luise Schotroff, *Lydia's Impatient Sisters: A Feminist Social History of Early Christianity*, trans. Barbara and Martin Rumscheidt (Louisville, KY: Westminster/John Knox Press, 1995); further: Kraemer and D'Angelo, *Women and Christian Origins*.

66. The problem can be seen with the naked eye by noting simply how the letter seems to conclude with 15:30–33. The oldest manuscript of Romans (P[46]) has the doxology in Rom 16:25–27 at the end of chapter 15, which would seem to close the letter formally, before including the rest of Rom 16, presumably a separate, attached letter. For the complex issues, see T. W. Manson, "St. Paul's Letter to the Romans—and Others," 225–41, in Manson, *Studies in the Gospels and Epistles* (Manchester: Manchester University Press, 1962), reprinted in Karl Donfried, *The Romans Debate*, rev. and expanded ed. (Peabody, MA: Hendrickson, 1991), 1–15. More recently the consensus has collapsed and many argue for the integrity of Rom 1–16 in its entirety. See, e.g., Peter Lampe, "The Roman Christians of Romans 16," in Donfried, *The Romans Debate*, 216–31 (= chapter 16 of Lampe's *From Paul to Valentinus: Christians in Rome in the First Two Centuries*, trans. Michael Steinhauser (Minneapolis: Fortress, 2003).

recommendation for a certain woman named Phoebe. Who was she? Paul says two things about her. First, he says that she is the *diakonon* of the church in Cenchreae,[67] the port town of the Greek city of Corinth. Then he says that she is the *prostatis* of many people, including Paul himself.[68] She was a church *diakonos* and a *prostatis*. What do these words mean?

A *diakonos* is a temple official in the Greek and Roman world. The Christian church adopted this term to refer to its leaders as well. Typically, we would translate it as "minister." Greek nouns, as we have seen, have a specific grammatical gender. *Diakonos* is a masculine noun. Nevertheless, most English translations of Romans 16:1 render the word here as "deaconess," as if the rarer, feminine version of the word—*diakonissa*—were being used. But it isn't. Paul calls Phoebe the *diakonos* of the church in Cenchreae, the plain sense being that she is an official of that church, or its "minister." So why translate it as "deaconess" here? In modern churches "deaconess" is a very different role from "minister." Usually a deaconess is a woman engaged, formally or informally, in duties related to spiritual care. In the eighteenth and nineteenth centuries, Protestant deaconesses also engaged in physical care, establishing some of the first hospitals in many European and American cities (Florence Nightingale was a deaconess). In any event, modern churches have female "deaconesses," but most do not have female "ministers." That is a male role—with the exception of a handful of modern American and European liberal Protestant denominations, which began to ordain women as "ministers" in the mid-twentieth century.[69] The vast majority of churches—Protestant, Catholic, and Orthodox—still do not ordain women as ministers or priests today. That is why no widely used translation of the Bible even yet calls Phoebe a "minister" of the church at Cenchreae.[70] What exactly the term *diakonos* would have implied about her duties is unknown—this is one of the earliest occurrences of the term in a Christian context. She was, however, that church's leader, its "minister," not its "deaconess."[71]

Paul also calls her a *prostatis*—she is the *prostatis* of many, and of Paul himself, he says. This is also a term with a fairly specific meaning in Roman

67. See Rom 16:1.
68. See Rom 16:2.
69. The first, actually, was Antoinette Brown, ordained in 1852 as minister of the Congregational Church of South Butler, New York. Most denominations did not begin to ordain women for another century.
70. The New Revised Standard Version, published by the National Council of Churches in the United States, comes close, rendering the word "deacon" (not "deaconess") and offering "minister" as an alternative translation in a footnote.
71. Schuessler Fiorenza, *In Memory of Her*, 170.

culture. It comes from the Roman custom of patronage and benefaction. A person's *prostatis* was his or her patron.[72] Typically, a patron was a person of means who could offer social and financial support to a client, or, often, many clients. Clients were in turn expected to honor the patron with obedience and, when needed, political support. The patron–client relationship was a semiformal one in Roman society, carrying certain expectations. That Paul calls Phoebe his patron means that she had supported and promoted him socially and financially and that he, in turn, was obligated to her. He owed her his allegiance. She was, in a sense, Paul's "boss." Why mention this fact here? It must be because her role as patron was part of her relationship to the Cenchreaen church. As churches originally came together in small groups to offer one another mutual care and support, they needed places to gather. Many of these nascent churches probably gathered in people's homes, or perhaps a home converted into a kind of clubhouse. Most of the people who participated in these early house churches were poor. But for things like houses, common meals, and emergency assistance they needed patrons—people of means who could pay for such things. Wealthier people gradually did find their way into these nascent Christian churches, and when they did, they fell into the established role of patron. This was Phoebe's role. She was a patron of the church at Cenchreae. Eventually the patron–client relationship would provide the basic pattern of social hierarchy used by churches to organize themselves more formally. Bishops were originally Roman-style patrons. You might say, then, that Phoebe was a proto-bishop. Because Paul traveled extensively and had a large network of acquaintances, one of the loyalties he could offer Phoebe was a letter of introduction, which allowed her to bring her social capital along wherever she traveled.

Was Phoebe a unique or rare example of female leadership in these early churches? Judging from the rest of Romans 16, certainly not. The rest of the recommendation—most of it, really—consists of a long series of flatteries. The writer of such a recommendation would need to show its recipients his *bona fides*, his *gravitas*. Paul was vouching for Phoebe, but

---

72. Traditionally this word has been rendered as "helper" in English translations, on the grounds that women could not function as patrons in Roman society. But we now know that this was not so. The closest parallel to Phoebe's role as *prostatis* in Cenchreae is from a third-century inscription from ancient Aphrodisias (not far from modern Izmir in western Turkey), which refers to a woman named Jael, who was the patron (*prostatis*) of a local synagogue. See Robert Jewett, *Romans: A Commentary*, Hermeneia (Minneapolis: Fortress Press, 2007), 946–47, originally published by Joyce Reynolds and Robert Tannenbaum, *Jews and God-Fearers at Aphrodisias: Greek Inscriptions with Commentary* (Cambridge: Cambridge University Press, 1987), 41.

who would vouch for Paul? This is the reason for all the name-dropping: to ensure that Phoebe would be received as an important person, Paul needed also to establish himself as an important person. His personal greetings to people like Epaenetus, "the first convert in Asia" (Rom 16:5), do precisely this. If he knows these important people, then he must be important too. Social Intercourse 101.

What is striking about the names that begin to roll off Paul's tongue in Romans 16 is the fact that many of these important people are women. The first person he mentions is Prisca, along with her male counterpart, Aquila—but note that Prisca's name comes first in the pair. [73] Important? After mentioning Epaenetus, he goes on to greet "Mary, who has worked hard among you" (Rom 16:6). Mary was a common Jewish name, so this is probably not any other known Mary—just an important person in the church to which this letter was originally sent. Then he greets another pair, "Andronicus and Junia" (Rom 16:7). Many older translations—and even some modern ones—refer to this Junia as "Junias," as though the name were masculine rather than feminine. This is because Paul goes on to characterize these two as "prominent figures among the apostles" (Rom 16:7b). That a woman could have been an apostle, let alone a *prominent* apostle, just seemed impossible, so translators made up the masculine name "Junias" to refer to her. But Junias is not an actual name in antiquity. No, the plain sense of the text is that Paul here gives a shout-out to a prominent woman apostle named Junia (some manuscripts have "Julia").[74] Then, after mentioning several men and their families, he greets two "workers in the Lord, Tryphaena and Tryphosa" (Rom 16:12a), both women, and then, another woman, "the much loved Persis, who has worked for many things in the Lord" (16:12b). Then, finally, in a list of several names, most of which are male, he mentions (another) "Julia" (16:15).

What does all of this mean? Paul was part of a nascent Christian missionary movement that included many women in prominent roles. People knew these women and respected their judgment. By calling them out, Paul ensured that his letter would be well received and respected. Perhaps Paul had recruited some of these women. But Phoebe was his patron, not the other way around. And of Junia he says explicitly that she and Andronicus were "in Christ" before him.[75] Therefore, women were obviously involved in

73. See Rom 16:3–5a.
74. For more on this early apostle, see Bernadette Brooten, "'Junia . . . Outstanding Among the Apostles (Romans 16:7)," in *Women Priests: A Catholic Commentary on the Vatican Declaration*, ed. Leonard Swidler and Arlene Swidler (New York: Paulist, 1977), 141–44.
75. See Rom 16:7.

the leadership of the Jesus movement before Paul joined it. It was part of what he signed on to, and he embraced it thoroughly (in spite of his squeamishness over the transvesting androgynes of 1 Corinthians 11).

If the book of Acts can be relied upon to provide a realistic—if not historically accurate—account of Christian origins, Paul, it seems, relied heavily on women as he traveled from place to place. Of the several churches he is said to have created, most of them were founded through the agency of women, or women working together with men. The church at Philippi, for example, was founded by Lydia.[76] In his letter to Philippi, Paul mentions two other women designated as "fellow workers," Syntyche and Euodia.[77] In that letter he appeals to them to settle their differences. This probably means that they were among that church's leaders and their disagreement was having consequences for the community. In Athens, Paul's first comrades were a man, Dionysus, and a woman, Damaris.[78] Prisca (Priscilla) and Aquila, whom Paul greets in Romans 16, were, along with Paul, the founders of the Corinthian churches,[79] and later, when Paul went back east to Syria, they stayed behind and founded the community in Ephesus.[80] Back in Corinth, a woman named Chloe became an early leader, sending emissaries to Paul with the report that occasioned the letter known as 1 Corinthians.[81] Paul, it seams, was simply surrounded by prominent women who were—as he so often calls them—"fellow workers in the Lord." But Acts doesn't mention the most colorful woman associated with Paul and the early Jesus movement in these early years.

ST. THECLA

If you travel much around modern Syria and Lebanon today you'll soon begin to encounter a strange saint among the Christians there. Her shrines are everywhere, and on many Aegean islands as well, where pious women gather to pray to their patron saint for health and various favors, many of which will be commemorated in the form of votive offerings tacked to the walls. A miniature tin breast, an eye, an ear. In these places her feast day, September 24, is well celebrated. Her traditional icon conveys little: in her right hand she holds a cross, while in her left, a book or scroll. But behind

76. See Acts 16:11–15.
77. See Phil 4:2.
78. See Acts 17:34.
79. See Acts 18:1–4.
80. See Acts 18:18–23.
81. See 1 Cor 1:11.

this modest image is a great story—the story of the first woman to follow Paul, Thecla. Her story is told in a poorly preserved text known as the Acts of Paul and Thecla.[82] The church father, Tertullian, condemned it as a forgery,[83] but the legends it contains probably circulated for generations before the text itself was written down sometime in the second century.[84]

Thecla was a follower of Paul, entranced by the great apostle when he came to preach in her hometown of Iconium—modern Konya in south central Turkey. We first meet Thecla perched in a window, listening, spellbound by Paul's voice.[85] For days she is transfixed. This worries her mother. Why is she attracted to this new stranger? What will Thamyris, her fiancé, say when he hears about it? Thecla's mother fetches him to come pull her away. But Thecla will not be moved. Instead, she is persuaded by Paul's message of perpetual virginity. She won't marry Thamyris after all. What happens when a woman refuses to marry in the ancient world? What would happen if she tried to travel about, teaching and holding forth like a wandering philosopher? Could a woman be an apostle? This is the imaginative territory explored in the legends and stories about Thecla.

Thecla, it turns out, is not free to reject her fiancé. For this, in fact, she is condemned to be burned alive.[86] This is her first test. Boys and girls bring the kindling, the executioner tells her to climb onto the pyre and she does, they light the fire, the flames blaze up, but alas, Thecla is not harmed. "God has compassion on her," clouds gather, the earth rumbles, and a great storm pours down rain and hail to put out the fire. So Thecla is saved.[87]

Her next trial is in Antioch, where she travels with Paul.[88] No sooner have they arrived than Thecla is approached by another man, Alexander, who is smitten by her extraordinary beauty. Paul? Paul says he doesn't know her—she isn't mine! So Alexander tries to abduct her. But Thecla throws a tantrum—rips his cloak, throws the wreath from his head, and humiliates this new suitor. But girls aren't supposed to reject the advances of men. So alas, Thecla is condemned to the beasts. Just so is the scene set. Thecla is led to the arena, accompanied by a wealthy local woman who befriends her and offers her comfort.[89] This is Tryphaena (named in Rom

82. A fine introduction to the Acts of Paul and Thecla is Dennis MacDonald's *The Legend and the Apostle: The Battle for Paul in Story and Canon* (Philadelphia: Westminster, 1983). In what follows, I will follow MacDonald much of the way.
83. Tertullian, *On Baptism* 1.17.
84. As shown by MacDonald, *The Legend and the Apostle*, 17–33.
85. Acts of Paul and Thecla 7.
86. Acts of Paul and Thecla 20–21.
87. Acts of Paul and Thecla 22.
88. Acts of Paul and Thecla 26.
89. Acts of Paul and Thecla 31.

16?), a kind of second hero in the story, who protects Thecla and keeps her pure. In the procession, Thecla is bound to a fierce lioness, but—here's some foreshadowing—the lioness does not harm her. They arrive at the arena, Thecla and Tryphaena say their tearful goodbyes, and Thecla is led into the ring. What happens next, and the way the story is told, is so important to our point in this chapter that I can only let the text speak for itself:

[32]Then there was a tumult, the roaring of the beasts and the shouting of the people, including the women, who sat together, some saying: "Bring in the sacrilegious one!," but the women saying: "Away with the city for this lawless act! Away with all us, proconsul! This is a bitter sight, an evil judgment!"

[33]But Thecla was taken from Tryphaena and stripped. A girdle was put upon her and she was cast into the arena. Then lions and bears were released against her. But a fierce lioness ran to her and lay down at her feet, and the crowd of women cheered. And a bear charged her, but the lioness ran and met him and tore the bear apart. And another lion charged her, a trained man-eater that belonged to Alexander, but the lioness wrestled with him and it died along with him. And the women wept all the more, seeing that the lioness, which had protected her, was dead.

[34]Then they sent in many beasts, while she stood and stretched out her hands and prayed. And when she had ended her prayer, she turned and saw a great tank full of water, and said: "Now is it time for me to bathe." And she dove in, saying: "In the name of Jesus Christ I baptize myself on the last day." And all the women saw it and everyone wept, saying: "Do not dive into the water," and even the governor wept that such great beauty should be devoured by seals. So, then, she dove into the water in the name of Jesus Christ. But the seals, seeing a bright flash of fire, floated up dead on the water. And a cloud of fire surrounded her, so that the beasts did not touch her, nor was she seen naked.

[35]Now, when other more fearsome beasts were sent in, the women cried aloud. And some cast leaves, and others nard, and others cassia, and some balsam, so that there was a cloud of perfume. And all the beasts that were hit by it were held as if in sleep and did not touch her. So Alexander said to the governor: "I have some very fearsome bulls. Let's bind the criminal to them." And the governor frowned, but allowed it, saying: "Do what you wish." And they tied her by the feet between the bulls and put hot irons under their bellies so that they might be enraged and kill her. Then they lept forward, but the fire that burned around her burned through the ropes, and she was freed.[90]

90. Acts of Paul and Thecla 32–35; trans: adapted from Rodolf Kasser's translation in *New Testament Apocrypha*, 2 vols., rev. ed., ed. Edgar Hennecke and Wilhelm Schneemelcher, trans. R. McL. Wilson (Cambridge: James Clarke & Co, 1991/ Louisville, KY: Westminster/John Knox Press, 1991).

Just then Tryphaena, who turns out to be a relative of Caesar, faints dead away and everyone thinks she's dead. That sends everyone into a panic and the whole scene stops. As people try to revive Tryphaena, the governor turns to Thecla and says, "Who *are* you?" She replies, "I am the handmaid of the living God."[91] In the end, Thecla is sent on her way to find Paul and continue her quest to become an apostle.

What strikes most people about this text is the way it seems to reflect the perspective and interests of women. All the heroes are women. All the villains are men. Even Paul comes off as cowardly and smug. Thecla, by contrast, is humble, yet bold and courageous. A gallery of women provide commentary as a female lion protects her against Alexander's surrogate attack lion. The women perfume the other animals into submission. And men, if you came just to see the naked lady, you're out of luck. God's very own cloud of fire protects her from your lecherous eyes. Dennis MacDonald, whose study of this text, *The Legend and the Apostle*, is still the best way to get to know it, argues that the legends strung together to create this story were probably cultivated by generations of women who saw Thecla as their patron apostle.[92] Indeed, we know from Paul's authentic letters that from the very beginning of the Jesus movement, there were women who did as Thecla did: eschewed marriage, refrained from sex, and lived as Paul did, as an apostle.[93] Paul calls them "widows."[94] Their path was not easy. In the end, Thecla only manages to get on with her vocation when she dons male clothing and begins to present herself as a man.[95] This must have been the way many of these women got away with the crime of refusing to become a wife and mother. Others, like Prisca, may have posed as conventional women with *ersatz* husbands, like Aquila. Was this Junia's strategy with Andronicus? And what of the two women, Tryphaena and Tryphosa? Did one play the role of husband and the other of wife? Paul once speaks of the apostles having the authority to travel abroad accompanied by "sister wives."[96] The most reasonable interpretation of this reference imagines that the apostles traveled around with women ("sisters") posing as their wives.[97] The purpose would have been to enable women to share in the apostolic life without risking reproach for having chosen to live unmarried

91. Acts of Paul and Thecla 37.
92. See note 80, earlier.
93. See the discussion, later, of 1 Cor 7 and 1 Tim 5.
94. See 1 Cor 7:8.
95. See Acts of Paul and Thecla 40.
96. 1 Cor 9:5.
97. Schuessler Fiorenza argues that these women were not real wives, but comissionaries with the men with whom they traveled (see *In Memory of Her*, 172–73).

and chaste. The women of the Jesus movement must have tried various strategies to gain exemption from the normal life course of ancient women. But alas, they still lived in a patriarchal world.

THE DEMISE OF THE WIDOWS

So what happened to all these women? Where did they go, and how did the church become the great bastion of patriarchy that it remains, for the most part, today? While some of Paul's second-century admirers were trying to preserve the legacy of early women apostles in the Pauline churches by writing down the legends of Thecla, others were busy trying to quash it. We find their efforts in a collection of letters known as the Pastoral Epistles—1 and 2 Timothy and Titus.[98] These New Testament texts are attributed to Paul, but most critical scholars regard them as pseudepigraphical, that is, forged by someone in the first half of the second century.[99] The someone—we'll follow convention and call him "the Pastor"—had a very different vision of what the nascent Christian church should become in the second century. The social radicalism of the legends, he believed, would be the undoing of the church. Instead, he thought that the church should model itself on the typical patriarchal household of the Roman Empire. We encountered him, you'll recall, in the last chapter, in his views on slavery. "Let all who labor under the yoke of slavery regard their masters as worthy of all honor" (1 Tim 6:1). This was what Romans expected of their slaves. What did they expect of their women?

> Let a woman learn in silence with all submission. I permit no woman to teach
> or to have authority over men; she is to keep silent. For Adam was formed first,
> then Eve; and Adam was not deceived, but the woman was deceived and became
> a transgressor. Yet, a woman will be saved by bearing children, if she continues
> in faith and love and holiness, with modesty.
>
> 1 Tim 2:11

---

98. MacDonald, *The Legend and the Apostle*, 54–77, argues that these letters were in fact composed to counter the effect of the legends preserved in the Acts of Paul and Thecla.

99. Most critical introductions to the New Testament offer the straightforward evidence of this conclusion: their language and usage is different from Paul's, their manner of argumentation and formal features are different, and the situation and organization of the Pauline churches they presuppose cannot be squared with what is apparent from the authentic letters. For a standard, uncontroversial treatment of the issue, see Raymond Brown, *An Introduction to the New Testament*, Anchor Bible Reference Library (New York: Doubleday, 1997), 662–68.

One who fills the role of *diakonos*, he says, "must be the husband of one wife," who can "manage their children and their households well" (1 Tim 3:19). So much for Phoebe, the *diakonos* of the church at Cenchraea! Her path in this later generation would have been a much more conventional one.

In chapter 5 of 1 Timothy, the Pastor goes after those women who had taken up the role of "widow" in his jurisdiction. Recall, Paul referred to the ascetical women in the Corinthian churches as "widows." These were women who, like him, refused to marry and instead lived the celibate life.[100] They were not actual widows—though perhaps the office began among younger women widowed by older husbands. Speculation. In the days of the Pastor, though, the role of "widow" had taken on certain elements of formality. These women were "enrolled," that is, formally recognized by the church.[101] There was a ceremony, in which widows pledged their allegiance to Christ.[102] The role also must have merited financial support, so the widow would be free to carry on with her duties.[103] The precise nature of these duties is unclear. The Pastor offers only a sarcastic caricature of them: "gadding about from house to house . . . saying what they should not" (1 Tim 5:13). One might imagine them as something like itinerant teachers, moving from house to house and sharing their ideas, caring for the sick, perhaps. But the Pastor despised them. They were women and should have taken up the life course expected of women then. He was a social conservative. The social radicalism of the earlier Jesus movement embarrassed him and he worried that these unconventional women would attract the attention of critics.[104] So he planned their demise through the ruse of forgery.

Timothy and Titus were real colleagues of Paul in the middle of the first century, when the Jesus movement and the Pauline mission were yet young. Ironically, Paul mentions Timothy in Romans 16, the letter of recommendation for Phoebe, the minister of Cenchreae.[105] Timothy probably would have vouched for her authority, had he been asked. In the second century, though, the Pastor made Paul and Timothy the architects of a new regime. Widows were to be "real" widows, not "widows" in the figurative sense.[106] They must have been married and they must be old—not less than sixty years of age.[107] Since the life expectancy for women was roughly thirty

---

100. See 1 Cor 7:8.
101. See 1 Tim 5:9, 11.
102. See 1 Tim 5:11–12.
103. Inferred from 1 Tim 5:16.
104. See esp. 1 Tim 5:14b.
105. See Rom 16:21.
106. See 1 Tim 5:3.
107. See 1 Tim 5:9.

years, this alone would have eliminated most of the widows, both real and figurative. They were no longer to be "enrolled," which must mean that they would no longer receive financial support from the churches.[108] Perhaps most galling to the women who had chosen this vocation, they were to marry and have children, like most women did.[109] The Pastor was shutting down the office.[110]

But what about Paul's authentic letters? Didn't they authorize the lives of these women? Hadn't Paul himself advised that it was better for women not to marry and to remain celibate?[111] Yes, but the record on Paul is not as clear as we would like. In 1 Corinthians 14:34–36, there is a notorious passage that poses a number of challenges. It reads like this:

> As in all the churches of the saints, let women keep silent in the churches. For they are not permitted to speak, but should be subordinate, just as the Law says. If there is anything they wish to learn, let them ask their husbands at home, for it is shameful for a woman to speak in a church. Or did the Word of God begin with you, or are you the only ones it has reached?

For years, centuries really, these verses have overshadowed Romans 16, and even the passages in 1 Corinthians itself that indicate women were not silent in Paul's churches. As we have seen, in 1 Corinthians 11 Paul deals with women who were far from silent in the churches. They were praying and prophesying. In chapter 7 we learn of other women who were joining Paul in the life of asceticism, with no husbands to consult at home! How shall we square all of that with 14:34–36?

Many modern scholars of Paul have noticed something slightly off about these verses. First, they are not topical. They do not really fit their context. In chapter 14 Paul is talking about spiritual gifts, especially speaking in tongues—a common practice in the communities he founded. These verses have nothing to do with that. Second, they are not necessary. If you stop reading at the end of 14:33 and jump directly to 14:37, you don't miss a beat. Perfect continuity. Third, Pauline scholars have always been troubled by verse 34b, where Paul says women should be subordinate to men, "even as the Law says." That is not a very Pauline way of arguing. Paul thought that the Jewish Law was not binding on these new communities. Finally,

---

108. See 1 Tim 5:11.
109. See 1 Tim 5:14.
110. See esp. Deborah Krause, *1 Timothy*, Readings: A New Biblical Commentary (London and New York: T & T Clark, 2004), 96–109.
111. See 1 Cor 7:8.

there are some ancient manuscripts of 1 Corinthians that do not include verses 34 and 35 here, but place them later, after verse 40. This last detail is something of a telltale. It indicates that these verses might have begun as a marginal note inserted by a scribe into some early manuscript of 1 Corinthians. In subsequent copies, one scribe slipped them into the text after verse 33, and another after verse 40. In other words, these verses are not authentic. Scholars call them a later "interpolation" accomplished by someone other than Paul.[112] But who? Who wished that Paul had hewed to a more traditional Roman standard when it came to the women in his communities? The Pastor. It may be that the Pastor was not content with forging new letters of Paul that would turn the apostle to his own point of view. He also reached back into the authentic letters themselves and changed them to silence the women in his own context. "Let women keep silent in the churches."

As the Pastor was engaging in these literary shenanigans, women were still participating in the leadership of churches in many places. A second-century movement originally known as the New Prophecy, and later as Montanism, featured the prophecies of two prominent women, Prisca and Maximilla. Marcion, another second-century teacher now regarded as heterodox, may have ordained women as priests and bishops. And on his side, the Pastor was certainly not alone. When he wrote the Pastoral Epistles, there was already a long tradition of rewriting Paul to be more accommodating to common Roman social practice, as the pseudo-Pauline letters, Colossians (see 3:18–4:1), and Ephesians (see 5:21–6:9) clearly attest. But in retrospect, we can now see that the Pastor's words became a kind of final curtain for the female leaders of the Jesus movement. The widows did disappear. Nuns would one day replace them. Ministers like Phoebe would be replaced by deaconesses. But these were all subordinate roles. The church became a reflection of the world around it: a male-dominated patriarchy. A woman with male power? *Hermaphroditus stante*? Preposterous.

---

112. The theory that 1 Cor 14:33b–36 is a late interpolation into Paul's original letter goes back to the German scholar Wilhelm Bousset, "Der erste Brief an die Korinther," *Die Schriften des neuen Testaments* (Göttingen: Vandenhoeck & Ruprecht, 1908), 141–42. It was widely held at one time, but now may be more disputed. Some scholars have cried foul, saying that this is simply a liberal attempt to cleanse Paul from a view distasteful to many moderns (though certainly not to Bousset). Others have argued that Paul wrote these words but meant them ironically, adding, "What! Did the word of God originate with you?" in verse 36. For a discussion of the alternatives and their relative merits, see Antoinette Clark Wire, *The Corinthian Women Prophets: A Reconstruction Through Paul's Rhetoric* (Minneapolis: Fortress Press, 1990), 229–32. My view is that it is clearly an interpolation.

Conclusion

You Are All One

You are all one. There are a lot of ways one could construe the meaning of this, the final line of our creed. Does it mean we should all be the same? Or is it that difference doesn't matter? Or is it still something else altogether? Like so much else about the creed, its final claim is less obvious than its familiar-sounding phrasing would lead us to believe.

WE ARE ALL THE SAME

Are we all the same? This was the question that stood at the heart of ancient debates about slavery. Aristotle did not think so.[1] Slaves were different. They were servile in mien and yet powerfully built. What they lacked was a free, or rational, soul. Oh, of course, there were exceptions. Among the captives sold into slavery on the battlefield was the occasional leader of men, whose superior qualities were accidentally betrayed by circumstance. But this was the exception. On the other side, though, there must have been opponents of Aristotle, against whom his arguments were aimed. Slaves were no different from us, they must have said. We are all victims of circumstance. Centuries later Epictetus, the former slave, made exactly that case—that the slaves over whom we rule are really no different: "Don't you

---

1. *Politics* 1.1253b–1255b.

remember who you are, and they over whom you rule . . . that they are your kin, brothers and sisters by nature, the offspring of Zeus?"[2] Epictetus knew the world, and the fact that there would always be slaves. But if it were in his power to do so, he would have eradicated slavery as a violation of the laws of God. For Epictetus, "you are all one" might well have meant "you are all the same."

The problem is that we are not all the same in every respect. Are Jews and Greeks the same? Are women and men? In the things that counted most for Epictetus, they were and are. But there are other things: language, custom, culture, physiology. These are the things that worried Daniel Boyarin as he contemplated the meaning of this creed.[3] If "you are all one" means "you are all the same," what becomes of difference? Are those things that make us uniquely and distinctly who we are also to be eradicated? Since we aren't really all the same, oneness as sameness can only be achieved by force of will. The imposed identity of the powerful, the winners, the colonizers yields a certain "oneness" too. Christians would eradicate Jews. The native born would eradicate the foreigner. And if eradication is too much, then subordination offers enough oneness: women to men; gay, bi, and trans to straight; children to fathers. Sameness can be measured in degrees— degrees of separation from the norm: white, male, Christian, straight. Oneness as sameness is worth worrying about. Unity by exclusion and subordination is nothing to celebrate. "You are all one" should not mean, then, "You are all the same." It works for "slave and free," but for "Jew and Greek" and "male and female," it's a disaster.

WE ARE ALL DIFFERENT

The Apostle Paul, as we have seen, was worried most about Jews and Greeks. And while it may well be the legacy of Paul that Christian Gentiles have come to assume that the only good Jew is an assimilated Jew, Paul himself was actually better than this on the issue of diversity and difference. There is a very telling passage in 1 Corinthians where Paul responds to a group in the Corinthian churches that go by the slogan, "It is good for a man not to touch a woman" (1 Cor 7:1). To this, Paul replies, ever so humbly, "I wish that everyone were just like me" (1 Cor 7:7), that is, full of self-control, devoted to prayer, and so forth. But then, now wisely, Paul goes on

2. *Disc* 1.13.4.
3. Daniel Boyarin, *A Radical Jew: Paul and the Politics of Identity* (Berkeley: University of California Press, 1994).

to say something that sounds remarkably modern in an ancient world that was still unapologetic in its bigotries. Everyone should live the life they are given to lead, he says. Don't change; remain as you are. If you're Jewish, be Jewish. If you're Greek, be Greek. If married, stay married. If celibate, stay celibate—if you want. But if you change your mind and want to be sexually active, go ahead, knock yourself out. Being part of that Corinthian community did not require anyone to change who they were. It's all good. Yes, Paul actually says all of this and more (see 1 Cor 7, *passim*). If, in modern liberal discourse, "oneness" has come to mean "sameness," Paul actually arrives at a fairly postmodern insight: people do not all have to be the same to live together in one community of mutual caring. He actually preferred diversity to sameness. Remain as you are. That is his guiding principle.

That is, until he bumps up against a troubling hypothetical: what if you are a slave?[4] That hypothetical really does expose the limits of the postmodern turn. As long as we are talking about cultural expression in a benignly pluralistic setting, it's all good. But when real distinctions of power and privilege come into play, then "remain as you are" is no longer benign. "Be who you are" now becomes "know your place." When difference really makes a difference, when issues like food and income, and the ability to be secure in one's own body, indeed, to be more than a body, a mere object without real agency, a "tool with a voice"—when these matters of essential well-being are at stake, it's not all good. No slave ever celebrated the difference between slave and free. The celebration of difference is not enough by itself. Identity politics is still politics, and the powerful still win in the end. Democracy can be hell. Oneness as tolerance is no match for numbers when crowds elect demagogues, bigots, and bullies.

WE ARE ALL ONE

Here, then, is another approach. Think about Pliny's letter—that first time *Christiani* appear in the public utterances of the Roman Empire.[5] When Pliny captured for interrogation two of the leaders of the nascent church in Pontus, they were both women and they were both slaves. He doesn't mention their ethnicity. But he does say what they were doing—or *not* doing, in this case: they were not participating in the public rites of sacrifice. Public sacrifice was in the ancient world a very communal affair, a celebration

4. See 1 Cor 7:21.
5. Pliny the Younger, *Letters*, 157 10.96.

of oneness. The whole community gathered on such occasions, men and women, first citizens and peasants, freeborn and slaves. Aristocrats served as priests; men gathered in close; women, children, and slaves stood on the periphery. The ox or pig or sheep was slaughtered, then cooked and eaten. Each in his or her turn received a portion. Priests and aristocrats, the patrons of the feast, received their due—the finer cuts. Then the lesser portions went out, shoulder, ribs, tail, hooves, until all had received their due. If your family was a shoulder family, you got a shoulder; a rib family, a rib; a tail family, a tail. Women and children and slaves received from their husbands and fathers and masters their share, their food, their sustenance. By the end of the feast, everyone knew his and her place in the greater scheme of things. And all gave thanks.

Why did those female slaves of Pontus abstain? In their newly forming community, they were not female slaves, standing on the periphery waiting for their portion. They were leaders. They knew their place and they had rejected it. In their new community they had discovered like-minded people who would recognize their decision to do that. Pliny's problem was that this idea was catching on. Too many people no longer knew their place. The sacrifices—the glue that held the ancient world together[6]—were languishing. This chaos, he correctly saw, would ultimately undermine his authority, and so he cracked down on the dissidents. He invited people to recant and fall back into line. Those who didn't, he executed.

"There is no Jew or Greek, no slave or free, no male and female" was not about overcoming difference for the sake of sameness. Nor was it a celebration of difference and cultural diversity. It was about overcoming the distinctions that commonly underwrite the human tendency to denigrate the other, to disempower, disenfranchise, dehumanize, and even enslave another person on the flimsy grounds that he or she is different. It was about denying a caste system. The creed, recall, was composed on the basis of a cliché: I thank God I was born a native not a foreigner, a Roman not a barbarian, a Jew not a Greek. I thank God I was born a man not a woman, free not a slave. Why? Because in the caste system of the Roman Empire, native, freeborn men had all the advantages, all the power. The creed must have been, finally, about imagining a world in which that was no longer so, in which female slaves could be leaders of free men, where foreigners and native born stood with equal power and equal rights. "You are all one" signifies *solidarity*.

---

6. Stanley Stowers, "Greeks Who Sacrifice and Those Who Do Not," in *The Social World of the First Christians: Essays in Honor of Wayne Meeks*, ed. L. Michael White and O. Larry Yarbrough (Minneapolis: Fortress Press, 1995), 328.

Human beings are social animals. We desire one another, the company of others, a community in which to live our lives together. But being together is hard. We try to make it easier. We find people who are like us, and exclude those who are different. We find clarity in our relationships by creating hierarchies of power, using race, class, and gender—and anything else we can make to count for something it isn't. We have done this in every time and every place since the day we first walked out of the steppe and forest and swamp and into fields and towns and nation-states. This is who we are.

But here is a credo that claims another truth: this is not how we must be. Difference does not have to count in this way. It was once a Christian creed, perhaps even the first creed. It says nothing a creed should say. It is not about God. Nor is it about the nature of Jesus Christ or how he saves us from our sins. It is about us. And perhaps that is why few have ever really believed it. It is easier, it turns out, to believe in a higher power, a God, a savior, who will save us from our sins of hatred and violence than to think, to believe, that human beings are capable of the miracle of solidarity: of reaching out beyond one's own interest to see the interests of another, to live with and for another in the hope only of a common redemption from the tears in the human fabric that have come from difference. Oneness can never be achieved by eradication, and only a little by tolerance. Real oneness comes only when we realize we are all deeply connected and stand with one another in solidarity as "offspring of Zeus," children of God.

And this was what baptism meant, once upon a time. This creed, recall, was originally a baptismal creed. Baptism, then, was about solidarity in the knowledge that everyone is a child of God. Neither race, nor class, nor gender, nor any other category of difference we might dream up to signify *the* difference between *us* and *them* could withstand the restorative powers of baptism so conceived. Baptism restored its recipients to the state of primordial perfection once enjoyed by Adam. In this common kinship all could stand as one. There is no Jew and Greek, no slave and free, no male and female. In Adam these things simply do not exist. Baptism meant an end to otherness and othering, estrangement, and contempt for difference.

Over time, this was forgotten. Perhaps a critical moment came when baptism became, for Christians, the signal rite of initiation. Once baptism became the thing that marked Christian from non-Christian, or even one kind of Christian over all other kinds, it became a new boundary that spawned all over again a new us and a new them. The Apostle Paul didn't like baptism when he first encountered it because it could prove divisive (1 Cor 1:14–17). There is no us, no them, is a very hard thing to believe.

As I write this on the eve of 2018, all over the world race, gender, and class differences are once again exploited to divide and denigrate foreigners, women, and the poor. After debating for a generation about how best to recognize and appreciate difference, we find ourselves thrown back into a struggle many had thought we could count as settled. The celebration of difference has, alas, drawn hostile fire. This raw and public display of racism, sexism, and scapegoating is shocking, and the success with which these ancient demons reward their purveyors is more shocking still. And as all of this unfolds in Western civilization, its dominant religious tradition seems powerless to oppose it. To the contrary, conservative Christians are among the most enthusiastic partisans of the new populist bigotry. In the United States they even elected a president who rode to power on a foul wave of racist, sexist rhetoric.[7]

To this, our ancient baptismal creed speaks a very clear word: *there is no us, no them.* Everyone is a child of God, made one in a common kinship that goes back to our mythic, hoary past. Adam is the whole human family. Every tribe and clan belongs to Adam, in whom there is no class, no gender. It is tragic that this creed, its myth, and its ritual were so soon abandoned by the Christian church and never, henceforth, got a hearing in the civilization we still inhabit. Christendom has been constructed around the very conventional human instinct to identify the "us" and the "them." Race, class, and gender have been and are still the categories of difference that make a difference in the real world of power and privilege. It is worth remembering this ancient creed as one of those rare cultural and religious resources that might be turned against the instinct to draw back from difference, to "other," to denigrate and to dominate those whom we fear. This forgotten creed stands on the side of solidarity, of oneness, of universal kinship. To recall it now is to recall a future once dreamt, defined by this simple claim: "You are all children of God."

---

7. White evangelical Christians voted for Donald J. Trump by a margin of 81 percent; see the Pew Research Center, "How the Faithful Voted," last modified on November 9, 2016, http://www.pewresearch.org/fact-tank/2016/11/09/how-the-faithful-voted-a-preliminary-2016-analysis/.

WORKS CITED

Aune, David E. *Prophecy in Early Christianity and the Ancient Mediterranean World.* Grand Rapids, MI: Eerdmans, 1983.

Balsdon, J. P. V. D. *Romans and Aliens.* London: Duckworth, 1979/Chapel Hill: University of North Carolina Press, 1980.

Bartchy, S. Scott. *First-Century Slavery and the Interpretation of 1 Corinthians 7:21.* Society of Biblical Literature Dissertation Series. Atlanta: Scholars Press, 1973.

BeDuhn, Jason. *The First Testament: Marcion's Scriptural Canon.* Salem, OR: Polebridge Press, 2013.

Bell, H. Idris. *Jews and Christians in Egypt.* London: Oxford University Press, 1924.

Belser, Johannes. "Die Frauen in die neutestamentliche Schriften." *Theologische Quartalschrift* 90 (1909): 321–51.

Betz, Hans Dieter. *Galatians: A Commentary on Paul's Letter to the Churches in Galatia.* Hermeneia. Philadelphia: Fortress Press, 1979.

———. "Transferring a Ritual: Paul's Interpretation of Baptism in Romans." In *Paul in His Hellenistic Context.* Edited by Troels Engberg-Pedersen, 84–118. Minneapolis: Fortress, 1995. Reprinted as pp. 240–71 in Hans Dieter Betz, *Paulinische Studien. Gesammelte Aufsäzte III.* Tübingen: Mohr/Siebeck, 1994.

———. "The Sermon on the Mount (Matt. 5:3-7:27): Its Literary Genre and Function." *Journal of Religion* 59 (1979): 285–97. Reprinted as pp. 1–16 in Hans Dieter Betz, *Essays on the Sermon on the Mount.* Philadelphia: Fortress, 1985.

Bousset, Wilhelm. *Die Schriften des neuen Testaments.* Göttingen: Vandenhoeck & Ruprecht, 1908.

Boyarin, Daniel. *A Radical Jew: Paul and the Politics of Identity.* Berkeley: University of California Press, 1994.

———. *Borderlines: The Partition of Judeo-Christianity.* Philadelphia: University of Pennsylvania, 2004.

Bradley, Keith R. *Slavery and Rebellion in the Roman World, 140-70 BC.* Bloomington: Indiana University Press, 1989.

Brisson, Luc. *Sexual Ambivalence: Androgyny and Hermaphroditism in Graeco-Roman Antiquity.* Translated by Janet Lloyd. Berkeley: University of California Press, 2002.

Brock, Ann Graham. *Mary Magdalene, the First Apostle: The Struggle for Authority.* Harvard Theological Studies 51. Cambridge, MA: Harvard Divinity School, 2003.

Brooten, Bernadette. "'Junia . . . Outstanding Among the Apostles (Romans 16:7).'" In *Women Priests: A Catholic Commentary on the Vatican Declaration.* Edited by Leonard Swidler and Arlene Swidler, 141–44. New York: Paulist, 1977.

Brown, Raymond E. *An Introduction to the New Testament.* Anchor Bible Reference Library. New York: Doubleday, 1997.

Bultmann, Rudolf. "The History of Religions Background of the Prologue to the Gospel of John." In *The Interpretation of John*. Edited by John Ashton, 18–35. Philadelphia: Fortress, 1986 (German orig., 1922).

———. *History of the Synoptic Tradition*. Rev. ed. Translated by John Marsh. Oxford: Blackwell, 1963.

———. "Ignatius and Paul." In *Existence and Faith: Shorter Writings of Rudolf Bultmann*. Edited and translated by Schubert Ogden, 267–77. New York: Meridian, 1960.

———. *Theology of the New Testament*. 2 vols. Translated by Kendrick Grobel. New York: Charles Scribner's Sons, 1951, 1955.

Burrus, Virginia. *Chastity as Autonomy: Women in the Stories of the Apocryphal Acts*. Studies in Women and Religion. Lewiston, NY: Mellon, 1987.

Callahan, Allan. "Paul's Epistle to Philemon: Toward an Alternative Argumentum." *Harvard Theological Review* 86 (1994): 357–76.

Cameron, Alan. *Circus Factions: Blues and Greens at Rome and Byzantium*. Oxford: Clarendon, 1976.

Cartledge, Paul. *The Greeks: A Portrait of Self and Other*. Rev. ed. Oxford and New York: Oxford University Press, 2002.

Collins, Adela Yarbro. "The Origin of Christian Baptism." In *Cosmology and Eschatology in Jewish and Christian Apocalypticism*, 218–38. Supplements to the Journal for the Study of Judaism 50. Leiden: Brill, 1996.

Conzelmann, Hans. *1 Corinthians: A Commentary on the First Epistle to the Corinthians*. Translated by James W. Leitch. Hermeneia. Philadelphia: Fortress, 1975.

D'Angelo, Mary Rose. "Reconstructing 'Real' Women from Gospel Literature: The Case of Mary Magdalene." In *Women and Christian Origins*. Edited by Ross Kraemer and Mary Rose D'Angelo, 105–28. New York and Oxford: Oxford University Press, 1999.

Davies, Stevan. *The Gospel of Thomas and Christian Wisdom*. New York: Seabury, 1983.

DeBoer, Esther. *Mary Magdalene: Beyond the Myth*. Harrisburg, PA: Trinity Press, 1997.

DeConick, April. *Seek to See Him: Ascent and Vision Mysticism in the Gospel of Thomas*. Supplements to Vigiliae Christianae 33. Leiden: Brill, 1996.

Donaldson, Terrance. *Judaism and the Gentiles: Jewish Patterns of Universalism (to 135 CE)*. Waco, TX: Baylor University Press, 2008.

Downey, Glanville. *A History of Antioch in Syria from Seleucus to the Arab Conquest*. Princeton, NJ: Princeton University Press, 1961.

Dudley, Donald R., and Graham Webster. *The Rebellion of Boudicca*. London: Routledge and Kegan Paul, 1962.

Ehrman, Bart. *Forged*. San Francisco: HarperOne, 2011.

———. *Forgery and Counterforgery: The Use of Literary Deceit in Early Christian Polemics*. Oxford and New York: Oxford University Press, 2012.

Eisenbaum, Pamela. *Paul Was Not a Christian*. San Francisco: HarperOne, 2009.

Eliade, Mircea. *Mephistopheles and the Androgyne: Studies in Religious Myth and Symbol*. Translated by J. M. Cohen. New York: Sheed and Ward, 1965.

Fantham, Elaine, et al. *Women in the Classical World: Image and Text*. Oxford and New York: Oxford University Press, 1994.

Fee, Gordon. *The First Epistle to the Corinthians*. New International Commentary on the New Testament. Grand Rapids, MI: Eerdmans, 1987.

Ferguson, Everett. *Baptism in the Early Church: History, Theology, and Liturgy in the First Five Centuries*. Grand Rapids, MI: Eerdmans, 2009.

Ferris, Iain. *Enemies of Rome*. Stroud: Sutton, 2000.

Freedman, Harry, and Maurice Simon. *Midrash Rabbah*. 10 vols. London: Soncino, 1939.

Friesenbruch, Annelise. *Caesars' Wives: Sex, Power, and Politics in the Roman Empire*. New York: Simon and Schuster, 2010.

Gager, John. *Reinventing Paul*. Oxford and New York: Oxford University Press, 2000.

Gambetti, Sandra. *The Alexandrian Riots of 38 CE and the Persecution of the Jews: A Historical Reconstruction*. Supplements to the Journal for the Study of Judaism 135. Leiden: Brill, 2009.

Glancy, Jennifer. *Slavery in Early Christianity*. Minneapolis: Fortress Press, 2006.

Goodenough, E. R. *The Politics of Philo Judaeus*. New Haven, CT: Yale University Press, 1938.

Goodman, Martin. *Rome and Jerusalem: The Clash of Civilizations*. New York: Random House, 2007.

Grant, F. C. *Hellenistic Religions*. New York: Liberal Arts Press, 1953.

Harrill, J. Albert. *Slaves in the New Testament: Literary, Social, and Moral Dimensions*. Minneapolis: Fortress Press, 2006.

Hellholm, David, Tor Vegge, Øyvind Norderval, and Christer Hellholm, eds. *Ablution, Initiation and Baptism: Late Antiquity, Early Judaism and Early Christianity/ Waschungen, Initiation und Taufe: Spätantike, Frühes Judentum und Frühes Christentum*. 3 vols. Beihefte zur Zeitschrift für die neutestamentliche Wissenschaft 176/1–3. Berlin: DeGruyter, 2010.

Hengel, Martin. *Judaism and Hellenism: Studies in Their Encounter During the Hellenistic Period*. Translated by John Bowden. Philadelphia: Fortress Press, 1974.

Hennecke, Edgar, and Wilhelm Schneemelcher, eds. *New Testament Apocrypha II*. Rev. ed. Translated by R. McL. Wilson. Cambridge: James Clarke & Co, 1991/ Louisville, KY: Westminster/John Knox Press, 1991.

Hezser, Catherine. *Jewish Slavery in Antiquity*. Oxford and New York: Oxford University Press, 2005.

Hunt, A. S., and C.C. Edgar. *Select Papyri*. LCL. Cambridge, MA: Harvard, 1932.

Hurd, John C. *The Origin of I Corinthians*. Macon, GA: Mercer University Press, 1983.

Hurtado, Larry. *Lord Jesus Christ: Devotion to Jesus in Earliest Christianity*. Grand Rapids, MI: Eerdmans, 2003.

Isaac, Benjamin. *The Invention of Racism in Classical Antiquity*. Princeton, NJ, and Oxford: Princeton University Press, 2004.

Jeffreys, Elizabeth, et al. *The Chronicle of John Malalas*. Byzantina Australiensia 4. Melbourne: Australian Association for Byzantine Studies, 1986.

Jewett, Robert. *Romans: A Commentary*. Hermeneia. Minneapolis: Fortress, 2007.

Joshel, Sandra. *Slavery in the Roman World*. Cambridge Introductions to Roman Civilization. Cambridge: Cambridge University Press, 2010.

Kahl, Brigitte. *Galatians Re-Imagined: Reading with the Eyes of the Vanquished*. Paul in Critical Contexts. Minneapolis: Fortress Press, 2010.

Käsemann, Ernst. *Commentary on Romans*. Translated by Geoffrey W. Bromiley. Grand Rapids, MI: Eerdmans, 1980.

King, Karen. *The Gospel of Mary of Magdala: Jesus and the First Woman Apostle*. Salem, OR: Polebridge Press, 2003.

Kloppenborg Verbin, John. *Excavating Q: The History and Setting of the Sayings Gospel*. Minneapolis: Fortress, 2000.

Kondoleon, Christine. *Antioch: The Lost City*. Princeton, NJ: Princeton University Press, 2000.

Kraeling, Karl. "The Jewish Community in Antioch." *Journal of Biblical Literature* 51 (1932): 130–60.

Kraemer, Ross Shephard, and Mary Rose D'Angelo. *Women and Christian Origins.* Oxford and New York: Oxford University Press, 1999.

Krause, Deborah. *1 Timothy.* Readings: A New Biblical Commentary. London and New York: T & T Clark, 2004.

Kvam, Kristen et al., eds. *Eve and Adam: Jewish, Christian, and Muslim Readings on Genesis and Gender.* Bloomington: Indiana University Press, 1999.

Labahn, Michael. "Kreative Erinnerung als nachosterliche Nachschöpfung. Der Ursprung der christliche Taufe." In *Ablution, Initiation and Baptism: Late Antiquity, Early Judaism and Early Christianity/Waschungen, Initiation und Taufe: Spätantike, Frühes Judentum und Frühes Christentum.* Vol. 1. Edited by David Hellholm, Tor Vegge, Øyvind Norderval, and Christer Hellholm, 337–76. Berlin: DeGruyter, 2010.

Lampe, Peter. "Keine 'Sklavenflucht' des Onesimus." *Zeitschrift für neutestamentliche Wissenschaft* 76 (1985): 135–37.

———. "The Roman Christians of Romans 16." In *The Romans Debate.* Rev. and expanded ed. Edited by Karl Donfried, 216–31. Peabody, MA: Hendrickson, 1991. Reprinted as chap. 16 of Peter Lampe, *From Paul to Valentinus: Christians in Rome in the First Two Centuries.* Translated by Michael Steinhauser. Minneapolis: Fortress, 2003.

Leenhardt, Franz. *La place de la femme dans l'église d'après le Nouveau Testament.* Études théologiques et religieuses 23/1. Montpelier: La Faculté Libre de Théologie Protestante, 1948.

Lefkowitz, Mary R., and Maureen B. Fant. *Women's Life in Greece and Rome: A Source Book in Translation.* 3rd ed. Baltimore: Johns Hopkins University Press, 2005.

Lieu, Judith. *Marcion and the Making of a Heretic: God and Scripture in the Second Century.* Cambridge and New York: Cambridge University Press, 2015.

Lopez, Davina. *Apostle to the Conquered: Reimagining Paul's Mission.* Paul in Critical Contexts. Minneapolis: Fortress Press, 2008.

MacDonald, Dennis. *The Legend and the Apostle: The Battle for Paul in Story and Canon.* Philadelphia: Westminster, 1983.

———. *There Is No Male and Female: The Fate of a Dominical Saying in Paul and Gnosticism.* Harvard Dissertations in Religion 20. Philadelphia: Fortress Press, 1987.

Manson, T. W. "St. Paul's Letter to the Romans—and Others." In *Studies in the Gospels and Epistles,* 225–41. Manchester: Manchester University Press, 1962. Reprinted as pp. 1–15 in *The Romans Debate.* Rev. and expanded ed. Edited by Karl Donfried. Peabody, MA: Hendrickson, 1991.

Martyn, J. Louis. *Galatians: A New Translation with Introduction and Commentary.* The Anchor Bible 33A. New York: Doubleday, 1997.

———. *History and Theology in the Fourth Gospel.* The New Testament Library. 3rd ed. Louisville, KY, and London: Westminster John Knox Press, 2003.

Mayor, Adrienne. *The Amazons: Lives and Legends of Warrior Women across the Ancient World.* Princeton, NJ: Princeton University Press, 2014.

McCoskey, Denise Eileen. *Race: Antiquity and Its Legacy.* London and New York: Oxford, 2012.

McGinn, Thomas. *The Economy of Prostitution in the Roman World: A Study of Social History and the Brothel.* Ann Arbor: University of Michigan Press, 2010.

Meeks, Wayne. "The Image of the Androgyne: Some Uses of a Symbol in Earliest Christianity." *History of Religions* 13 (1973–74): 165–208.

———. "The Man from Heaven in Johannine Sectarianism." *Journal of Biblical Literature* 91 (1972): 44–72. Reprinted as pp. 141–73 in *The Interpretation of John.* Edited by John Ashton. Philadelphia: Fortress, 1986.

Meeks, Wayne, and Robert L. Wilken. *Jews and Christians in Antioch in the First Four Centuries of the Common Era*. Society of Biblical Literature: Sources for Biblical Study 13. Missoula, MT: Scholars Press, 1978.

Mingana, Alphonse. *Commentary of Theodore of Mopsuestia on the Lord's Prayer and the Sacraments of Baptism and the Eucharist*. Woodbrooke Studies 4. Cambridge, MA: Heffer and Sons, 1933.

Munro, Winsom. *Jesus, Born of a Slave*. Lewiston, NY: Mellon, 1998.

Murphy O'Connor, Jerome. "Sex and Logic in 1 Cor. 11:2–16." *Catholic Biblical Quarterly* 42 (1980): 482–500.

———. "1 Corinthians 11: 2-16 Once Again." *Catholic Biblical Quarterly* 50 (1988): 265–74.

Musurillo, Herbert. *The Acts of the Pagan Martyrs: Acta Alexandrorum*. Oxford: Clarendon, 1954.

Nissinen, Martti. *Homoeroticism in the Biblical World*. Minneapolis: Fortress, 1998.

Osiek, Caroline. *Philippians and Philemon*. Abingdon New Testament Commentaries. Nashville: Abingdon Press, 2000.

———. *Shepherd of Hermas: A Commentary*. Hermeneia. Minneapolis: Fortress, 1999.

Parsons, Peter J. *The Oxyrhynchus Papyri*, vol. 50: *Graeco-Roman Memoirs*. London: Egypt Exploration Society, 1983.

Patterson, Orlando. *Slavery as Social Death*. Cambridge, MA: Harvard University Press, 1982.

Patterson, Stephen J. "From John to Apollos to Paul: How the Baptism of John Entered the Jesus Movement." In *Christian Origins and the Establishment of the Early Jesus Movement*. Early Christianity in Its Hellenistic Context 4. Edited by Stanley Porter and Andrew Pitts. Leiden: Brill, 2016.

———. "Jesus Meets Plato: The Theology of the Gospel of Thomas." In *Das Thomasevangelium, Entstehung—Rezeption—Theologie*. Beihefte zur Zeitschrift für die neutestamentliche Wissenschaft 157. Edited by J. Frey et al., 181–205. Berlin: DeGruyter, 2008. Reprinted as pp. 33–60 in Stephen J. Patterson, *The Gospel of Thomas and Christian Origins: Essays on the Fifth Gospel*. Nag Hammadi and Manichaean Studies 84. Leiden and Boston: Brill, 2013.

———. *The Lost Way: How Two Forgotten Gospels Are Rewriting the Story of Christian Origins*. San Francisco: HarperOne, 2014.

———. "Motion and Rest: The Platonic Origins of a Mysterious Concept." In *Scribal Practices and Social Structures among Jesus Adherents: Essays in Honour of John S. Kloppenborg*. Bibliotheca Ephemeridum Theologicarum Lovaniensium 285. Edited by William E. Arnal et al., 251–61. Leuven, Paris, and Bristol: Peeters, 2016.

Pew Research Center. "How the Faithful Voted." Last modified on November 9, 2016. http://www.pewresearch.org/fact-tank/2016/11/09/how-the-faithful-voted-a-preliminary-2016-analysis/.

Pleket, H. W. *Epigraphica II: Texts on the Social History of the Greek World*. Leiden: Brill, 1969.

Pomeroy, Sarah. *Goddesses, Whores, Wives, and Slaves: Women in Classical Antiquity*. New York: Schocken, 1975.

Reinhartz, Adela. "From Narrative to History: The Resurrection of Mary and Martha." In *The Feminist Companion to the Hebrew Bible in the New Testament*. Feminist Companion to the Bible 10. Edited by Athalya Brenner, 197–224. Sheffield, UK: Sheffield Academic, 1996.

Reynolds, Joyce, and Robert Tannenbaum. *Jews and God-Fearers at Aphrodisias: Greek Inscriptions with Commentary*. Cambridge: Cambridge University Press, 1987.

Ricci, Carla. *Mary Magdalene and Many Others: Women Who Followed Jesus*. Translated by Paul Burns. Minneapolis: Fortress Press, 1994.

Riesner, Rainer. *Paul's Early Period: Chronology, Mission Strategy, Theology*. Translated by Doug Stott. Grand Rapids, MI: Eerdmans, 1998.

Robinson, James M. "LOGOI SOPHŌN: On the Gattung of Q." In James M. Robinson and Helmut Koester, *Trajectories Through Early Christianity*, 77–113. Philadelphia: Fortress Press, 1971.

Robinson, James M., Paul Hoffmann, and John S. Kloppenborg, eds., Milton Moreland, managing ed. *The Sayings Gospel Q in Greek and English, with Parallels from the Gospels of Mark and Thomas*. Minneapolis: Fortress Press, 2002.

Rothschild, Clare K. *Baptist Traditions and Q*. Wissenschaftliche Untersuchungen Zum Neuen Testament 190. Tübingen: Mohr Siebeck, 2005.

Sanders, E. P. *Paul and Palestinian Judaism: A Comparison of Patterns of Religion*. Philadelphia: Fortress, 1977.

Schaberg, Jane. *The Resurrection of Mary Magdalene: Legends, Apocrypha, and the Christian Testament*. New York and London: Continuum, 2002.

Schnackenburg, Rudolf. *Baptism in the Thought of St. Paul*. Translated by G. R. Beasley-Murray. Oxford: Blackwell, 1964.

Schoedel, William R. *Ignatius of Antioch: A Commentary on the Letters of Ignatius of Antioch*. Hermeneia. Philadelphia: Fortress Press, 1985.

Schotroff, Luise. *Lydia's Impatient Sisters: A Feminist Social History of Early Christianity*. Translated by Barbara and Martin Rumscheidt. Louisville: Westminster John Knox Press, 1995.

Schuessler Fiorenza, Elisabeth. *In Memory of Her: A Feminist Theological Introduction*. New York: Crossroad, 1983.

———. "A Feminist Critical Interpretation for Liberation: Martha and Mary: Luke 10:38–42." *Religion and Intellectual Life* 3 (1986): 21–35.

Scroggs, Robin. *The Last Adam*. Philadelphia: Fortress Press, 1966.

Sherwin White, A. N. *Racial Prejudice in Imperial Rome*. Cambridge and New York: Cambridge University Press, 1967.

Sim, David, and James S. McLaren. *Attitudes to Gentiles in Ancient Judaism and Early Christianity*. London: Bloomsbury, 2013.

Smith, Jonathan Z. "The Garments of Shame." *History of Religions* 5 (1966): 217–38.

Stendahl, Krister. "The Apostle Paul and the Introspective Conscience of the West." *Harvard Theological Review* 56 (1963): 199–215.

———. *The Bible and the Role of Women: A Case Study in Hermeneutics*. Philadelphia: Fortress, 1966.

———. *Paul Among Jews and Gentiles*. Philadelphia: Fortress Press, 1976.

Stroker, William D. *Extracanonical Sayings of Jesus*. Society of Biblical Literature: Resources for Biblical Study 18. Atlanta: Scholars Press, 1989.

Stowers, Stanley. "Greeks Who Sacrifice and Those Who Do Not." In *The Social World of the First Christians: Essays in Honor of Wayne Meeks*. Edited by L. Michael White and O. Larry Yarbrough, 312–25. Minneapolis: Fortress Press, 1995.

Suter, Ann. "The Anasyrma: Baubo, Medusa, and the Gendering of Obscenity." In *Ancient Obscenities: Their Nature and Use in the Ancient Greek and Roman Worlds*. Edited by Dorota Dutsch and Ann Suter, 21–43. Ann Arbor: University of Michigan Press, 2015.

Tcherikover, Victor. *Hellenistic Civilization and the Jews*. Translated by S. Applebaum. Philadelphia: Jewish Publication Society of America, 1959.

Thompson, Cynthia. "Hairstyles, Headcoverings, and St. Paul: Portraits from Roman Corinth." *Biblical Archaeologist* 51 (June, 1988): 99–115.

Thurmon, Howard. *Jesus and the Disinherited*. Boston: Beacon Press, 1976 (orig. publ. 1946).

———. *With Head and Heart: The Autobiography of Howard Thurmon*. New York and London: Harcourt, Brace, Jovanovich, 1979.

Thurn, Johannes. *Ioannis Malalae Chronographia*. Corpus Fontium Historiae Byzantinae 35 (Series Berolinensis). Berlin: DeGruyter, 2000.

Townsley, Jeramy. "Paul, the Goddess Religions, and Queer Sects: Romans 1:23–28." *Journal of Biblical Literature* 130 (2011): 710–16.

Tyson, Joseph. *Marcion and Luke-Acts: A Defining Struggle*. Columbia: University of South Carolina Press, 2006.

Uro, Risto. "The Bridal Chamber and Other Mysteries: Ritual System and Ritual Transmission in the Valentinian Movement." In *Sacred Marriages: The Divine-Human Sexual Metaphor from Sumer to Early Christianity*. Edited by Martti Nissinen and Risto Uro, 457–86. Winona Lake, IN: Eisenbrauns, 2008.

Weinel, Heinrich. *Paulus. Der Mensch und Sein Werk*. Tübingen: J. C. B. Mohr (Paul Siebeck), 1904.

Wiedemann, Thomas. *Greek and Roman Slavery*. Baltimore: Johns Hopkins University Press, 1981.

Williams, Demetrius. "'No Longer a Slave': Reading the Interpretation History of Paul's Epistle to Philemon." In *Onesimus Our Brother: Reading Religion, Race, and Culture in Philemon*. Edited by Matthew Johnson, James Noel, and Demetrius Williams, 11–46. Minneapolis: Fortress Press, 2012.

Winter, Sara. "Paul's Letter to Philemon." *New Testament Studies* 33 (1987): 1–15.

Wire, Antoinette Clark. *The Corinthian Women Prophets: A Reconstruction Through Paul's Rhetoric*. Minneapolis: Fortress Press, 1990.

World Health Organization. "Women's Health Fact Sheet #334." Last updated September 2013. http://www.who.int/mediacentre/factsheets/fs334/en/.

Zetterholm, Magnus. *The Formation of Christianity in Antioch: A Social Scientific Approach to the Separation Between Judaism and Christianity*. Routledge Early Church Monographs. London: Routledge, 2003.

Zöckler, Thomas. *Jesu Lehren im Thomasevangelium*. Nag Hammadi and Manichaean Studies 47. Leiden: Brill, 1999.

INDEX OF MODERN AUTHORS

INDEX OF ANCIENT TEXTS